W9-AQB-907

SOFTWARE PEOPLE

An Insider's Look at the Personal Computer Software Industry

DOUGLAS G. CARLSTON
President, Brøderbund Software

Computer Book Division/Simon & Schuster, New York

To
Gary and *Cathy Carlston,*
without whom Brøderbund would never have existed.

Published by the Computer Book Division
Simon & Schuster, Inc.

Simon & Schuster Building
Rockefeller Center
1230 Avenue of the Americas
New York, New York 10020

SIMON AND SCHUSTER and colophon are registered trademarks
of Simon & Schuster, Inc.

Design by Shirley Covington

Manufactured in the United States of America

1 2 3 4 5 6 7 8 9 10

Library of Congress Cataloging-in-Publication Data
Carlston, Douglas G.
  Software people.

  Includes index.
  1. Computer software industry—United States.
I. Title.
HD9696.C63U51487   1985   338.4'700536'0973   85-18355
ISBN 0-671-50971-3

Contents

Acknowledgments

I want to thank John Brockman, who conceived of this book, and Frank Schwartz, who believed in the project and gave me the confidence to tackle the job. I'd also like to thank Howard Rheingold, who helped me write much of this book and whose knowledge of his craft made the rest as intelligible as it is. Without his gentle prodding, I never would have succeeded in committing anything to paper. I'd like to extend my appreciation to my assistant, Janetta Shanks, whose humor and organizational skills helped bring the book together. Many software industry people contributed their time and let me pick their brains for the book: Paul Lutus, Ken Williams, Ed Auer, Margot Tommervik, Bill Budge, Messrs. Son, Hoshi, Kudo, and Gunji, and Bill Baker. Thank you all. My gratitude extends to all the Brøderbunders who kept our company on such a steady course that I could spend weekends working on the book: Gary Carlston and Cathy Carlston, Ed Bernstein, Bill McDonagh, Stu Berman, Debbie Hipple, Jane Risser, Jon Loveless, Brian Eheler, Brian Lee, Al Sonntag, Allan Kausch, and all the others. The three outside groups whom we most credit for our early success are Dave Wagman and Bob Leff of Softsel, Al and Margot Tommervik of *Softalk* magazine, and Minoru Nakazawa of Star Craft. Finally, I thank my wife, Mary, for her patience and support on this project during our first year of marriage.

Introduction

When my brother and I started Brøderbund Software in 1980, we had no idea that it would become one of the largest home computer software companies in the world. In fact, we originally entered the software business by accident. We had no business plan, no scheme to make our fortunes. We were just trying to come up with a way to pay our next month's rent.

In most ways, we were unlikely candidates for the roles we assumed. Neither of us had any business experience to speak of, neither of us knew very much about computers, and neither of us lived anywhere near those centers of innovation where so many high-technology firms were springing up. Before we started our company, I was a lawyer, practicing my trade in rural Maine. My brother Gary had just returned from Sweden, where he had spent five years working as a coach for a women's basketball team. He was now living in Oregon, where, after a stint as field director for the March of Dimes, he became involved in an importing business that proved to be unsuccessful.

What we had was computer fever—a malady we shared with all the other entrepreneurs who were forming similar companies. Of the two of us, I was the one who was more heavily stricken. Programming can be an addiction—those who get drawn into it often forget jobs, family, and friends in their absorption with these fascinating machines. My own addiction began in 1978 when I took the fateful step of entering a Radio Shack store in Waterville, Maine, in order to take a closer look at the computer that was displayed in the window. I ended up walking out with a TRS–80 Model 1 tucked underneath my arm. My life has not been the same since.

I wasn't a complete stranger to computers, however. In the mid-1960s, as a teenager, I had taken a summer course on computers at Northwestern University. In the following years I found a few programming jobs, first at the University of Iowa in Iowa City (where my family lived when I was in high school) and later at the Aiken Computation Lab of Harvard University, where I was an undergraduate. My fellow programming fanatics and I used to jam chewing gum into the locks on the doors of the chemistry building just so we could sneak in after midnight and play with the big IBM 1620. But college was an exciting place for me, and there were lots of other distractions, so my interest in computers waned. By the time I saw that computer in the Radio Shack window ten years later, I had forgotten everything I once knew about computers—except how much fun they were.

When I obtained my TRS–80, I was a lawyer in Newport, Maine, a small town that had fewer than 5000 residents and was close to my parents' summer place. Having grown tired of practicing corporate law in Chicago, I had retreated to Maine in 1977, opened a law practice with a friend, and divided my time between lawyering, building houses, and skiing. All of this had been fun at first, but rural life was starting to bore me, and I began looking for a distraction.

I bought the computer because I thought it would be fun to use. I also had a notion that I could computerize a lot of the routine work around my law office. At that time I knew of a lawyer in Northern Maine who traveled around the area in a Winnebago camper that was fully equipped as an office and that included a microcomputer system; he was able to crank out wills, trusts, and deeds in a fraction of the time normally required for such work and at a fraction of the cost that most lawyers charged. Our law office needed to be able to compete with him, I thought. We needed to computerize.

I know now that those thoughts were purely rationalizations. As I started to play with the computer, all my old fascination with the technology returned. These tiny machines could do almost as much as the huge, expensive models I had first encountered! My interest in the law business declined, and I spent more and more of my spare time learning the tricks of programming. I did eventually write the legal software for my firm, but we never really used it. At the same time I also wrote a game. Although I saw it as a weekend amusement, that game was actually the beginning of the end of my law career.

The game was a simulation—a science fiction fantasy called *Galactic Empire.* I wrote the program in a couple of weekends for my personal enjoyment. And when I say a couple of weekends, I mean a programming marathon that started Friday afternoon and wrapped around to Monday morning, relieved only by occasional catnaps and snacks. When the game was finished, it turned out to be a lot of fun to play, and so I started adding more and more features to it, until I finally ran out of space in the computer's memory. Even these powerful new microcomputers can hold only so much in their electronic memories before they cry uncle and refuse to run a program.

I then began to look for ways to make my programming code more compact so that I could add just one more feature. Like minuets and mathematical equations, programs should be elegant as well as formally correct, and it takes a very skilled, experienced programmer to tinker with a program without destroying its elegance. My own program structure ended up looking like a tangled ball of spaghetti, but only another programmer would have noticed how ungainly it was. For those who were just playing the game, the programming code was invisible.

Imagine you're playing the game. What you see on the screen is the cockpit of a spaceship. You're at the helm, where you see, in the upper left corner of the screen, a window that looks out into interstellar space. If a planet comes into view, your onboard computer identifies it for you. Below the viewport you see a computer screen (after all, spaceships are bound to have computers on board, so I included a "computer within the computer"), and off to the right is your fleet detail that tells you at a glance how many fighters, transports, and scout ships you have at your disposal. The objective of the game is to conquer a cluster of twenty planets that had unlikely names like "Javiny" and "Ootsi." To accomplish your goal within the 1000 years that you are allotted (people live longer in the future) requires considerable logistic sophistication.

In fact, the game was a fascinating intellectual exercise. It was far more fun to play than I had ever thought it would be. What made it so special was that I had never been able to play anything like it before. Without computers it would have been impossible to create such a simulation. In other words, a whole new area of entertainment had just been created. It's hard to describe how excited I felt. I love games of all sorts. The idea that the world might suddenly be filled with hundreds of brand-new games was unbelievably thrilling.

At that time, however, I owned very little software, and Radio Shack carried almost none. It was then that the store manager told me about a wonderful chess program published by a Boston-based company called Personal Software; eventually, I drove all the way to Boston to get a copy. But one program simply wasn't enough to satisfy my appetite. I then discovered *80-NW*, a home-printed four-page computer magazine that was dedicated to users of the TRS-80. I bought a subscription to the magazine and was treated every other month to an ever thicker book filled with programming tips and advertisements for microcomputer-related products. Dozens of programs were available, and I could have bankrupted myself in a week simply by ordering all the software that struck my fancy. So one day I thought up a scheme to get more games.

I sent a copy of *Galactic Empire* to four companies that had runs ads in *80-NW*. Would they be interested in publishing my program?, I asked. And, by the way, would they consider sending me their line of software, *gratis*, as part of the deal? To me, creating a game and trading it for other games promised to be an intensely satisfying transaction. It would be great fun if I could get away with it.

The scheme succeeded beyond my wildest dreams. Scott Adams of Adventure International sent me his whole line of adventure games from Florida. Art Canfil of Cybernautics sent me his program *Taipan* from San Francisco. The Software Exchange (TSE) in Milford, New Hampshire, sent me a huge pile of games. And in return, everybody wanted to publish my program, a procedure that was a little different in the late 1970s than it is now. Then, programs were stored on cassette tape—a fairly slow and clumsy medium that was eventually replaced by floppy disks. Moreover, in those days no one thought to ask for *exclusive* publishing rights to a program, so with my permission Adventure International, TSE, and Cybernautics all published my game, with varying degrees of success. I was in seventh heaven, having never imagined that writing software could be profitable!

Compared with the effort of writing software, the activity of selling it was not only profitable but also remarkably fast-paced, right from the beginning. Four days after I sent *Galactic Empire* to Scott Adams in Florida, I received a call from Scott's wife, Alexis. Yes, they loved the program, she said. In fact, they already had orders for it, and if I would give her oral permission to publish, they would start shipping later that day. The contract would follow later. Scott and Alexis were as good as their word. I received my first royalty check, for a couple of hundred dollars, two weeks later. I was astonished. People were actually paying me to have fun!

I started to take the whole programming business a little more seriously, and in time my obsession with the TRS–80 began to destroy my law practice. I couldn't help myself. Even in the courtroom, I'd suddenly find myself thinking of a more efficient way to write a particular piece of code, or I'd realize that there was a logical defect in a program that wasn't doing what I wanted it to do. My legal briefs ended up with bits and pieces of programming code scribbled in the margins, and I could hardly wait to get back to the office to key my ideas into the machine to see whether they worked.

Finally, in October 1979, I dissolved my law practice. I

was having a lot more fun writing computer games than I was drawing up wills. The fact that I was also making a modest but steadily increasing income from my programming efforts had something to do with my decision, but at the time it wasn't at all clear that this was a prudent career move. I had no idea whether the freelance programming business was going to continue to be financially viable, but I abandoned my law career anyway because the microcomputer software world drew me in a way that I found irresistible.

It immediately struck me—when I realized just how possible it was to make a living at my kind of programming—that I had an opportunity to lead an altogether different way of life. It took me a while to accept that I had stumbled upon such a beautiful loophole in the rules of life, but once I did I knew that my job for the immediate future was to create fantasies and translate them into computer programs. If you think that sounds a lot more like play than work, you know how I reacted to the prospect of this new career. The kind of fascinating sci-fi sagas that had occupied my spare hours—flying interstellar craft to a thousand strange planets—was now my profession as well as my avocation.

It didn't take long for my new career to change the way I lived my life. Something very different from everything I had previously planned for myself suddenly became possible, and I was still young enough to be tempted by the prospect of a romantic journey into an uncertain future. So I went along with the opportunity to become an electronic-age vagabond.

I didn't need an office or more equipment than I could fit into the trunk of my car. In fact, I could write my fantasy programs from wherever I could plug in my computer, so I started traveling across America. With my dog in the front seat and my computer and a few other possessions in the back seat, I headed in the general direction of Oregon. I stopped along the way to visit friends and relatives, play with the computer, and shed the three years of Harvard Law School and four years of the juridical practice. I was free, for the first time in years.

Three thousand miles later, I arrived in Eugene, Oregon, where my brother Gary lived. He had given up his job with the March of Dimes and was now investing all his time and energy in his ill-fated importing business. One day when he was feeling particularly broke, I suggested that he try to sell some of my programs; after all, everyone else seemed to be making money doing it. By this time, I had followed up my first simulation program with another, *Galactic Trader;* eventually, I finished four programs in the *Galactic Saga* series. On the morning of February 20, 1980, Gary called a fellow named Ray Daly, owner of The Program Store in Washington, D.C., and talked him into ordering $300 worth of our products. We then officially formed a company, and, using a name from one of my science fiction simulations, we called ourselves Brøderbund. A software company was born.

That evening, Gary and I had a celebration dinner at a local restaurant to fortify us for the arduous task of filling Daly's order. Computer software was still sold in the form of cassette tapes, and so we spent most of the next day with three cassette tape recorders, dozens of cassettes, plastic packing bags, and staplers strewn all over the living room floor as we frantically tried to copy enough programs to fill the order on time. Our efforts were successful. We packed the cassettes into the plastic bags and sent them off. At the top of each bag was our (hastily produced) business card and a punched hole that retailers used to hang the bags on the pegboard racks that passed for point-of-purchase displays in those days.

Things moved very quickly from that point. We had some financial problems in our first year, but by the third year of operation, we had moved from Eugene to San Rafael, California, a community in Marin County, twenty minutes north of the Golden Gate Bridge. We had hired more than forty people to help us and were occupying a fairly large building. Our company was selling millions of dollars' worth of software annually. Software pioneers who had been only names in magazines or the heroes of hobbyist legends were now my colleagues, competitors, and, in some cases, friends.

Brøderbund is now around the tenth largest software publisher in the microcomputer industry, while the software industry itself has become a significant slice of the gross national product. Indeed, the software business, and particu-

larly software people, seems to have attracted a disproportionate amount of attention from the general public.

Most people are not particularly interested in investment
bankers or manufacturers of pantyhose. But the readers of
magazines as different as *Time* and *Ms.*, *Fortune* and *Playboy*,
Forbes and *Cosmopolitan* have been eagerly following the
tales of Adam Osborne and Steve Jobs, Bill Gates and Mitch
Kapor. Perhaps the sudden fascination with microcomputer
Wunderkinder is a result of the youth of these entrepreneurs.
Perhaps it is because people sense (or are told) that this mysterious, intangible, and volatile new commodity promises to
have an unprecedented impact on America and the world. It
also could be due to an interest in Horatio Alger stories like
ours and those of people who have made a lot more money
than Gary and I have.

Or perhaps it is because people are always intrigued by
extraordinary characters who do what they do because they
love doing it and, almost unintentionally, end up changing the
face of our society in the process. I know that I continue to be
fascinated with software people, many of whom happen to be
my relatives, my friends, my employees, and my business
associates. Some of them think and behave in ways that have
to be labeled eccentric. Some of them are no more eccentric
than an insurance salesman. Many of them are extremely
bright, even geniuses, when it comes to thinking up the intri-
cate codes that cause computers to serve as video games, software tutors, or electronic accountants. Some of them know little about programming but a great deal about marketing
products. All of these people share, in varying degrees, an
obsession with personal computer software—an obsession that
in fact led to the birth and phenomenal growth of an entire
industry.

The primary reason for this book is to tell the stories of
the remarkable people who created and have been the driving
force behind the microcomputer software industry. Although
I make no claim to being an official historian of the industry,
I hope to convey something of its unique nature by describing

the people I know or know about who have played major roles in the evolution of the software business from its infancy to its coming of age.

Time is highly compressed in the software business because computer technology changes so quickly. The period during which the events in this book took place, from the age of the first hobbyist computer, the Altair, to the present era of Apple and IBM, lasted only around ten years. The first, strictly hobbyist phase of the personal computer industry began in 1975, when a few intensely devoted hobbyists began to put together their first Altair kits. By 1978, the hobbyists were putting together companies to sell the first generation of home computers that didn't have to be assembled from kits. By 1980, the newborn video game and personal computer companies had grown at a dizzying speed into a billion-dollar industry.

For a time, it seemed that all who dipped their pans in the software stream came up with a few nuggets, if not an entire lode. The software gold rush began in 1980, the first of several years in which teenage programmers and software entrepreneurs who were still in their early twenties made personal fortunes.

Until the middle of 1983, companies continued to proliferate and prosper, riding the unprecedented annual rates of growth in the computer industry. Then the personal computer market began to level off, and people who had been making fortunes for years suddenly found themselves losing fortunes in months. This period, which extended through 1984, is the era generally referred to as "the shakeout." In examining the shakeout, which was at least as important to the history of the software industry as was the gold rush (albeit less glamorous), I have attempted to point out some of the underlying causes of several of the business disasters that occurred during that period.

In this book are the stories of people who lived the events of these various software eras. Although the individual stories overlap, the overall order of their presentation is roughly chronological, progressing from the hobbyist days through the early years, the gold rush period, and beyond the shakeout to the present.

Each of the people profiled in this book helped to shape the extraordinary character of the software industry. Intense, volatile, creative, lucrative, adventurous, and regularly eccentric—it is an industry that, in terms of its spirit and complexity, is quite unlike most other contemporary American businesses. Moreover, it is dominated not by a single type of individual but by a variety of people. The hobbyist-programmers might have started the whole thing, but the sudden blossoming of the home computer software industry came about as a result of the efforts of many different kinds of people who played very different roles—programmers, entrepreneurs, publishers, developers, and marketers. And the nature of their products varied just as widely across different software genres that addressed very different markets, from games to business productivity tools to educational programs. If anything, the software community is an eclectic collection of different interests, linked only by the personal computer that makes the market possible.

Some of the people I've written about here were included because of their importance to the software industry. Some people are included because they exemplify a certain kind of software legend. Some of them are my friends or acquaintances whose stories are closely related to mine. There are many stories I did not tell, including those of many friends. To them I apologize—my intent was more to give a feeling for the industry than to provide the definitive history.

Many of the principals in the industry, whom I did not know personally when the events described here happened, were interviewed for the purposes of this book. In other cases, where I did not interview the subject in person, I have done my best to sift the most likely true stories from the vast and contradictory lore of software legends, which are already becoming embellished with each retelling as the age of the Altair recedes into history.

Bill Gates and and Paul Allen are foremost among the people who are included here. Their names cannot be omitted from any history of the software industry—partially because of the continued success of their company, Microsoft, and partially because they were present at the beginning of the microcomputer era, during the pioneering Altair days. Gates was nineteen years old when he left Harvard to join Allen in New Mexico to create software for the first hobbyist microcomputer. Less than ten years later, the company they founded topped $100 million in sales.

Other major figures in the founding of the microcomputer software industry include Dan Bricklin and Bob Frankston, who came up with the first microcomputer spreadsheet, *VisiCalc*, and Dan Fylstra and Peter Jennings, whose company, VisiCorp, marketed Bricklin and Frankston's product, making it the first phenomenal best-seller in the micro market. Their program made the four principals millionaires, established personal computers in the business world, and ensured the early success of Apple because so many business people bought Apples to run *VisiCalc*.

Without programmers, there would be no software industry. The legendary programmers of the gold-rush years number in the dozens. I chose three for this book. One of them, Bill Budge, is not only an example of the new breed of programmer as fine artisan, but also an old friend of mine. His programs *Raster Blaster* and *Pinball Construction Set* were milestones in software history, acclaimed for their artistry as well as the sheer dollar volume of their sales.

Then there's Paul Lutus, the fabled programmer–hermit of the Oregon wilderness. Paul exemplifies the legend of the eccentric character with a knack for programming who made himself a millionaire by writing a best-selling program while living in his backwoods cabin.

The third programmer profiled here is another one of those who can't be excluded from any history of the software industry, although I don't know him personally. John Draper didn't make himself a millionaire like Lutus, or create a masterpiece of programming elegance like Bill Budge, but he was perhaps the first of the maverick techno-wizards because of his past career as a colorful anti-hero known as "Captain Crunch," king of the "phone phreaks" (until he was busted for playing with the phone company's switching network without paying for the privilege). Years later, a program he wrote led to one of the first and biggest entrepreneurial coups of the software gold rush.

Indeed, aggressive entrepreneurship has been one of the major forces behind the phenomenal growth of the software industry. Most of the early software entrepreneurs were programmers who discovered that they could make a lot of money marketing their own programs. Others saw the opportunity to make fortunes by marketing other people's products. Bob Leff and Dave Wagman, for example, founded a software distribution business that went from a shoestring budget to a $150 million annually in a little over four years. They distributed Broderbund's products when we first started publishing, and they even bought us disks when we couldn't afford to fill their orders.

Unlike me, Bob and Dave are the kind of successful entrepreneurs who take advantage of all the high-life perks of their occupation—from the champagne they gave away to their suppliers to the matched Porsches they bought for themselves. Like all the most successful entrepreneurs in the software Wild West show, they also work twelve to eighteen hours a day.

My friend Ken Williams has a different kind of entrepreneurial story altogether. Still living out his own brand of fantasy up in the Sierra foothills, he and his wife/partner, Roberta, and their tribe of well-heeled programmers make up the single largest component of the workforce in Oakhurst, California, and are the dominant cultural element in a territory where the last big action was the gold rush of 1849. Less than four years after Roberta convinced Ken to program the adventure-fantasy game she had designed, their company, "Sierra Online" (now called "Sierra"), reached a level of more than $6 million in annual sales.

Ken and Roberta's company was one of the first and most successful of the software publishers—companies like Microsoft, Brøderbund, Sirius, Synapse, and a dozen others profiled here, that concentrated on marketing products created by in-house or freelance programmers. A small number of these companies, most of them associated with Apple-oriented products, most of them located in California, were, along with Brøderbund, part of a loose group of friendly competitors I've called the Brotherhood.

Then there are the developers, who came along a little later than the first publishers. Developers come up with the ideas for new programs and hire programmers to create these products, which will then be sold or licensed to software publishers for marketing. Some of these developers, like Joyce Hakansson, concentrated on a specialized segment of the industry, such as educational software. Others specialized in games or productivity software. Some developers were either started by or backed by venture capitalists—groups of investors who often guided (and occasionally took over) the management of the companies they invested in.

Not all the software entrepreneurs were programmers, distributors, publishers, or developers. There were those like Al and Margot Tommervik, founders of *Softalk* magazine, whose focus was on the personal computer culture. In the case of the Tommerviks, their market and their community encompassed that segment of the computer subculture who were devoted to the use of Apple computers. The Tommerviks, who started their first magazine with the money Margot won on a television game show, were among the more prominent casualties of the software shakeout.

Because the computer revolution is a worldwide phenomenon, and because my own company in particular has had a long history of dealing with Japanese software companies, I have also written about Japan's software community and industry. Even as the companies mentioned in the foregoing paragraphs struggled to create an industry in the United States, a parallel struggle was taking place in Japan. There, hobbyists followed the development of microcomputers with every bit as much interest and enthusiasm as their American counterparts. And in response to the growing market in Japan for products made with or for microcomputers, a small group of Japanese entrepreneurs emerged to build a fledgling industry in their country.

Computer addiction knows no national boundaries, it

seems, and it appears that Japanese hobbyists are no more immune than Americans to the lure of entrepreneurship. Consider Masaaki Hoshi, who founded *I/O*, now the largest microcomputer magazine in Japan, strictly as a part-time enterprise to help him keep in touch with other hobbyists. As so many of the cottage entrepreneurs did here in the United States, he started small in 1976 and got caught up in a wholly unexpected wave of consumer enthusiasm for what had, until then, been interesting only to a small group of hobbyists.

Or consider Akio Gunji and Kazuhiko "Kay" Nishi, who worked with Hoshi until they saw an opportunity to compete with him. In 1977, they started their own magazine, *ASCII*, which they then used as a base to turn their operation into an empire that included one of the largest software publishers and distributors in Japan, and several of the most successful magazines in the industry as well.

One of the people who occasionally wrote articles for *I/O* and *ASCII* was Yuji Kudo, an amateur photographer and avid collector of model steam locomotives. When he started his own software company, he named it after his favorite locomotive and turned Hudson Soft into Japan's largest microcomputer software publisher. Another successful entrepreneur in Japan's software world was Jung-Eui Son, a software distributor and publisher who started his own magazine when his competitor's magazines wouldn't take his advertising. His distribution company, Soft Bank, which he started when he was a teenager, ended up as the largest microcomputer software distributor in Japan.

More than a few other software people have not yet been introduced, although their stories are told in later chapters: Among these are Mary Carol Smith and Don Fudge of Avant Garde Productions; Nasir Gebelli, the first superstar programmer; Scott Adams of Adventure International, my own first publisher, whose business has been eclipsed by those companies founded by many of his former employees; and Bill Baker, the twenty-one-year-old deal maker who built a company on the basis of one of John Draper's creations, then sold the company for $10 million on the eve of the shakeout.

There are still more whose stories we'll encounter along the way. For now, we'll start at the beginning of the personal computer era, way back in the "ancient" days of the mid-1970s, when the first microcomputer kits were assembled by many of the people who were to become the leaders of today's microcomputer software industry.

THE BIRTH
OF AN INDUSTRY

1

The Age of the Altair

In the beginning was the IBM mainframe. The microworld was formless and devoid of software. On the first day, Intel brought forth the 4004, fashioned from the Silicon of the Valley. MITS said 'Let there be Altair,' and the microcomputer was created. Then Microsoft, created in the image of Gates, begat the microcomputer software industry. The hackers were the first prophets, and the homebrewers were the patriarchs, but the children of Intel remained in bondage until the Woz led them to the promised Apple with one bite missing. . . .

The idea of a Scripture of the Microcult is not entirely a joke. The origins of the microcomputer industry are indeed spoken of in quasi-mythological tones by many people in the personal computer culture, even though the events upon which the myths are based occurred no more than a decade ago. Gates and the Woz are real people who happen to have created multimillion-dollar companies before they were thirty. MITS was a real place that symbolizes to computer freaks what Kitty Hawk means to aviation fanatics. And there is a definite evangelical streak to be found beneath the entrepreneurial surface of the founders of the earliest microcomputer businesses.

Many of my colleagues started out as hobbyists and ended up as industrialists, and although their fortunes have diverged in a dozen unlikely directions over the past ten years, many share a reverent nostalgia for the 1975–76 era—the Age of the Altair. Indeed, for many, that era represents a kind of magical time, but in reality it was directly experienced by only a rare few survivors who still tell the tales of Altair to the multitudes of recent converts.

Altair was the name of the first widely used hobbyist computer based on the new microprocessor technology. It was a do-it-yourself kit that preceded the factory-assembled Apples and Commodores and IBM PCs. Compared with today's personal computers, the Altair was computationally puny and unbelievably difficult to program. But it inspired a group of people who believed it was possible to have computers for their own personal use. They were solitary, garage-based computer tinkerers who called their avocation "home-brewing" and who were all surprised when they discovered how many others were fiddling with Altairs, or patiently waiting for Altair parts to be shipped to them.

But these Altair users were more than the forerunners of the personal computer enthusiasts who were to buy Apples and PCs five or six years later. They were the spearhead of the microcomputer revolution, and although some of them even knew it, none of that first wave could have predicted how much money, power, and attention would come their way over the course of a decade.

Out of that hobbyist network of a few thousand people, a dozen or so ended up creating the personal computer technology we see today in millions of homes and offices. Some of those people are still tinkering—happily or not. A few of them are personally worth tens or hundreds of millions of dollars. Not all of them are on speaking terms with one another any longer, but in the beginning, all were unified by their one common interest: the microcomputer. In fact, the microcomputer industry is the only major one in the world that started out as a club for teenage enthusiasts.

Both the hardware and software branches of the industry were directly influenced by these enthusiasts who, as relatively small groups of hobbyists, gathered in the mid-1970s to share ideas. Of those groups, two are most notable. The first included the now-legendary amateur computer builders in the San Francisco Bay Area who called themselves the Homebrew Computer Club and who ended up being the founding fathers of the microcomputer hardware industry. The second group consisted of a pair of very young but decidedly professional programmer–entrepreneurs from Seattle. It was their creation that was the beginning of what has become today's microcomputer software industry.

Until recently, the better known story behind the microcomputer revolution has been on the *hardware* side of things, and yet, as a mathematically minded programmer would say, hardware is necessary for making a computer, but it isn't sufficient. You need more than circuitry to make a computer do anything useful. You need *software*—coded instructions that turn a computer into a word processor or spreadsheet, telecommunication terminal or video game. The lesser-known chapters of this story, then, are about software, and they're chapters where people like me step into the scenario.

Still, it wasn't until the waning days of the homebrew era that software people started to become important. When the Age of Altair gave way to the eras of Atari and Apple, the software epoch had only just begun. Its dawning marks the point in history where the physical components of computers became less important than the human ability to think of new things to do with these machines. Nevertheless, no book about microcomputer software people can exclude the Altair story or a discussion of microcomputer hardware, nor can it leave out an early tribute to Ed Roberts, Paul Allen and Bill Gates, Steve Wozniak, and the other legendary homebrewers whose hobby unexpectedly gave birth to a new and unprecedented kind of industry.

Although I know several of these founding fathers, my own roots in the industry do not go as far back as the Altair Era. I was a young attorney working in Chicago when the era began and the first microcomputer kits were marketed by a company located between a laundromat and a massage parlor in a shopping center in Albuquerque. I didn't write my first line of microcomputer code until three years after the now-famous January 1975 issue of *Popular Electronics* told of a wondrous new toy for electronic enthusiasts. That new toy was an affordable computer, and the company that sold it by mail order was called Micro Instrumentation and Telemetry Systems—fondly remembered as "MITS."

A brief discussion about the technology and history of the microprocessor and microcomputer is necessary in order to explain what was so important about the mail-order microcomputers sold in the 1970s by a small company that no longer exists. Computers are not as hard to understand as they have been made out to be. You might need to know esoteric details of electronic circuit design if you intend to build a computer, and a healthy knowledge of how the computer operates is helpful if you want to successfully program one. But you need to know only a few simple, general principles to understand how computers work.

The first principle has more to do with economics than electronics, and it is also the hardest to believe: Computers get smaller, more powerful, and less expensive as time passes. Computers and software change very quickly because the electronic technology on which computers are based also changes quickly. Most of these changes are triggered by the continuing miniaturization of computer components. In fact, the computer revolution has been strongly influenced by the electronic miniaturization revolution, the importance of which lies in the relationship between the size of electronic components and the efficiency of computers built from those components.

To understand the power of software, you need to know only two essential facts about computing machinery. First, a computer is a machine for interpreting instructions, especially instructions that tell it how to imitate other machines. Second, both the machine that interprets the instructions and the instructions themselves are built from very simple elements—electrical switches that can be turned on and off. In essence, a computer is a collection of switches, which can be vacuum tubes, transistors, integrated circuits, or any other technology that can create a network of devices that are either on or off.

The real power of a computer lies in *how* and in *what patterns* you turn those switches on and off—the *software*. When you want to create switching patterns that can accomplish complex tasks like calculating the results of physics equations or storing census statistics or creating pictures on a screen, you need lots of switches—very fast ones.

The faster those switches can operate, and the more switches you can put into a computer, the more things you can do with the computer. And smaller switches can operate at higher speeds than large ones. At the heart of the microprocessor revolution is the fact that the switches got smaller and faster. As the speed of the computer's fundamental elements increased, so did the sheer informational volume—the "memory," or the amount of coded on-and-off information that the computer could store. Over the four decades since the first electronic digital computer was invented, computing power increased more than a millionfold.

But the speed and number of switches are not the only aspects of computers that are affected by the size of the basic components. The heat generated by all that switching is another aspect, and it is also a major problem in computer design. Big components tend to get hot, especially when packed together in large numbers in an enclosed space, and that means that electronic computers are limited in their size and power. The first computers were built out of vacuum tubes, which were very hot and very big. No computer with a capacity that surpassed a certain threshold amount of computing power could be devised by using vacuum tubes. Such machines would melt before anything substantially useful could be done with them.

Not long after the first tube computers reached their heat limit, however, a discovery in the field of subatomic physics made considerably more efficient switching elements possible. In the late 1940s the transistor was invented, and that meant that computers could be constructed from elements that were much smaller and much cooler than the old tube technology. As a consequence, "smarter" computers could be built—computers that could follow more complex strings of instructions.

Besides their cool and rapid manner of operating, transistors had another advantage over the old computer elements—they were cheaper than tubes. Indeed, a paradoxical phenomenon has governed the evolution of computer technology: As computer components became smaller, cooler, and more powerful, they also became cheaper. They also happened to come along at the perfect time. The pressure to develop electronics and computer technology to their furthest limits, and substantial financial resources to support large-scale research and development efforts, were provided by two of the most powerful institutions in history—the Defense Department of the United States government and IBM. In the years that followed World War II, this fortuitous combination of fundamental scientific breakthroughs, breakneck engineering, and unprecedented economic benefits eventually made computer technology an integral part of all the levels of society.

Computers are valuable because they multiply the power of the human brain, in the way levers are useful tools for multiplying the power of the human arm. A lever, however, is only for moving a large object, but a computer can do much more than that. It can command machines to move large objects, or it can perform mathematical calculations, or it can put words on a screen. It is an all-purpose tool that empowers anyone who can afford to use it. In fact, the sudden empowerment made possible by available computers has happened so fast that our society has barely begun to feel its impact. As computers have become cheaper, in terms of computations per dollar, the computer-using population has expanded dramatically.

In the 1950s, computers more powerful than those used previously by the Defense Department were being installed by large institutions like banks and corporations. By the 1970s, computers of even greater power were being used by small businesses. Now, in the 1980s, middle-class households can afford computers that only the national government could afford to build thirty years ago, and it is reasonable to expect that people thirty years from now will be able to afford computers that are as powerful as the mightiest supercomputers being used today.

While computers kept getting smaller, more powerful, and cheaper throughout the 1950s and 1960s, they were still too expensive to be made accessible to the exclusive use of one person. By 1970, a computer still couldn't be called an affordable device for individuals, but its cost had fallen from millions of dollars to thousands. By the early and mid-1970s, another series of breakthroughs in miniaturization was underway. Researchers for electronic companies had already discovered ways to put thousands of components into ultra-miniature circuits known as "integrated circuits"—or, as they came to be known, "chips." These chips made all kinds of electronic devices possible—satellite communications, cheap color televisions, stereos, and radios, as well as personal computers.

In 1969, engineers at Intel Corporation designed a chip that had all the switching elements needed for a computer's central processing unit—the historic 4004 chip. In 1972, a somewhat more powerful version—the 8008—was developed by the same engineers. While the 4004 could handle information only in 4-bit chunks, the 8008 was a true 8-bit processor, and this boosted the device's potential applications from the realm of calculators to the world of true computers.

The 4004 and the 8008 were the first *microprocessors*—electronic devices capable of processing information—but they were not quite *computers*, which are information-processing machines that must possess specific capabilities. The 8008 had the basic information-processing capability and the built-in "language" of instructions that could enable it to become a computer, but other devices had to be connected to the chip in order for people to actually create and use programs. This wasn't a simple matter; you had to have a pretty advanced knowledge of electronics to assemble the different parts of the computer.

Still, a subtle but crucial shift in the course of events was triggered by these devices, although only a few people recognized their significance when they were created. In fact, neither the world at large nor the electronics world in particular heralded the arrival of the Intel 4004. Intel was just looking for a new kind of chip that the company could sell to all the other companies that make consumer devices out of microelectronic chips.

In any case, at this point in the story we are still talking about hardware expertise, but now we are beginning to talk about *computer* designers, not just electronic component manufacturers, for the microprocessor was the first electronic computer technology cheap enough to make it possible for ordinary people to afford relatively powerful computers (although, as we shall soon see, the first people to use these homebrew computers were far from ordinary).

The microprocessor has often been called "a computer on a chip," which is slightly misleading, since it isn't possible to use one of these chips as a real working computer without connecting it to additional electronic equipment. That is where MITS and the homebrewers came in. Ed Roberts, the owner of MITS, entered the annals of computer legend when he decided to build a kit for putting a microprocessor together with all the other necessary components. Little did he know that there was a vast, previously unknown market for these devices. Hundreds of young computer enthusiasts across the country were fiercely determined to get their hands on real working personal computers. The year was 1974.

Roberts hadn't started out to be a computer entrepreneur. He had originally wanted to be a doctor, and last I heard, about a year ago, he actually was in medical school in Florida. But he received electronics training in the Air Force, and in the late 1960s he started his own company and sold radio equipment to model airplane hobbyists—hence the name "Microelectronic Instrumentation and Telemetry Systems."

Before the Altair kit came along, MITS faced some rocky times, especially when Roberts decided to get into the calculator business at precisely the wrong time to compete with the Texas Instruments juggernaut. But he moved on to microprocessors and shopped around for a better chip than the 8008. The problem with the 8008 was the way its instruction set hampered the efforts of programmers. He finally purchased a quantity of Intel's successor to that chip, the 8080, for $75 apiece. The price was right, and the 8080 instruction set was far more amenable to computer software design.

A man named Les Solomon, who was the technical editor of *Popular Electronics* magazine, heard about Roberts's devices and convinced MITS to provide the original working model for a cover article on the first affordable computer kit. In January 1975, the article appeared. The mail-order kits sold for $397, and Roberts was hoping for a few dozen orders so that he could keep the business going. The first day he checked his mail after the article appeared, he found more orders than he had hoped for in a *year*.

Nobody could have predicted how many people were eager to spend $400 on a computer kit. Roberts was swamped. Within a few weeks, MITS' bank balance went from nearly half a million dollars in the red to a quarter of a million in the black. But his small company couldn't ship the kits fast enough to satisfy some of Roberts's most fanatical early customers. Some of them actually went to Albuquerque, prepared to camp out on his doorstep until their Altair was ready!

The origin of the name *Altair* is also a microcomputer legend. According to Roberts and Solomon, they were speculating on the phone about possible names for the kit before the article appeared. Solomon asked his daughter, who was watching "Star Trek" at the time, what Roberts ought to call the device. She replied that in that evening's episode the starship *Enterprise* was heading for a star called Altair. So Roberts put the world *Altair* on the cover of the machine, in those hard-to-read "computer letters" that were considered "futuristic" in the 1970s.

Still, programming an Altair was an almost inconceivable tedious business at first. Nowadays, people program by using their keyboards and video screens to write the symbols for a program in what is known as a "high-level language" (for example, BASIC). After they write their program, they enter it into the computer, and then another program known as a compiler or interpreter translates the high-level program to the kind of language—the patterns of on-and-off impulses—that the machine understands. Back in 1975, an Altair owner had to create even the simplest program by laboriously turning switches on and off by hand.

The lack of a high-level language was a big handicap, but there were other problems with the Altair besides that. You can't run complicated software unless the hardware has a certain information-handling capacity. The memory of the earliest model was infinitesmal. The first Altair held 256 bytes of information—approximately 2000 on or off impulses. By contrast, most home computers today have 256 *kilo*bytes of information—a memory that is a thousand times as large as the Altair's. There was no way to feed information to the processor other than by setting the switches, one a time, by hand—and if you made a mistake you had to start from the beginning.

A volunteer army of garage tinkerers set out to solve these problems by creating software, memory expansion devices, and input–output devices. From all accounts, and from the many innovations that came forth from the homebrew reign, it was an open, enthusiastic, brilliant, intense, esoteric, fun, and exuberant effort—the finest days of the hacker tradition.

Although all the homebrewers of the mid-1970s started out as orthodox members of the Altair cult, they quickly developed their own patriarchs, their own legends, their own shrines. The homebrew mythology started shortly after the birth of the Altair and centered on northern California, rather than New Mexico. The Apple empire, the ill-fated but revolutionary Osborne Computer Corporation, and almost all of the earliest microcomputer-related companies trace their origins back to an anarchistic, ragtag group of computer zealots, the Homebrew Computer Club, who started meeting in the auditorium of Stanford University's Linear Accelerator building in the spring of 1975.

Lee Felsenstein, a veteran of the Free Speech Movement, a former reporter for *The Berkeley Barb*, a lifelong electronics freak, and the "anarche" who presided over the early Home-brew Computer Club meetings, later became famous, if not rich, by designing the Osborne I—the first "portable" personal computer. Steve Wozniak, barely out of high school, was another homebrewer whose attempts to outdo the Altair led to a company that grew from a garage to a billion-dollar opera-tion in a few swift years. Dozens of other members of the Homebrew Computer Club started their own companies in the post-Altair, pre-Apple era—with varying degrees of success.

Important as they might have been to the personal com-puter revolution, the entrepreneurial success and engineering brilliance of the homebrewers is not as directly relevant to our story as is the history of two other Altair enthusiasts who launched the microcomputer software industry. These two homebrewers-turned-industrialists were teenagers at the time, as were many of the early Altair fans. They were far from inexperienced in either the computer world or the busi-ness arena, however, and their creations marked the transi-tion of microcomputer programming from a freewheeling amateur affair to a full-fledged business enterprise.

Paul Allen and Bill Gates were their names, and when the Altair came along they were already professional pro-grammers. In the 1960s, when they first met at Seattle's exclusive Lakeside School and began their long, profitable partnership, Paul Allen was fifteen and Bill Gates was thir-teen. They rode bicycles to work years before they owned a company car. Despite their youth, their ability to find the flaws in adult-sized minicomputer programs got them their first job.

A company in Seattle had just received a new minicom-puter from Digital Equipment Corporation (known as DEC). The Seattle firm, a company called the Computer Center Cor-poration (known to the young hackers as "C cubed"), made a deal with DEC: As long as C cubed could uncover bugs in the new computer's system software, it wouldn't have to start pay-ing for its use of the computer. This was a mutually profitable arrangement, since both the inventor and the user of the computer had a practical need to track down and eliminate all the programming errors that could cause the system to "crash" and stop working. Gates and Allen were therefore employed by C cubed, which offered them an equivalent deal: These exceptionally bright kids would be allowed to play with the computer, free of charge, for as long as they could come up with new bugs. They did their job so well that they were soon earning real pay.

After several months, DEC, fearing that these hot young bug hunters might find flaws in the system indefinitely, backed down on its original arrangement with C cubed and demanded payment for use of the computer. Meanwhile, Gates had grown so adept at the black art of computer crashing that he had learned to defeat the security procedures of several well-known computer systems. Crashing systems was something of an accomplishment back then, since it proved that one could out-think the people who had designed the system security. The practice had not yet earned the notoriety it found fifteen years later, when the movie *WarGames* brought the stereotype of the mischievous hacker to public awareness.

By 1971, when Bill Gates had finished his sophomore year of high school and Paul Allen had graduated, their reputation as bug hunters had spread. They were soon hired by a major company, TRW, which was in need of troubleshooters who knew how to find software flaws in exactly the same kind of DEC system that Allen and Gates knew so well. TRW had been contracted to develop the complex and critically important computer system that would control the electrical power generated by the Bonneville dam on the Columbia River. The reliability standards for such a system were, understandably, extremely high. The young troubleshooters ended up making a significant contribution to the project.

Eager to capitalize on their expertise, Gates and Allen developed a computer program for analyzing the traffic-flow data collected by those rubber tubes that transportation departments stretch across highways. Under the company name Traf-O-Data, the young entrepreneurs tried to sell their service to various municipalities; these efforts failed to make them rich. By this time, Bill was in his last year of high school while Paul was studying at Washington State. They got together again during their summer vacation, when they secured summer jobs at another computer giant—Honeywell.

Meanwhile, the miniaturization revolution was proceeding at such a rapid pace that Allen and Gates both knew that affordable computers were going to arrive sooner or later. When they did, these two young entrepreneurs wanted to get in on the ground floor of what they suspected would be a major revolution within the computer industry. In fact, Allen tried to convince Gates that they should write a BASIC interpreter for Intel's 8008 microprocessor, but Gates felt that the chip's built-in language was too clumsy.

Their entrepreneurial speculations were based on their knowledge of the way microprocessor chips were set up to receive instructions from programmers. When a microprocessor chip is built, certain circuits are put into it to perform elementary information-processing operations. One such circuit would take two inputs and add them together, for example. Another such circuit could perform an elementary logical operation such as opening a circuit when either one of the two inputs was on. These wired-in elementary commands are known as the *instruction set* of that chip, and they constitute the "words" of any higher languages that communicate instructions to that kind of chip. Each chip has its own instruction set, but all instruction sets are written in the same code, known as *machine language*, which is based on an "alphabet" of on-and-off switches.

A BASIC interpreter for the Intel 8008, then, would be a program written in the language of the chip's hardwired instruction set. The purpose of such a program is to make life easier for programmers. In the machine's native language of ones and zeroes (the numerical equivalent of the on-or-off states of the switching elements) it would take literally dozens of machine instructions to perform a simple arithmetic operation like multiplying two times three. First, the numbers each have to be assigned specific positions in the processor's memory. Then the built-in multiplication procedure has to be directed to first multiply the contents of one memory location by the contents of another memory location and then to put the product of the operation in yet another specific memory location.

Programming anything of significant complexity with such a nit-picking and endlessly specific code is like writing a novel with alphabet blocks. The interpreter program would enable the BASIC programmer to write a command like "PRINT 2*3," then enter it into the computer along with the BASIC interpreter program, which would translate the command into the proper 8008 instructions, apply it to the data, and return the correct answer on the screen or printout.

After Allen and Gates decided to pass up the 8008, Allen quit Washington State to continue working with Honeywell and moved east to Honeywell's Boston office. In the fall of 1974, Gates was at Harvard, just across the Charles River. The next time they contemplated the state of microprocessor-based software was the afternoon Allen saw the historic Altair issue of *Popular Electronics* at a Harvard Square newsstand. This new computer kit was based on the Intel 8080 microprocessor, an improved version of the 8008 chip they had originally rejected as the target for a commercial software effort. This was it—their opportunity to expand their entrepreneurial venture, begun with Traf-O-Data, into the software business.

Although they didn't even have an Altair, they called Ed Roberts and asked if he was interested in a BASIC interpreter. Roberts told them that several other programmers had already made the same proposal, and as far as he was concerned he would buy the first BASIC that would actually run on an Altair. Gates and Allen promised him delivery of their interpreter in three weeks. They then programmed a larger computer to simulate an Altair, and by using the simulation rather than the actual hardware, they created the BASIC interpreter they promised. It took twice as long as they had expected—not an unusual turn of events in the software business.

Six weeks after their conversation with Roberts, Allen finally delivered a paper tape that contained, in a code consisting of a pattern of holes punched into the paper, his and Gates's version of BASIC for the Altair. This was before disk drives were cheap enough for small computers, so punched paper tape (as ancient as that technology sounds) had to be used to feed the program to the computer. After a tape reader converted the pattern of holes into on and off impulses that automatically set the Altair's memory-location switches, the Altair was ready to receive BASIC commands. The remarkable thing about that tape is that it worked the first time—a virtually unheard-of event in the bug-prone world of software. It was an especially noteworthy feat, considering the fact that they didn't have an Altair to test it on!

Within a month, Roberts had hired Paul Allen away from Honeywell. Bill Gates stayed at Harvard while Paul Allen went to New Mexico to become MITS' software director. In the meantime, they had renamed Traf-O-Data Micro-Soft, later to be shortened to Microsoft. Then Gates took a leave of absence from Harvard (in fact he never returned) and moved to Albuquerque. He and Allen hired a programmer by the name of Monte Davidoff to help them enhance their BASIC interpreter. MITS was in ferment. The Altair freaks were already drifting in to check on their orders and become involved in the operation. Gates and Allen, perfectionists since their days as consultants for TRW, didn't exactly mesh with Roberts, who was strictly a seat-of-the-pants guy. But they were on to something hot.

Gates wrote the disk operating system program for the first Altair disk drives in a famous marathon session in February 1976. According to one of the legends that have since become a prerequisite for homebrew software immortality, he apparently sequestered himself in a motel room with a computer, pencils, and notebooks until the task was complete. The same story is told of Wozniak and the creation of Apple's first disk operating system. In any case, 1976 was also the year that Roberts's competitors began to appear, in the form of companies like IMSAI, Processor Technology, and Cromemco—all founded by members of the Homebrew Computer Club. Given the increasing competition, Allen and Gates's BASIC interpreter became a major selling point for the Altair.

But in the meantime, it had also become a source of conflict between MITS, Microsoft, and the homebrewers. A lot of people objected to the idea of selling software—especially for $500, which was the price of Microsoft BASIC. Some people refused to pay for it. Others made copies of the punched paper tape and distributed them for free. A $500 BASIC interpreter was simply a philosophical affront to the inner circles of the personal computer cult. The hacker tradition went back to the early 1960s, when similarly obsessed computer enthusiasts at MIT created the software for the kind of interactive computers that led to personal computers. And hacker tradition dictated that software was supposed to be free.

Gates didn't agree. In February 1976, at the same time he was creating the Altair disk operating system, he also wrote a now-infamous manifesto titled "Open Letter to Hobbyists," which was published in the Homebrew Computer Club newsletter. He pointed out that "as the majority of hobbyists must be aware, most of you steal your software. Hardware must be paid for, but software is something to share. Who cares if the people who worked on it get paid?" A lot of the homebrewers didn't react kindly to this bluntly worded accusation by a nineteen-year-old programmer who was clearly interested in becoming a successful entrepreneur.

In retrospect, that rift between two factions of an obscure group of highly technical young amateurs appears to have been the birth pang of an infant industry. But very few people, other than maybe Paul Allen and Bill Gates, were thinking of industries or fantasizing about software empires back in 1976 and 1977. Most were content at the time to keep their hobby—and whatever differences of opinion they might have about that hobby—to themselves. Their arguments were still in the family, for they were all part of a single community. But in a very short time, these amateurs would find that they were no longer obscure.

2

From VisiCalc
to Activision:
The Beginning of
the Software Industry

The year 1977 marked the beginning of an entirely new era in
the computer revolution. In the spring of 1977, both the Apple
II and the Commodore PET were born in the same place—the
first West Coast Computer Faire. The Faire was an unexpectedly popular, totally enthusiastic convergence and celebration
by thousands of disciples of the new doctrine of the personal
computer. The man responsible for convening the Faire was
one of the most mischievous and skillful social organizers of
the personal computer culture, a somewhat older, definitely
more radical associate of the homebrewers—Jim Warren.

Warren already had a reputation as a flamboyant social
organizer by the time he got hooked on computing and
decided that everybody else ought to get in on the thrill.
Before that he had been chairman of the mathematics department at a Catholic women's college on the fringe of Silicon
Valley. After five years, he was fired in the midst of a scan-
dal. It seems that the college administration was not amused
by the reports from *Time*, the BBC, and *Playboy* that had
documented the wild parties that he was having at his home.
In Warren's words, these parties ". . . were rather sedate by
any common standards, except people didn't have to have
clothes on."

Following his dismissal from the college, he looked
around for new employment and happened upon a job at

Stanford University that required programming skills. He was not particularly qualified for the position. But he learned quickly while on the job, and like many others, he found that he had a talent and an enthusiasm for the art and science of programming. He was soon involved in a crusade to "bring computing to the people." He edited an enthusiasts' magazine, one with a social conscience and sense of humor as well as pages of technical jargon. Its title, *Dr. Dobb's Journal of Computer Calisthenics and Orthodontia*, was a programmers' joke based on the magazine's subtitle, *Running Light without Overbyte*, which referred to the limited memory capacity of early microcomputers.

By 1976, computer hobbyists were beginning to attend national shows in New Jersey, Denver, and Detroit. Warren, who had attended several of these shows, thought that the organizers had not done justice to the spirit of the movement and that the shows lacked what he felt was an essential element: a party-like atmosphere. One thing they know about out in California is how to throw a party, and with Warren's own slightly scandalous credentials as a socializer, he became determined to throw his own bash for computer enthusiasts. He saw his show as a potentially joyous event, a celebration of the liberating advent of personal computing. He envisioned organizing something like the Renaissance Faires that at the time were immensely popular in the San Francisco Bay Area. He then formed a company, signed up exhibitors at $300 apiece, and, renting the San Francisco Civic Auditorium for the event, convened the first West Coast Computer Faire in April 1977.

The event was a milestone, remembered with reverence and glee by those who participated—a Woodstock for the personal computer generation. People who would be running multimillion-dollar operations a few years later were manning their booths and talking about their products. The Apple II made its debut. Companies were born. Introductions were made. Visionaries traded crazy predictions about how there would soon be millions instead of thousands of people in this personal computer community.

In the aftermath of the Faire, and by one of those twists of fate that are called "history" long after they happen, Microsoft grew overwhelmingly in its importance while MITS disappeared. Roberts's company, whose Altair had been worth $13 million in gross sales in 1976, was sold in May 1977 to a company called Pertec for what Roberts said was "essentially 6 million dollars." Gates and Allen decided that their BASIC interpreter would not be part of the acquisition—thus signaling the end of their relationship with Ed Roberts. Pertec management brought in some three-piece-suit types who immediately alienated the fanatically devoted MITS employees. The Altair was facing stiff competition in the market at just the time MITS' original crew was departing.

By late 1977, the first wave of home computers like the Altair, the Sol, and the IMSAI were sharing the marketplace with Commodore's PET and a model put together by a couple of homebrewers, both named Steve, who decided to give their elegantly garage-engineered product the unlikely name of *Apple*. The hardware hobbyists were building an industry right in the backyard of the mainframe giants. And the software entrepreneurs were coming up with programs for those new, small, affordable computers—programs that would quickly change the way offices operated, businesses were run, and teenagers entertained themselves.

Microsoft in particular continued to turn out different versions of BASIC as the different brands of personal computer grew in number, diversity, and power. Allen and Gates eventually moved to Bellevue, an affluent, woodsy suburb of Seattle, to expand a company that would in time become a major force in the software business.

From 1975 through 1977, personal computers were mostly for hobbyists who were willing to learn how to program in BASIC or even get down to circuit boards and soldering irons to put their equipment together. Homebrew computers were exciting only to that tiny minority who loved to work with their hands as well as their heads. The far vaster audience of people, however, didn't care how computers were put together. They became owners primarily because they were drawn to what computers could *do* for them. And by the late 1970s, personal computers could do more than ever before, thanks mainly to the development of video displays and the development of better software. It was, in other words, the creation of spreadsheets, word processors, and adventure games—*programs*—in conjunction with improved hardware technology that turned computers into consumer items.

In the late 1970s, prior to my own entry into the software industry, three different programs virtually created the mass market for personal computers. First, there was *VisiCalc*, which convinced businesspeople and everyone who worked with numbers that the potential pragmatic gains of being able to experiment with financial projections and to prepare business presentations made buying an Apple a worthwhile investment. Then *WordStar* showed typists, writers, and anyone who worked with words that a small computer could enable them to accomplish tasks that were either tedious or impossible to do with an old-fashioned typewriter. Finally, *Adventure Land* and other "fantasy simulation" games showed people of all ages that the small computer could be used as a fantastic toy and a means of amplifying the power of imagination. These games also advanced the notion that computers could be used in the home.

In many ways, *VisiCalc* created the Apple empire and gave it both a toehold in the small-business market for computers and a fanatic following in the hobbyist world. This program, the first electronic spreadsheet for microcomputers, was written in 1978 and 1979 by Bob Frankston and Dan Bricklin, who years before had been roommates at MIT. It originated when Bricklin, as a graduate student at Harvard Business School, was given a particularly onerous homework assignment—to prepare spreadsheet analyses of various hypothetical companies. The professor gave the students a mass of financial data and lists of assumptions, and the students had to make intricately cross-referenced calculations in order to project those companies' fortunes at specified times in the future.

Bricklin, a former professional programmer, suspected that the tedium involved in preparing these projections would be enormously relieved if their required calculations and cross-indexing were programmed for a microcomputer to do. He then took his idea to Frankston, an even more accomplished programmer. They worked on the program together, and the result, in October 1978, was the first prototype of *Visi-Calc*. Their enormously successful software development company, Software Arts, was born.

As it turns out, one of Bricklin's classmates at the Business School had his own small software publishing firm. His name was Dan Fylstra, and he had recently started Personal Software as a means of selling the *Micro Chess* program written by his partner, Peter Jennings. When Fylstra saw Bricklin and Frankston's creation, he invited them to a business meeting at a Chinese restaurant in Cambridge. There the cofounders of Software Arts agreed to produce an Apple-compatible version of *VisiCalc* that would be marketed by Fylstra and Jennings's firm.

Several years later, the two companies found themselves in a bitter conflict, the substance of which will be discussed later. But in the meantime, the early 1980s were exceptionally lucrative years for all parties involved. Apple, although initially skeptical about the usefulness of *VisiCalc*, ended up selling millions of computers to businesspeople who wanted to perform spreadsheet analysis and were interested in a tool that could help with their hardest task—predicting the future. Frankston and Bricklin made close to $10 million as a result of that agreement in a Chinese restaurant. And microcomputer software as a whole was becoming a far bigger business every week, largely as a result of their program.

At about the same time that the spreadsheet entrepreneurs were programming in Massachusetts, another enormously influential and lucrative program was created in California. Seymour Rubinstein, one of the earliest hardware entrepreneurs, had recently left the ill-fated IMSAI corporation (which folded in 1979, a victim of its marketing strategy, its erratic hardware, and competition from more advanced machines) to start his own company, MicroPro. Sometime after he published a filing program and a primitive word-processing program, he received several letters from people asking for a more powerful text editing program, like Michael Shrayer's *Electric Pencil*, which was the first commercial microcomputer word processing program.

Rubinstein, like any smart entrepreneur, responded to the needs of the market. He commissioned a top-notch programmer by the name of Rob Barnaby to create a word-processing program called *WordStar*. The program was released in mid-1979. It became an instant hit and was near the top of every best-seller chart until early 1985.

By 1983, MicroPro's revenues had exceeded $50 million, making it, by some people's estimates, the largest microcomputer software company in the world. But the question of whose estimates one wants to believe is a notorious trigger for heated debate among software people. Trying to arrange companies in rank order is a tricky exercise, especially in such a volatile industry. When this book was written MicroPro and Microsoft were running neck-and-neck for the number one spot, but MicroPro was facing internal problems and Microsoft was still coming on strong. By the time this book is published, the top slot on the charts may well have changed.

But regardless of this ongoing conflict over estimates, there is one point on which there has never been any dispute between the market gurus and prognosticators: In everybody's opinion, *WordStar* was an all-time runaway money-maker. The success of this program demonstrated that a single piece of intellectual property, created by a single individual, could bring in revenues of hundreds of millions of dollars in just a few years.

Word processing was a revolution unto itself. Indeed, because of word-processing software, a major change in society took place in a very short period of time. In 1979, only the largest business offices had computers—and those were always enclosed in special rooms, somewhere off in the data processing department, and were tended and administered to by computer experts. But some years later, there were in many offices more computers than typewriters, and you would be hard-pressed to find many businesses of reasonable size that didn't have at least one word processor. In the years following *WordStar*'s introduction, that venerable institution, the typing pool, began to disappear; and in general, the way people in offices and universities deal with text was irrevocably altered.

By the early 1980s, the business world was adopting word processing on a large scale. By the mid-1980s, with the advent of low-cost word-processing software like Broderbund's *Bank Street Writer*, word processing has begun to saturate the home market. And by the late 1980s, the typewriter may be on its way to the museum along with other obsolete curiosities like slide rules.

The third category of microcomputer software that took off in the late 1970s was geared for entertainment and was not business-oriented at all. The arrival of the first simulation games provided unexpected and, to many, far more exciting reasons for using a computer. A *simulation*, in terms of a computer, refers to a program that presents a realistic model of a process, an object, a series of events, a real world, or a hypothetical universe. Mathematical representations underlie all simulations, which is why computers are necessary to keep track of even a simple simulated universe. The model itself is presented on a screen or paper printout in the form of words and numbers or even in graphically displayed patterns.

Computer simulation techniques were originally developed for serious purposes like designing airplanes. That they could also be used as the basis for a particularly addicting variety of recreation—the fantasy simulation—was a fact initially recognized by a gleeful and talented bunch of young men who ran amok on MIT's computers more than twenty years ago. In fact, most software people agree that the term *hacker* originated with those early programmers, who seem to have discovered everything from the "serious" computerized gaming of chess programs to the purely recreational field of computer graphics games.

But these programmers, many of them MIT dropouts, had nevertheless been hired by MIT's computer development laboratories because of their prodigious programming ability. Not only was the software for the first interactive computer systems their creation, but artificial intelligence research, the construction of time-sharing software systems, and other landmarks in software development and computer science all came out of the hackers' headquarters in Cambridge's Technology Square. They were renowned for their accomplishments in advancing computer research and notorious for their irreverent attitudes and often unorthodox lifestyles.

And of course, while doing their more purposive work, they also delighted in finding ways to use computers to play games of various kinds. In 1961, for example, they got their hands on the first minicomputer, the PDP-1, which had a large, round video display screen, and they started playing around with different programs that would demonstrate the machine's graphic capabilities. One hacker, Stephen Russell, who was known to his cohorts as "Slug," came up with the idea of simulating spaceships on the screen. He had been reading science fiction novels about space battles, so he included a means of controlling the spaceship's flight patterns and a means of shooting down other ships. Meanwhile, another hacker by the name of Peter Samson created a realistic depiction of a star field as a background to the spaceships. The game *Spacewar* was born. Years later, *Spacewar*, as well as some other games that were originally designed by hackers at MIT and elsewhere, would form the basis of billion-dollar industries.

Although MIT was clearly the mother-temple of hacking, the Stanford Artificial Intelligence Laboratory (known as SAIL) became a West Coast shrine of the art. By the 1970s, a kind of party line for computers called the ARPAnet (developed by researchers for the Defense Department's Advanced Research Projects Agency) linked SAIL computers to those at MIT and hundreds of other institutions. This multi-computer long-distance network made it possible for programmers at various institutions to send messages and even programs to one another.

Games, of course, were one of the largest categories of community-shared programs on the ARPAnet. One day, a SAIL hacker and Stanford student by the name of Don Woods found a particularly intriguing game on the network—a nongraphic simulation of an adventure through a cavern-world that was replete with treasure, trolls, dragons, maidens, and flying horses. Woods contacted the game's creator, Will Crowther, because he wanted to add some refinements to the program. Crowther, a computer scientist in Palo Alto, had concocted the game as a means of amusing his children, and having once been a spelunker, he decided to create a fantasy in the form of an exploration of linked caves. He was working for a company that was connected to the ARPAnet, so he had simply posted the game on the network for other hackers to enjoy. Woods, however, came to the game with a sophisticated perspective, since he had been involved in role-playing board games like "Dungeons and Dragons." When Woods's refinements were added to Crowther's original version, the infamous game called *Adventure* was born.

I say that *Adventure* was infamous because research leaders and computer system managers very quickly discovered that many programmers were spending hours and days—even weeks and months!—on the game. It must be pointed out that as there were no graphics on the original *Adventure*, the game offered a different kind of thrill from the sensory addiction of the video games that would surface a few years later. Besides the fantasy aspect, it, and games like it, provided an intellectual challenge that caused otherwise rational programmers to spend days working their way through it.

The game is a puzzle in the form of a trip through a series of caves. Each cave poses a problem that must be solved before the player can progress to the next cave. As the player solves each puzzle and moves through the various caves, a narrative unfolds, describing the fantasy adventure. The player makes moves by typing in commands like "KILL TROLL" or "TAKE TREASURE," and sometimes the player must backtrack through several previous caves to pick up an object—such as a sword, a bag of food, or a jug of water—that is required to solve a problem in a later cave.

Adventure spread rapidly through the ARPAnet community and was played on the big mainframes and minicomputers that were available to the computer research labs where the hard-core hackers congregated. Such relatively sophisticated games, however, were inaccessible to the Altair hobbyists and homebrewers who were dealing with computer memory sizes far too small to contain the programming code for a fantasy simulation. Even when the larger-capacity machines like the TRS–80 and Apple appeared, it was widely believed that *Adventure* ate up too much memory to be programmed in one of the microcomputer languages used by those computers.

But software history is largely the story of people who accomplished tasks that had previously been considered impossible. In 1978, a young man named Scott Adams decided to take up the challenge of writing a simulation game for the TRS–80 microcomputer. He succeeded in solving this "insoluble" problem in the remarkable time of two weeks. His first game was *Adventure Land*, which was based on Crowther and Woods' *Adventure* and was totally nongraphic and text-oriented, like the original. It was an immediate success, and TRS–80 owners started buying it like crazy. Scott and his wife, Alexis, started a company, *Adventure International*, which grew into its own strange kind of game empire, and which seeded the software industry with Scott Adams protégés (Doug Carlston among them). In time, even Microsoft brought out a version of the original ARPAnet *Adventure*.

Just as *VisiCalc* introduced businesspeople to the benefits of computers, and *WordStar* showed wordslingers how computer programs could dramatically increase their productivity, *Adventure*-type games demonstrated to tens of thousands of nonbusinesspeople how much *fun* computers could be. And the idea, new at that time, that ordinary men, women, and children would find things to do with computers in their homes was buttressed by the success of *Adventure Land*.

But the home computer market had not yet blossomed, for there was a definite limit to the number of people who liked to solve puzzles by typing in primitive sentences like "PICK UP SWORD." The color television generation is very sophisticated when it comes to the matter of visual media, and the monotonous look of green alphabetic characters on a screen was far less attractive than the kind of fast-moving, high-resolution, brightly colored displays that most people were accustomed to watching.

Affordable personal computers cannot be built without microprocessors, but microprocessor-based computers would never have caught on if, in addition to having good software, they weren't also connected to television-like display screens. If computer output were still restricted to numbers and alphabetic characters printed on sheets of paper, as had been the case for decades, computers would still be confined to laboratories and data processing centers. Moreover, if it weren't for computer graphics technology, the home computer market would never have opened up as widely as it did and would instead have remained largely a community of hobbyists.

The reason for the importance of the video display is very simple: The visual sense is the way human beings assimilate information most efficiently. People can simply understand information far better if it is presented in a visual form. And games in particular are far more exciting if they have a visual component, especially if color and motion also are involved.

A computer processes information and presents it to humans in an understandable form. Census statistics, financial data, numbers, or text is entered via keyboards, punched cards, magnetic tape, or other input devices. The central processor of the computer compiles the statistics, sorts the data, performs calculations, and processes the text. All of this is a marvelous improvement over adding machines, ledger books, and typewriters, but it wouldn't have any meaning unless the processed information could be presented to people in an easily perceived form.

The idea that computer output could be presented in the form of images on a video screen seems natural today, but it was considered a radical innovation when it first came about in the late 1950s and early 1960s. Computer scientists might still be reading and interpreting esoteric printouts if the United States Air Force had not developed a computer that graphically displayed information about the state of the country's air-defense readiness. And the use of computer graphics might still be confined to the military if it weren't for those irrepressible hackers at MIT who created the first computer-based video games, like *Spacewar*, in the early 1960s. But *Spacewar* itself would not have been possible without the revolutionary breakthrough provided by a program called *Sketchpad*, written in 1961 by yet another brilliant MIT student, Ivan Sutherland. *Sketchpad* allowed computer users to produce and manipulate graphic patterns on video screens and to store the results in computers.

By 1976, the homebrewers began to experiment with various graphics devices for the Altair. They were able to produce kaleidoscopic effects and to devise very simple games, but the computers themselves were nowhere near powerful enough to recreate a minicomputer program like *Spacewar*. Ironically, then, the next step in the evolution of the personal computer industry did not come from the general-purpose computer technology of the Altair or its immediate successors, but from far less versatile machines.

In order for an electronic information-processing device to be called a computer, it has to be *programmable*. But by the mid 1970s, it was possible to build machines that, using "dedicated," nonprogrammable microchips, could create sophisticated graphic effects. These machines were called "video games," and although they didn't have much to do with microcomputers, they hastened the day when the personal computer cult would break through to infect the general population.

Video games resulted from the entrepreneurial combination of two different ideas that had been around for a long time. Since 1961 and *Spacewar*, it was obvious to those few people who knew about interactive computing and display technology that sophisticated games could be created by using video graphics and microelectronic controllers. Meanwhile, arcade games in the form of pinball machines had been a steady business for decades. It took another Silicon Valley entrepreneur by the name of Nolan Bushnell, along with several other partners, to decide to put these two factors together.

Forming a company that he initially named Syzygy, Bushnell tried to market the game machine *Computer Space*, a modified version of *Spacewar*, to bars and pizza parlors as an electronic substitute for pinball. The idea didn't catch on—only 2000 machines were sold. He then tried something simpler. In 1974, he unveiled *Pong* and marketed it to the same places. It was an absurdly simple game by *Spacewar* standards; using joysticks, the players moved light-paddles to bounce a ball of light back and forth across the screen.

Pong was a hit, to put it mildly. After his first test machines were installed, Bushnell received complaints from the proprietors of these establishments that his machines had broken down. When he followed up on the complaints, he discovered that the machines were malfunctioning only because their coin boxes had been jammed full before anybody had come back to empty them! In fact, when Bushnell approached a number of pinball-machine manufacturers in Chicago with the proposal that they might have a financial interest in his game, most turned him down. Bally Corporation, a giant pinball-machine manufacturer, was interested at first but then backed away from an agreement with him, largely because the corporation couldn't believe the financial statistics he was presenting on the basis of his experience with his test markets.

Indeed, it was Nolan Bushnell and his crude video games, launched a year before the Altair hobbyists and homebrewers began experimenting with personal computers, that triggered the huge influx of capital which would ultimately transform the hobbyist community into the sizeable home computer industry. In time, the success of the arcade games spawned home versions. The idea that small, inexpensive versions of arcade games could be connected to home television sets ultimately turned out to be just the beginning of the evolution of increasingly sophisticated microprocessor-based devices for home entertainment.

People started pouring quarters into Bushnell's arcade machines—to the tune of millions of dollars yearly. Bushnell followed up his first hit with another successful but slightly more advanced game, *Tank Command*, in which simulated tanks stalked through a video maze and hurled blobs of light at one another. Syzygy was then renamed Atari, after a move in the ancient Japanese game Go, and Bushnell hired creative young programmers and electronics wizards to think up new games. A young man by the name of Steve Jobs was one of Atari's early employees.

This new company combined electronic expertise that had previously been associated with defense contractors and consumer electronics manufacturers with the playfulness and love of games that characterized the hacker era. Two years after the company was born, it was doing $39 million worth of business. In 1976, Bushnell sold his increasingly profitable enterprise to Warner Communications for $26 million. For about six years, Warner's buyout of Bushnell was one of the smartest investments in history: By 1982, Atari's annual sales had swollen to more than $2 billion.

Atari in its Warner incarnation was to play an important role in the rise and fall of many other home computer companies. But in the 1970s, before the first home computer companies got off the ground, it was the sophisticated arcade games of Japanese manufacturers that turned the video game industry from a multimillion-dollar infant into a multibillion-dollar giant, unleashing an unexpected social phenomenon in the process. The key to the video game craze was in the "dedicated" hardware that enabled manufacturers to develop visual displays that were far better than those possible on the first programmable microcomputer systems.

Those games made possible an entirely new kind of sensory experience. In a real sense, they were even selling an experience—a means of ventilating primitive fight-or-flight reflexes through the various "zap the aliens" scenarios, through a visual and auditory encounter of hypnotic intensity, and through cognitive and perceptual gymnastics that offered immediate and quantitative rewards. The flashy high-resolution graphics ("high res," as it is known in the industry), the direct interaction via joysticks or buttons or trackballs, the electronic sound effects, and the way the games were designed to keep proficiency, difficulty, and level of reward in a delicate balance all seemed to precipitate an unnatural hunger in a large portion of every nation in the world—the youth.

The staid old pinball manufacturers who had turned away from Bushnell's video game simply had not foreseen the arrival and the nature of this vast, new, very different market. Nor could they have dared to predict how willing the game's customers would be to pay for their experiences. The rate of return on pinball machines had been holding steady for decades. Depending on the popularity of the machine, the weekly return per unit was measured, at best, in hundreds of dollars. The very first video games, way back in the *Pong* and *Tank* days, took in thousands weekly. But whereas the pinball manufacturers in Chicago might have not noticed the existence of this torrentially lucrative new market, the game manufacturers in Tokyo certainly did.

Japanese companies had been manufacturing coin-operated games since the late 1960s, and in the late 1970s they began distributing sophisticated video game machines to the Japanese market. The games were such a huge success that there was for a time a critical shortage of circulating coins in Japan. The devices were virtually sucking the money out of circulation. As a result of this almost shocking success, Japanese manufacturers of coin-operated games began to consider distributing their products to international markets.

The breakthrough of Japanese arcade games into the international market came in 1978, with *Space Invaders*, a fast-moving, colorful video game in which the player fires brightly colored "lasers" at swiftly descending "alien invaders" and tries to accumulate as many points as possible before the invaders destroy the laser bases. As the player gets a higher score, the invaders move more quickly and the electronic background music becomes more urgent. This kind of game, known as "shoot-'em-ups," quickly gained revenues of billions of dollars per year—all of it in coins. The video arcade games had become an enormous industry.

But in the meantime, in 1977, the Warner version of Atari was putting itself in a position to mine an even larger video game bonanza by building cheap game machines that could be plugged into home television sets; these devices, also "dedicated" rather than programmable, enabled people to play the enormously popular arcade games like *Pong* and *Tank*, and eventually *Space Invaders*, in their homes. The first versions of these devices sold extraordinarily well, but they were soon abandoned by their owners because they were limited in their capabilities and offered only one or two games.

Then, in the same year, Atari introduced the VCS 2600, which offered *replaceable* cartridges called ROMs. By plugging in a new ROM cartridge, it became possible to play the latest game on the old machine, instead of discarding the entire machine for the latest model. This is known in the industry as "giving away the razors and selling the blades," except in Atari's case it was *selling* both the razors *and* the blades. Although they were pieces of hardware, the ROMs were actually a form of software; inside each cartridge was the program that enabled the machine to play a new game. Their eventual success with consumers marked the beginning of a broadly based home video game industry and the point when software became a significant consumer commodity.

The home video game industry soon rivaled even the intensely profitable arcade game industry; Atari's revenues rose to more than a billion dollars per year. It was the most phenomenal rate of growth of any new industry in history, and an experience far beyond any CEO's wildest dreams. And Atari's CEO at the time was Raymond Kassar, who had recently been hired by the notoriously charismatic Warner chairman, Steve Ross. Sophisticated, sybaritic, highly cultured, Kassar had spent his entire career at Burlington Mills, a textile company, before coming to Atari. He wasn't a Silicon Valley entrepreneur and didn't care much for engineers or programmers, but for a while he happened to be in exactly the right place at exactly the right time.

After the Japanese introduced *Space Invaders*, they brought out *Galaxians*, which had even more variations on the "shoot the invaders" theme, and then *Pac-Man*, which created the "munch-'em-up" genre. Incredibly, people spent more than a billion dollars' worth of quarters a year simply to play this one arcade game. Then Atari licensed from the Japanese the rights to create the VCS (home) version of *Pac-Man*, and a programmer was hired to do a quick-and-dirty version for a reported $1 million. Ironically, the game programmer who created the original Japanese version of *Pac-Man* didn't make a penny in royalties.

By 1982, Atari had more than 80 percent of the huge and still growing home game hardware and software market. The VCS might not have been a computer, but those cartridges certainly were software, and a programmer was needed to create the code that was embodied in the cartridges. That meant that there were juicy royalties to be made. More than that, some programmers began to feel that they ought to get some personal recognition for their accomplishments.

While Kassar was buying apartments in the most expensive co-ops in the world and flying around in a luxury jet, a few of the programmers who were creating Atari's wealth decided that it was time for them to get their names printed on the cartridge's package. Kassar tried to ignore them, but they were persistent. In May 1979, four of Atari's best game designers, dressed in jeans, finally met with the elegantly tailored Kassar in his office. In an interview in an issue of *Info-World* (Vol. 5, No. 48), one of the programmers, Larry Kaplan, summed up the CEO's reaction: "He called us towel designers. He said, 'I've dealt with your kind before. You're a dime a dozen. You're not unique. Anybody can do a cartridge.'"

The following October, three of the four game designers— Dave Crane, Al Miller, and Bob Whitehead—left Atari to form Activision. Kaplan joined them a short time later. According to Kaplan, "Activision was started to prove that Kassar was wrong." But as an awesome collection of talent and a burning desire to succeed are still not sufficient to build a world-class company, the programmers soon got together with Jim Levy, a CEO whose previous experience had included involvement with a music and software company as well as with Time, Inc., and Hershey Foods. Eventually a venture capital partner—Sutter Hill, one of the hottest in Silicon Valley—joined Activision's effort.

As the first company in the video game business to concentrate exclusively on software, Activision was breaching the wall between the still financially puny but ever more sophisticated home computer software market and the relatively one-dimensional but monstrously profitable video game software market.

According to Levy, Activision's original business plan was based on three fundamental ideas. The first could be called the "appliance hypothesis"—a prediction that during the 1980s the computer would become as important in American homes as the television, radio, stereo, and automobile. "The second fundamental idea," Levy said in a June 1984 interview in Atari's *Antic* magazine, "was that software was going to drive the market." And the third idea was based on the premise that a software company requires an approach and focus different from that which a hardware company requires. This corporation, after all, was going to prove that programmers weren't towel designers.

Activision was an instant hit, and when the company went public, it made the founders Silicon Valley millionaires. By 1982, after only two years in the business, they topped $150 million in sales. Activision's best-selling product, a game called *Pitfall*, sold more than three and a half million units worldwide. In subsequent years, the company marketed four more games that sold more than a million units each. The Activision founders far surpassed their original goal of proving something to Atari: In effect, they created the concept of the software star. The company not only put the programmers' names on the game packages, it also put their pictures and bios in promotional materials and sent the programmers themselves on speaking tours.

Activision wasn't Kassar's—and Atari's—only problem. In 1981, when another group of game designers left Atari to form Imagic, Kassar called them "high-strung prima donnas," and afterwards many of the programmers who remained at Atari soon sported T-shirts with the words: "I'm another high-strung prima donna from Atari." But with annual sales figures approaching the billion-dollar mark, Atari was in no mood to listen to doomsayers who decried the erosion of their programming talent.

Atari's VCS was soon followed by other systems, including Odyssey, Intellivision, and Colecovision. Other game companies proliferated, and some of the country's largest companies became involved—notably Quaker Oats, CBS, and Mattel. By the time the video game business reached its peak, in the early 1980s, another up-and-coming industry was making inroads—the home computer market. Both the hardware and software components of personal computers had grown more powerful and less expensive since the days of the Altair. When microcomputers first became powerful enough to accommodate sophisticated game programs, complete with graphics, Brøderbund and I entered the story.

THE EARLY YEARS

3

The View from Brøderbund

I learned to program at the age of seventeen, which is a lot older than many of the current crop of programming stars were when they started. In fact, when I got my start in 1964, many of today's software luminaries were still in diapers. And now, a lot of the people in the software industry who are my age or older are taking orders from CEOs who are much younger than they are. Two prominent examples—Steve Jobs, co-founder of Apple Computer, and Bill Gates, co-founder of Microsoft, the largest microcomputer software company— were both under thirty years old in 1984, when I began writing this book.

But it isn't necessarily the extraordinary youth of these people that enabled them to rise to their celebrated positions in the industry. They rose because of pure talent. More specifically, most of the people who created this industry gained entrance because of their programming skills. And programming is something that can't be faked—the program either works or it doesn't. Computers are immune to all human prejudices. They are utterly literal and totally fair. They open their secrets to anyone, but only if that person can speak their language.

Indeed, until very recently, one of the major factors that kept the mysteries of programming closed to most people was *access*. Very few people ever had a chance even to try learning how to communicate with computers. The old-style machines were huge, extraordinarily expensive, and cloistered in air-conditioned, dust-free chambers; access to these inner sanctums was permitted only to a small priesthood of inter-mediaries.

I was one of the very few lucky ones who succeeded in gaining access to these machines in the early 1960s. My mother, father, two brothers, two sisters, and I moved from Dubuque to Iowa City, Iowa, in 1964, when my father, a Presbyterian minister, became professor of New Testament at the University of Iowa. My brother Gary, my sister Cathy, my mother, her sister, a cousin, and I became Brøderbund's founding shareholders, and Cathy and my mother both worked with Gary and me at Brøderbund at one time or another. But that was sixteen years in the future.

In 1964, I was a high school student. That summer I went to Northwestern University, in Evanston, Illinois, to attend a summer conference on engineering for bright high school kids. The conference included classes in calculus, physics, and engineering and, most importantly, a class entitled "Introduction to Digital Computers." It was then that I learned how to write programs in the programming language known as FORTRAN. The machine was an antique of laughably limited power, judging by today's standards: an IBM monster that filled an entire room.

Today's desk-top computers are far more powerful than that IBM machine and cost a fraction of the IBM's original price. But I had no idea then of what was to happen to computer technology in the near future. In those days, I was, like many others, simply seduced by the logical, gamelike, mathematical, and tactical challenges of writing, debugging, and running my own computer programs. It was like a cross between solving jigsaw puzzles, building models, and playing chess—the kind of fascinating activity that involved me for hours on end before I noticed the passage of time. I started cutting all my other summer classes in order to spend more time in the computer center.

The reason I had to hang out near the computer, and the very notion of "computer center" itself, were artifacts of the way computers worked in 1964. Computers in those days took in data and programs and then returned answers in the form of printouts; the system as a whole was known as "batch processing." First, all the programs and data had to be coded in terms of those square-shaped holes on small pieces of cardboard universally known as "IBM cards." If there was a missing instruction in the program, or if one of the cards had a hole punched in the wrong place, then the programmer would get back a printout full of mistakes (called "bugs") instead of solutions. That meant that the programmer would have to study the printout in order to discover the bug.

In practice, the programmer would bring a deck of cards down to the computer center, then wait five hours for the batch processing. But if any bugs turned up before the five hours elapsed, the programmer would simply copy the cards and submit them again. Because of the waiting time, several different programs would be run one after another, so that there would be a steady stream of output. This meant that I, as a programmer, was running down to the computer center every forty-five minutes to see if another batch of output was waiting for me. Before I realized what had happened, I had spent the entire summer immersed in printouts and decks of cards.

The following summer, I got a job at the University of Iowa computing center as a batch clerk who took in the decks of cards and gave them to the operators who ran them through the machine. As this procedure reflects, there was a definite hierarchy of access to the computer, and it is not wholly poetic license to refer to the top of the hierarchy as a priesthood guarding the holiest of holies. But I didn't mind my lowly position or the minimum-wage pay, partly because Iowa summers are hot and the computing center was one of the few air-conditioned buildings in the vicinity. I was also motivated by the prospect of getting a free account number to submit my own programs, and there were plenty of computer aficionados around—they weren't widely known as hackers yet—to teach me even more about the programming art. There weren't too many college programming courses, and none at the high school level, back in 1965. As far as I knew, the only way to really learn the ins and outs of the art was to hang around a university computer center and pick up tips from the experts.

This strategy soon paid off, and about halfway through the summer, the university started to use me as a programmer. One of the more interesting jobs I had was writing the program that computed the salaries of all the employees at the university. I got a sense of the real power that programmers held when I realized that my father was one of the employees whose salaries I was computing. At that time he was still teaching at the university, and out of curiosity I found out how much money he earned. This might not seem like a big deal today, but I remember being impressed with the fact that computer programmers were privy to a lot of information that would otherwise have remained under lock and key. They never would have been allowed access to it had they not performed the valuable and mysterious service of creating computer programs.

I went to Harvard the following fall. (In fact my brothers, Don and Gary, also attended Harvard, and at one point all three of us were there at the same time.) I worked as a programmer for two years as an undergraduate, but at that time computer science was hardly my burning ambition in life. Adventure, excitement, and novelty—qualities that others in my age group over at MIT found in the new time-sharing computers—were what primarily interested me. So I went off to Africa and ended up teaching math and geography in Botswana for a year.

When I returned to college, I became a more serious student and abandoned programming, which had been a personal hobby rather than a vocation anyway. I buckled down to study social psychology and was graduated with high honors in 1970. I went to graduate school on a fellowship at the Johns Hopkins School for Advanced International Studies in Washington, DC, and concentrated in African affairs and international economics. However, after I had attended school for a year, the school's funding was cut back unexpectedly, and it had to cancel most of its fellowships, including mine. Since I had no money, I took a job instead of returning to finish my masters degree.

American Express hired me as an editor for its language publications division, which was located in Washington, D.C. This division published basic texts, books to accompany teaching tapes, and readers that were used at its language centers. I edited French, German, Italian, and Spanish textbooks (I was pretty decent in French and German but had to rely on outside help for Italian and Spanish) and arranged the taping and manufacture of the language tapes.

With two languages out of four, I was apparently the best they could find—at least I was the best they could find for $7800 a year. I stayed at the job for only about seven months, however, before city life started to get to me. When a few more book contracts came my way, I talked my boss into letting me write the books instead of farming them out. Since authors didn't have to work at the office, I moved to Maine.

A few years previously, I had helped build a little ski chalet in Fryeburg, Maine, for my parents, and after making the arrangement with American Express, I fantasized that I could live in the chalet alone, deep in the woods, writing every other day and skiing the rest of the time. I had no worries about my ability to turn out the textbooks, which by nature had a prescribed format. And they weren't my first books, either—in college I had written a beginning Swahili textbook for a small publisher.

At first, the fantasy turned out to be a perfectly workable arrangement. I finished the books and skied a lot. But in time I got bored with this routine, too. Although I like being alone and am a serious bibliophile and daydreamer, I was developing a bad case of cabin fever. Because I had always enjoyed being a student, I decided to return to school, this time to try for a law degree. The only two places I knew were Iowa and Harvard, so I applied to the law schools at both universities.

Law school is one of the few graduate programs that one can get into without prerequisites (the only other one is business school, and I had no interest in business). Apparently my eclectic background was just what Harvard Law School was looking for, so I returned to Cambridge in 1972 and spent the next three school years at Harvard Law School attending classes and playing a lot of basketball; I spent the summers in Maine building houses, which I then sold to pay for law school. It was my first entrepreneurial endeavor, and although at first I learned a great number of ways to lose money, I eventually achieved my goal of making enough to help finance the completion of my studies.

After my graduation from law school I worked at a large law firm in Chicago. After three years, I quit the firm and moved back to Maine, where I set up my own office as a means of obtaining the general kind of experience a private practice could offer. I also planned to build houses in some entrepreneurial way while running my law practice. I ended up with a partner in the law practice and another partner who built houses with me.

In 1978 I obtained the TRS-80 to help with my law practice and (mostly) to have fun. It was then that I was drawn more and more back into programming. I continued to practice law, but eventually the housing recession depressed my construction business. Having a computer and some time on my hands, I began to develop my first game program, *Galactic Empire*, and before I knew it I was once again seduced by the sheer enjoyment of working with a computer. By the time I sent off that first program to Adventure International, The Software Exchange, and Cybernautics in hopes that they would publish it, I realized that I was looking for a way out of the law business and into the freelance microcomputer programming business.

As I recounted in the first pages of this book, my trip to Eugene, Oregon, in early 1980 eventually turned into the beginnings of Brøderbund. Gary was twenty-eight and I was thirty-two when we started the company. We still remember fondly those early frantic days of cassette recorders strewn about the living room of our house in Eugene. We recall not only the laughably casual way we did business then, but also the raw excitement we felt starting out on this crazy futuristic adventure. We did everything on the basis of instant decisions and ten-minute negotiations. Although many of the friendships and alliances we formed in those days are still part of our business, our business has changed considerably and has become more professional over the years. But back then, we did everything in a seat-of-the-pants manner.

Once, we found a printer in Eugene and said to him: "We don't have any money, but if you print up this documentation we think we'll be able to sell the program and pay you later." We must have looked honest, because the printer took us up on our offer, and the arrangement worked out, miraculously, just the way we said it would. The printer's name is Don Fast, and although we are no longer in Eugene we still do some business with him when we can.

Although by 1980 three companies in particular— Personal Software, Microsoft, and MicroPro—were on their way to establishing themselves as multimillion-dollar enterprises, it was still a time when most of the microcomputer software "industry" consisted of kitchen table operations like ours. And those were the days when most of the companies got together once a year in San Francisco for a strange kind of convention that was more of a cult-gathering and social get-together than a serious trade show like the huge ones we see nowadays.

Shortly after we got that first $300 order from the Program Store in Washington, D.C., Gary and I decided to attend the San Francisco convocation that we had heard so much about from other microcomputer folks. The event was the West Coast Computer Faire, and a week before it was scheduled to start, we called Jim Warren, the organizer, to see if we could get in on the action. For $200 we obtained a tiny space known as a "microbooth." In an excess of optimism we recorded almost a thousand copies of each of my TRS-80 programs, of which there were now three. We loaded the trunk of my car with sleeping bags, computers, and cassette tapes and headed for San Francisco in April 1980.

I remember that we arrived in the Bay Area on one of those clear, beautiful, days that seduce people into moving to northern California. Mount Tamalpais was a soft green, the bay was deep blue, San Francisco itself was a sparkling white, and the air was clear enough to see the treeline of the Marin hills from the Bay Bridge.

We crossed the bridge in high spirits, feeling very much in the tradition of the forty-niners and all the other half-crazy adventurers who had come to California in search of their fortunes. We headed for the auditorium where the Faire was held and found our booth, the size of which justified its name—six feet by six feet. In that rather restricted space we set up our TRS-80 and our newly purchased Apple on the fold-up table we had been provided. That was our entire hardware base and most of our capital investment at that time.

We had bought the Apple a week before the show in order to demonstrate my brother Don's game *Tank Command*. Don was married and employed as an associate professor at the University of Iowa, so he wasn't interested in moving west or switching careers in order to join Gary and me in our new enterprise. But he, like a great many others, was fascinated with the capabilities of the Apple II. He had originally created *Tank Command* for the Plato educational system and had later converted it for the Apple. His game and my three TRS-80 programs were Brøderbund's entire software line, and at the Faire, Gary and I had high hopes of selling many copies of all four programs in no time.

But unforeseeable events at the Faire ended up having more of a profound impact on Brøderbund's future than the events we had expected. Initially, we were just thinking about selling a ton of software and learning what all the big companies were up to. After the first couple of hours and no sales, however, we were hoping for enough cash to cover the cost of the microbooth. We had as yet no sense of community with any of the other companies at the Faire. As it turned out, our introduction to the community was literally right next door to us.

Our long-standing relationship with Japanese software companies started because the fellow in the booth next to ours didn't have an Apple. That booth was owned by an accountant named Jack Hatfield, who lived in Placerville, California, in the Sierra foothills, and who imported memory chips from Japan, offering packages that allowed people to upgrade the memory capacity of their computers. In the booth with Jack was a memory-chip supplier, a fellow named Mioshi, who was the president of a Japanese trading company. In addition to the memory chips, Mioshi had also brought to the Faire a couple of Apple arcade-type games that he had picked up in Tokyo from a company called Star Craft.

Since there was no Apple in their booth to demonstrate the games, Jack asked if we wanted to show the games in our booth. The only problem was that our machine had only 16 K memory, and we needed 32 K to demonstrate the programs. That was easy to solve—we just opened our Apple and put Mioshi's memory chips in. Mioshi agreed that after the show was over we could keep the memory chips as payment for letting them use the Apple. Those chips turned out to be a significant part of our profit from that show, along with about $200 we received from sales of our own games.

The way the games played and the way we felt when we played them, however, was far more interesting to us at that time than the profit-and-loss statements we'd face when we returned to Eugene. These were the first fast-action arcade games I'd ever seen on a personal computer. They were light years beyond anything I'd ever seen on the U.S. market so far. We played them ourselves because they were so tantalizing. Even though they weren't even our products, the Japanese games turned us on so much that we began pulling people out of the crowd to try them. But this became frustrating when everybody wanted to buy the games that weren't ours to sell in the first place. And Mioshi himself had brought only one copy of each game!

After the show, business began to look a little less fun. The TRS-80 games that had launched my programming and publishing careers gradually declined in sales. We were going broke fast. We then began writing versions of all our games for the Apple, having learned at the Faire that the Apple was an instant marketplace for new software in ways that we felt the TRS-80 was not. By June 1980, we had finished our first few Apple conversions.

Then we got an unexpected call from Mioshi, who was in Placerville. He wanted to fly to Eugene to discuss publishing arrangements. When he arrived, he brought ten copies of each of the games we had found so attractive in April. We then worked out an arrangement whereby we would buy one hundred copies at a time and store them in Placerville. From there Jack would ship them to us as we paid for them. Mioshi's price, was we were to discover, was very high. But we were so anxious to get those games for Broderbund's inventory that we were willing to lose money on the first ones we sold. One product cost us $10.50 each; when we started selling it to dealers we sold copies at 50 percent off the retail price of $19.95.

Our decision to start selling a product at a loss, in hopes of making the money back later in terms of a larger market base, was a fairly bold, if not ill-considered, strategem. By that time we had gone through all of the money I had saved from my law practices in Chicago and Maine (around $12,000), had borrowed $8000 from my relatives, and were approaching the limits on both my MasterCharge and VISA cards. The pressure was on, to say the least. Here were two promising Harvard graduates who were losing their money at an astonishing rate.

But at that point, another random event changed our fortune once again. In previous years, Gary had coached a women's basketball team in Sweden, taking it to the national championships twice. Three of his former athletes were now visiting the United States on vacation and were headed for San Francisco when they called Gary and asked him to join them there. Of course he had no money to finance such a trip, but then a friend of his from San Francisco bought him a plane ticket to the Bay Area. He took a lot of software with him, and as his friends drove him to the city from the airport, he convinced them to stop at a few computer stores along the way so that he could try to sell some programs.

Computer stores were fairly new enterprises in the summer of 1980—certainly not the international chains that they are today. They were hungry for any software to sell along with the Apple II. (The TRS-80 was sold only through

Radio Shack, not computer stores, and the IBM PC didn't exist yet.) The first day of Gary's venture into traveling software salesmanship, he racked up several hundred dollars' worth of sales. The next day he did even better. And since we sold on a cash-on-the-barrelhead basis, we were getting ahead of the game for the first time since we started the whole unlikely enterprise. Our sales had been less than $1000 a month since February and had sunk to zero in May. By the end of his stay in California, Gary had sold several thousand dollars' worth of software.

We used some of the money Gary brought back from San Francisco to buy a few hundred more cassettes from the Japanese, and to finance a sales trip I took across the country in August. I sold our software out of the car and stopped at Idaho Falls, Salt Lake City, Denver, Chicago, Boston, Washington, D.C., New York City—in fact, at every place I could find a computer store across the northern tier. I sold fifteen or sixteen thousand dollars' worth of programs on that trip, which really got things humming back in Eugene. No doubt about it, we were not only in the black, but it looked like we might actually be a viable company.

At about this time we realized that the higher-capacity and faster-running technology of disk-based software, which had been in existence for a while, would eventually become inexpensive and reliable enough to supersede the slower cassette-based programs in the marketplace. In fact, the disk format was becoming the standard medium for software by the end of the summer of 1980. With that in mind we began converting all of our own games from cassette to disk format and managed to convince our Japanese suppliers to do the same.

After I returned from my sales trip, a gentleman named Minoru Nakazawa showed up at our door in Eugene. He was the president of Star Craft, which created the software that Mioshi had been selling us. Nakazawa explained that Mioshi had kept a sizeable part of the money that we had paid for the product, a situation that was beneficial to Mioshi but not to either Star Craft or Brøderbund. Nakazawa asked us to make a direct arrangement with him, and as he didn't intend to sell any more software to Mioshi, we naturally went along with the suggestion. We worked out an arrangement that turned out to be much more profitable for us. We no longer had to store the programs in Placerville until we could pay for them; after our first check, he trusted us to pay him as we sold them.

In the last month of 1980, Brøderbund took off. With support from a distributing company called Robwin and later renamed Softsel, our sales never went below December's level of $55,000 again. The following January, Computerland started carrying our products. We were selling fewer and fewer strategy and simulation games and more and more of our video game–like programs. In the meantime, I was still trying to do the programming while Gary handled the sales. I was also doing the books, and we had a phone with call-waiting installed. We were still located in the same house in Eugene, but at least we had moved beyond the living room. My bedroom was the product development department, manufacturing still went on in the living room, and the kitchen became our shipping department.

But soon we moved into a house with a large garage and hired three people to help with manufacturing and shipping. My bedroom was still the product development headquarters, but the Ping-Pong table in the garage became the center for assembling and shipping the products. In the spring of 1981 we expanded our product line to include *Snoggle* (a *Pac-Man* imitation) and *Payroll*, our first nonentertainment package. At about that time, our sister Cathy, who was then living and working in New York, quit her job and moved to Eugene to join us. She started out as office manager and bookkeeper, then took over advertising as well. I wrote my last program that summer, having given up all hope of doing serious programming while running the business.

By the summer of 1981 we were also getting a lot of pressure from our Japanese colleague to move to a more convenient location. In Japan, a successful company wouldn't be located in a small town. For prestige value as well as operational convenience, a successful company in a small town would move to a major city. And if a Japanese company were serious about continuing its success, it would move to Tokyo. Of the major cities open to us, we were willing to consider only Seattle or the San Francisco Bay Area, both of which had better facilities for our Japanese friend. We chose the Bay Area because Gary and I hadn't forgotten the euphoria of our arrival there for the 1980 Computer Faire. So we packed up the entire enterprise and moved it south to San Rafael in August 1981.

There were five of us at the time we left Eugene—Gary, Cathy, Brian Ehler (who was a production worker and who is now director of Sales Administration), Chris Jochumson (an independent programmer and friend), and I. We set up operation in a house. We didn't know any better—we had always operated out of a house—and at first, our business consisted of a few phone calls, daily trips to the post office, and use of one Apple II computer (having long since abandoned the TRS-80). In the meantime, we were fairly oblivious to things like zoning laws and never suspected that our neighbors would report us, which they did the first week we moved in, when the UPS trucks started driving into our cul-de-sac to pick up our shipments.

The Planning Commission came by and we had a chat and decided to move the operation once again. We found an old liquor warehouse, also in San Rafael. We expanded throughout the building one chunk at a time, and after several months, we eventually filled the building and even the building next door. By 1983 it was time to move again, because we now had forty-five employees and no parking facilities. We were still violating most of the zoning ordinances, but as there were no neighbors we got away with it. Still, our accommodations were cramped and crowded, and the roof leaked like a sieve. In mid-1983 we moved into the building that we still occupy today. It still isn't spacious enough, but it is much nicer to work in. And it's in an industrial park in San Rafael, so we're legal now.

In the spring of 1982, we were approached by venture capitalists, as were several other formerly-small software publishers who had grown into multimillion-dollar businesses. Venture capitalists—sometimes known as "vulture capitalists"—

like to find million-dollar businesses, infuse them with money and guidance and even stick a few of their own people on the board of directors, and then take the companies "public" a few years later.

With the success of Microsoft, Micropro, Personal Software, and Digital Research, the big-money people were beginning to look a lot more seriously at the upside potential of this peculiar industry that had mutated from a bunch of hobbyists. We had one bad experience ourselves, with a venture firm that will remain nameless but that made us a very attractive offer of working capital in exchange for a healthy piece of the action. We almost agreed to do business with the firm until our lawyer pointed out that one term in their proposed contract gave the firm the power to fire us all and take over Brøderbund if we failed to show a profit two quarters in a row. We had no intention of ever failing to show a profit for even one month, but the idea of even taking the risk of losing our company was totally unacceptable. We eventually made a deal with a venture firm called Burr, Egan, and Deleage, and we've been happy with them.

By the time we moved to our present quarters, Brøderbund had already developed its own group of programmers—either in-house programmers or independent programmers who had a very close association with us. This development began after I had given up programming, when we realized that we had to find other product sources. Our most successful products, during the explosive stages of our growth, were the original programs that were submitted to us, like the Star Craft games. Then we began to work with original submissions that needed further development but nonetheless looked promising. Gradually, after a few years, we worked our way to a system that we found comfortable as well as profitable. We still use that system today, whereby we treat programs in development in a manner very similar to the way book publishers treat manuscripts in development. Later on in the book, when we take a look at the way different software publishers and developers create new products, we'll focus on the process of product development. For the time being, however, I think we've spent enough time discussing Brøderbund, which is hardly the one and only scene of action in the software world. It's time to enlarge the frame of reference to include other developments and other people in the burgeoning microcomputer software industry. Now that you know who I am and where I came from, its time to meet some other software people.

4

Legendary
Programmers

Without programmers there would be no microcomputer software industry today, and personal computers would have remained confined to the small fraternity of hobbyists knowledgeable enough to create their own programs. Without programmers like the ones discussed in this chapter, a software-using community never would have existed to make folk heroes out of these unlikely cultural explorers.

Some of them live like hermits, and others are as gregarious as rock stars. All of them love to tinker with abstractions. Some are intellectuals, many are artisans, and a few are true geniuses. I know dozens of these characters, but I've picked three to discuss here: Paul Lutus was chosen because of his outright eccentricity and the size of the fortune he made for himself; Bill Budge is included because of the artistry of his work and because he is a prime example of the software creator as pop star; John Draper's story shows up here because he was probably the first legendary software person, given his earlier notoriety as a different kind of technological folk hero.

Paul Lutus is either the most entrepreneurial of the software eccentrics or the most eccentric of the software entrepreneurs. Certainly he has one of the most unusual backgrounds of anyone in the software industry. In the late 1960s, he was a vagabond who spent several years actually living under the bushes in San Francisco's Golden Gate Park and, later, on various Lower East Side rooftops in New York City. He experimented with psychedelic drugs, was a street musician, and became a minor celebrity because of his skill at blowing soap bubbles. By the mid-1970s he was back in California, pursuing a relatively mainstream lifestyle and working for NASA. Then he moved to Oregon and lived alone in a tiny cabin on Eight Dollar Mountain. It was there that he taught himself how to program. In the early 1980s, he was still a hermit, albeit in a much more sumptuous retreat, and he had grown accustomed to receiving royalties of two or three million dollars a year from the sales of his programs.

Paul is an independent fellow, but he goes far beyond the normal bounds of independence one comes to expect from programmers, both in what he demands and what he succeeds in getting. He does his own carpentry, his own programming, and his own contract negotiations. He loves music and plays a number of musical instruments. He loves to fly and even pilots his own plane. He even grows his own food, and his brain still seems to generate ideas far faster than he is able to articulate them. To this day he wears clothes that would best be described as "comfortable." His once-tangled head of hair is thinning, but his beard is full and bright red, and he still talks as fast and as passionately as humanly possible when he really gets wound up.

I've seen Paul only a few times, but of course I knew all the Lutus legends long before I first met him. Hearing about Paul Lutus was one of the mandatory initiation rituals in the software industry. Not long ago, I finally saw him on his own turf and asked him, face to face, which of the Lutus stories are true and which are fictional. In the summer of 1984, he invited me up to his latest mountaintop retreat, in southern Oregon. When I got there, he told me the highlights of his strange story.

To get to Paul's place I flew into the small airport in Medford, Oregon. Had he not picked me up in a four-wheel-drive Subaru station wagon, I never would have found his house myself. We got off a main highway and headed for the nearest forested hills, where we crossed a covered bridge, followed a steadily deteriorating roadway that runs alongside a stream, turned off through an inconspicuous and unmarked gate onto a gravel road, and drove straight across a rough landing strip. Then we drove past a "No Trespassing" sign and a "Warning: Protected by Guard Dogs" sign, and after the "Radiation Hazard" and "Mine Field: Contact Commanding Officer for Map of Area" signs, we finally arrived at a large house built into a mountain—Lutus Central.

Paul claims that his independence and his reclusiveness began during his unpleasant childhood in San Jose, California. "My family is very peculiar," he told me. "Even when we were living in the same house, we didn't talk with each other." Paul's father, a machinist, worked for IBM, and when Paul was young his father sometimes brought home obsolete computer parts. Paul remembers retreating into his workshop and his imagination, putting the components together in different combinations and pretending that they made a real computer. In the fifth grade, when his teacher wanted to put him in a class for slow learners because he always seemed to be dreaming or doodling in some world of his own, a test revealed that he had a genius IQ.

In high school, he was the classic example of a brilliant but emotionally tortured nerd. Only a few years before, he had been considered "slow," and now he found himself regarded by his peers as a "brain," which made him more of an outsider than ever before. Although he did have a few friends, he was pretty much of a loner who entertained himself. He built his own ham radio and an oscilloscope that he traded to a friend for a used bicycle. He remembers riding his clunky bike to and from school whereas his classmates drove their cars to football games and dates. "I was the most socially unacceptable person who ever went to that high school" is the way he remembers it now.

At sixteen he dropped out of school and got a job as a television repairman. Then, some years later, attracted by the countercultural ethic, he decided that making money wasn't a decent goal in life and quit the television repair business to live on the streets and make it as a folksinger during the height of the Haight-Ashbury and East Village scenes of the 1960s. Several years later, facing a winter on the streets of New York, he finally decided that having a job and a regular address wouldn't be so indecent after all. Establishing a *modus operandi* that was to serve him well for years to come, he walked into the instrumentation laboratory at New York's Mount Sinai Hospital and, with typical verbal persuasiveness, talked his way into a job building electronic equipment for medical research.

In the spring of 1974, after about a year at Mount Sinai, Lutus decided to ride his bicycle from New York to California. He was twenty-seven years old. He had no attachments and no particular plans for the rest of the year, to say nothing of the rest of his life. In Boulder, Colorado, he took some time out to learn hang-gliding, then bought a motorcycle and continued westward. The motorcycle and his money gave out somewhere around Sacramento. He hitchhiked to San Francisco, picked up a newspaper, and saw an ad for a job he knew he could do. He cleaned himself up as much as possible and performed a bit of his patented verbal razzle-dazzle on the personnel officers of an aerospace contractor.

He told a tale about a technical education he never had, but, showing that he knew what he was doing when it came to electrical and electronic design, he talked his way into a contract to design part of the complicated lighting system for the first Space Shuttle. His brilliant solution to this technical problem won him a bonus and a certificate of recognition from NASA. The aerospace contractor offered him other projects, but Lutus declined and in fact quit the job right then and there.

The subcontractor was reluctant to see him go, since he had turned out to be the star performer whenever NASA officials showed up to see how the lighting project was progressing. He had a knack for filling blackboards with equations and deftly fielding all technical questions with extemporaneous dissertations on the details of his design. But Paul was determined to get himself some breathing and thinking space. He had lived on the streets and in the parks, he had been a hobo and an aerospace engineer, he had traveled and dealt with too many people, and now it was time to find a place to be alone with his thoughts. And so he took his NASA money, told his former employers that he would be back to work for them as soon as he needed more money, and left San Francisco for the deep back country of Oregon.

In the spring of 1976, Lutus backpacked construction materials to the top of Eight Dollar Mountain, a wooded ridge 400 feet above a wilderness valley in Oregon, and hand-built a 12- by 24-foot cabin. After the cabin was finished, the provisions and modest furnishings were packed in, and the wood was chopped for the winter, the one thing he had in abundance was spare time, so he taught himself programming. At the time, he undoubtedly fit the classical definition of a poverty-stricken "hermit," but eventually his self-taught programming skill would eliminate his poverty and make him a rich hermit instead.

To most people, hackers are just the latest and perhaps the scariest variety of mad scientist. Weird computer guys, in the minds of the nonprogramming majority, are exactly like other weird technocultists. But people like Paul Lutus turned a much more favorable light on the public image of the programmer when they showed how much their arcane skill was worth on the open market. Some of the early entrepreneurial hackers of the microcomputer age came up with something that no previous variety of obsessed scientist had procured— vast amounts of money. As for Lutus himself, it is ironic that after he painstakingly worked himself into a position of bucolic solitude and lived a lifestyle that took a lot of manual labor to maintain but paid him very little in terms of money, one of the first things he did to amuse himself ended up making him rich.

That first winter, when he found himself alone with his thoughts in his wood-heated, waterless cabin, Paul started toying with one of the few items he had brought with him—a sophisticated battery-powered Hewlett-Packard electronic calculator. He told me that he had brought the calculator up to the cabin in the first place to help him with basic arithmetic. Higher mathematics had always interested him, but he had never bothered to memorize even the multiplication tables.

"The law said I had to attend school, so I was physically present in the classroom after the seventh grade" is the way he puts it, "but I wasn't there in any intellectual sense. I was in the back of the room with my own books. At home I built radios. I didn't know my multiplication tables, but I sure as hell knew how to think."

And as it happened, by setting up equations in proper sequences, he figured out how to create a limited variety of programs on the calculator. As an exercise, he made a pocket-calculator model of the solar system and wrote an article about it for publication in an electronics hobbyist magazine. The Jet Propulsion Laboratory wrote Lutus to tell him they were using his calculator model to help perform their own calculations for the *Viking* Mars-lander mission.

"I realized that my calculations were more than exercises," Lutus told me. "I saw a way to capitalize on my unique way of thinking about things. Programming started out as fun, but I certainly didn't object to making money from it."

(This is a familiar refrain. Many other software entrepreneurs, me included, were disbelieving when we first learned that people were actually willing to *pay* us to mess around with programming. I remember how I felt when I saw my first royalty check for *Galactic Empire*.)

Paul then became more and more interested in programming for microcomputers. Although eventually he would write a little science fiction software himself, he was mostly interested in building *tools* for computer owners—word processing programs and graphics programs that people could use to make their own discoveries. Tools of this nature help people win their independence and offer a very attractive kind of profession to someone like Paul, for whom making his own discoveries has been one of the most dominant themes of his life and work.

And so, after the HP calculator, Paul bought himself one of the early Apples, which he connected to his generator. Having low serial numbers is quite a status symbol among Apple fans, and Paul always points out that his Apple II was number sixteen. One of the things he thought about in his mountaintop retreat was how to create programs that were compact enough to fit into the very limited memory space of these early machines. It was the perfect kind of intellectual puzzle for him: After a life of drifting between art, technology, and vagabondage, he had finally found a pursuit so absorbing that he could pass entire nights solving a programming problem without noticing that sunset had turned to dawn. He sent more than thirty cassette-based programs to Apple, which bought most of them—for anything from $100 to $500 each.

But few of the programs Apple purchased were ever distributed. Of the few that were published, one of them, strangely enough, had initially been rejected by Apple. It was a simple music program—a tone generator. It was finally printed and attributed to Paul, whose name was nevertheless misspelled in Apple's famous "Red Book"—their first, terribly written, technical reference manual. (Software publishing was a lot looser back then; nowadays, a mistake like that would lead to a lawsuit.) Lutus then sold some programs to other companies, but he never made more than a few hundred dollars per program until the spring of 1978, when he returned to the San Francisco Bay Area to work on another Space Shuttle job. He brought with him a cassette that would enable the Apple to understand a few spoken commands. He asked Apple for a thousand dollars up front. Apple offered him one of their new disk drives in return for the program.

When he got back to Oregon, late in the spring of '78, Paul turned out a variety of small programs for different manufacturers, and he thought he would attempt a more ambitious program—a word processor. He had been trying to write an article about Albert Einstein and resented all the time he lost retyping drafts. What he needed was a computerized writing tool—a program that would enable his Apple to do what fancier word processors on bigger computers could do. By the end of the summer, he had a crude working version of *Apple Writer*. He didn't know it at the time, but this was the first version of the program that would make him a millionaire.

Lutus took this version of *Apple Writer* down to Apple and demanded a flat fee of $7500—far and away the most money a programmer had ever asked for thus far. Having sold only about 5000 of the new Apple IIs by the fall of 1978, Apple was still a small enough company to consider $7500 to be an issue for serious deliberation. The Apple people finally agreed, but they kept asking him to make changes, additions, and fixes on the program. After a while, he decided that he had no obligation to continue fixing the program until he ended up upgrading it to a new version (something every programmer has a right to charge for) for free. He then began to conceive of new features for a completely revamped word processor, and he started writing the program that eventually became *Apple Writer II*.

By 1979, Lutus programs were selling for between $5000 and $10,000 apiece. He was now earning more money in a single month than he had made in all of his vagabond years combined. Over a year had passed since he had sold the first version of *Apple Writer*. At about this time he had completed another word-processing program that he claimed was a radically new product. Because Apple still paid flat fees instead of the royalty arrangement Lutus now wanted, he began to look around for a publisher. Having once met Peter Jennings of Personal Software, publishers of *VisiCalc*, Paul wrote him a letter and proposed that Personal Software publish the new Lutus word-processing program under the name *LexiCalc*. Dan Fylstra, whom Lutus had not known previously, immediately took over and asked Paul to "refrain from serious negotiations with anyone else" during Personal Software's forty-five-day evaluation period.

Lutus was to receive $1500 for the waiting period, during which, according to Lutus, Fylstra asked for various modifications in the program. He began to sense that he was creating a whole new version before he even had a contract. Although he swears that he never initiated negotiations during the option period, Paul was contacted by Apple, which told him they had heard about his program via a friend inside Personal Software. The software people at Apple, who were not willing at first to meet Paul's demand for a royalty arrangement rather than a flat fee, were nonetheless eager to see his program. Somehow, word of this traveled back to Fylstra, who immediately launched into an acrimonious dispute with Lutus over the phone and via letter.

Lutus eventually sold his program to Apple, but this time he received an advance against royalties instead of a fee. Since Apple was selling considerably more than a few thousand machines by this time, Lutus started receiving royalties that soon amounted to more than $5000 a day. Whereas *Apple Writer* had been only a modest success, *Apple Writer II* remained the best-selling word processor for the Apple for five years; his 25 percent royalty on this one program made Paul a millionaire.

The first wave of successful Apple programmers made more money in a few years than almost any mainframe or minicomputer programmer normally makes in a lifetime. For example, Paul Lutus earned more than a million dollars a year during the 1980–83 boomtime, and the word-processing program he created with his generator-powered Apple earned him nearly 3 million dollars in royalties in a single year.

Before long he had enough money to indulge his longtime dream of flying his own plane. He even moved out of his old cabin at Eight Dollar Mountain and donated it, along with his first airplane and thousands of dollars, to The Nature Conservancy, a wilderness preservation group. He became the sole source of financial support for Planned Parenthood in southern Oregon. (Because, he claims, his own childhood was so miserable.) After building a series of progressively larger cabins he finally moved to a real house—one that he didn't even pack in and assemble himself. He has an airstrip now, as well as two airplanes. He writes articles, continues to support charitable ventures, flies around making speeches to school children, publishes slim volumes of poetry, and is still one of the best programmers in the business.

Paul's current house—the one he invited me to recently— is a rambling, white stucco and terra cotta tile affair in the Spanish style, with a central courtyard and a thick, ornately carved front door. If you can envision a slightly scaled-down version of President Nixon's Western White House in San Clemente, and put it in rolling hills surrounded by Douglas firs instead of on a cliff that overlooks the Pacific, surrounded by palm trees, you get the picture. The house, which was originally built by a survivalist, even had a moat around it when Paul first moved in, but he filled it in and planted a garden.

If the original cabin on Eight Dollar Mountain was the epitome of spartan, his latest place could easily be described as luxurious. There are massive rock fireplaces and high ceilings; he has electricity now, and a state-of-the-art stereo with speakers in every room. Not exactly the kind of hermit he once was, he now entertains an occasional friend. He even has girlfriends but retains a passionate distaste for the institution of marriage. He still makes his own music—I saw a recorder, a lute, a guitar, and a piano at his house—and one night during my stay he and a girlfriend treated me to a flute duet for several hours. When he needs more intensive solitude, he takes off in one of his planes.

I spent a morning flying around southern Oregon in his Super Cub with him. While he practiced "touch and gos" on isolated mesa tops and tiny airstrips, we talked about his future in the software industry. Or at least, I tried to talk to him about it. Lutus, like many programmers, avoids thinking about long-term or large-scale strategies for securing his position in the industry. Job security was never his goal in the first place. The computer is a device with which he and many programmers have an intensely personal relationship—a relationship that exists independent of their relationship with the software marketplace. They program because programming is in itself pure entertainment for them, and because real life seldom produces the kind of immediate feedback and instant rewards that programming can provide.

Paul needs that kind of relationship, but only as long as it continues to be a liberating rather than a confining force. For that reason, he absolutely rejects any attempt to stereotype or pigeonhole him. That's why he devotes so much of his time proving both to himself and to others that he is much more than a rich programmer. He is an aviator, a musician, a political activist, an outdoorsman, a poet. He is utterly himself—irascible, brilliant, iconoclastic—and will not be trapped by the expectations or preconceptions that others may have about him.

One way people liberate themselves from others' expectations is by acting in as idiosyncratic a manner as possible. Once people define that behavior, however, even idiosyncracy becomes a cage. The existence of rich programmers like Paul proved that unorthodox people who relate to machines better than they get along with people still can be valued by our society. But Paul understands that the myth of the programmer can estrange him from the actual role of programmer. As he says, he is fortunate. His savings permit him to do whatever he likes. He doesn't have to program for the marketplace, and that feels good because he's not at all sure that he wants to create for the market, at least not the market that exists now.

Paul has his own inner vision of what the future holds for the software industry, and he'd just as soon program for *that* market. If the world catches up to him, that's fine with Paul. But if it doesn't, that's okay too. He never specified what the software market of the future looked like in his vision, and in our conversations he didn't talk about one specific kind of software he planned to produce. We'll all just have to wait to see what he comes up with next, I guess.

"The rich are different from other people," Scott Fitzgerald reputedly said. "Yes," Ernest Hemingway allegedly replied, "they have more money." By the same token, programmers are different from other people because they know how to write computer programs. For many people, the programming skill is as difficult to grasp and as distant from their daily experience as is fluency in Swahili or the ability to assemble a pocket watch.

But this difference between programmers and nonprogrammers will probably become very blurred in the near future because programming will no longer require facility with the arcane amalgamation of abstruse mathematical calculations and painstaking logical puzzle solving. One key that will help to open the door to this coming populist revolution in software design is an exciting new kind of program, known in the trade as a program generator, that is already on the market. A lot of people in the software industry see these innovative products as the first step toward the creation of a programming-literate population that will number in the millions instead of in the thousands.

Program generators are partially tool-like, partially game-like, and partially lesson-like. A program generator brings the nonprogramming computer user to an intermediate stage between using a computer program that was written by someone else and generating a computer program of one's own. This stage is reached not through any formal education in programming principles but by means of a kind of transitional metaphor between the thinking involved in playing a video game and the kind of thinking needed to create a program.

One of the best and most successful program generators was written by a friend of mine named Bill Budge, who has been a legend among Apple programmers since the earliest days of commercial microcomputer software. He is also probably the quintessential representative of the new breed of programmers who see themselves as teachers and artists as well as technicians and craftsmen. He is, in fact, a programmer raised to the level of a pop star. Bill's current publisher, Electronic Arts, is even promoting him in much the same way that record companies promote their artists—with personal appearances, posters, even full-page magazine ads that display photo portraits of the programmer as culture hero. In one of the first magazine ads on Bill, the copy next to his photograph claimed: "In a bedroom in a frame house in Berkeley, California, a guy who looks like he might have stepped out of a TV series family is playing with some ideas that could change your life."

Bill does indeed look like he stepped out of "Leave It to Beaver." He could be one of Wally's friends, the kind of gangly but good-looking guy who is usually depicted with a basketball under one arm. He could even pass for one of the non-blond minority in a surf movie. Although there is a certain truth to the "nerd mythology" that microcomputer technology was first invented by a bunch of MIT types with thick glasses, bad complexions, and unsuccessful social lives, Bill

Budge is evidence of the fact that an obsessive love of computer programming can strike even the tall, dark, and handsome boy next door. (*Softalk*, the magazine for Apple owners, once published a fan letter that described Bill as a "hunk." The letter was later revealed to be a hoax—composed by Corey Kosack, a sixteen-year-old programmer who happened to be doing some work for Brøderbund at the time.) As for the frame house mentioned in the Electronic Arts ad, it too exists, although it is considerably more than the humble student dwelling implied by the ad, and it is actually located in Piedmont, an affluent neighborhood a few miles away from Berkeley.

It is also true that Bill is playing with ideas that are likely to change your life. His tools will put the power of computer programming into the hands of ordinary people. And he has yet to come up against the limits of his abilities. He's the kind of synthesizer and innovator who takes ideas from dozens of places and weaves them into brilliant and startlingly unexpected patterns. His past programming achievements, and the way he always seems to have his antennae out for sources of new ideas of every kind—from the Egyptian Book of the Dead to theories of dance notation—lead me to expect something even more spectacular from him in the near future. Certainly, Bill will be among those people who are going to make the next decade of the microcomputer software industry even more interesting than the past decade.

Bill was a famous programmer (in programming circles) before I ever owned an Apple—in fact, before I had even seen an Apple computer. I first learned of his name when on my journey west to visit my brother Gary—the trip that turned into a career—I stopped in Chicago to visit my aunt, who had an Apple II. Several diskettes containing demonstration programs came with the machine. One of the diskettes contained a game called *Penny Arcade*, which had a beautiful graphic opening sequence that struck me as a particularly provocative example of what one could do with an Apple. *Penny Arcade* had been written by Bill Budge.

The first time I met Bill was at the West Coast Computer Faire in 1981. Since then we've spent a lot of time together, talking about the art and science and business of developing software, and on several occasions we have even talked about becoming business partners. I can remember one particular occasion when a conversation between Bill, me, and some other programmers actually led to Bill's program generator and masterwork—*The Pinball Construction Set*, about which more will be said later on.

Like most great programmers, Bill got into software at a young age. He was in exactly the right place at the right time to join the first generation of programmer–entrepreneurs. But unlike today's youngest programmers, who have learned to program with the more advanced computer languages that have come along in the past few years, Bill started out the hard way. At sixteen, as a precocious student at Piedmont High, Bill was introduced to computers by his math teacher, who put a few exceptional students together with an old IBM 1401. The 1401 didn't have an easy-to-learn high-level language like BASIC, or even an older, harder-to-learn language like FORTRAN. Bill had to create his first programs in a language called 1401 Autocoder, a very primitive assembly language.

An assembly language consists of three-letter commands (like JMP or LDA) that tell the computer to perform very simple one-step-at-a-time operations. For example, where a command in a high-level language like BASIC might be able to say PRINT X + Y − Z, an assembly language program might require a dozen instructions to perform the same task. Assembly language instructions, however, can be converted into machine language—the code of zeroes and ones that instruct the computer to produce the on-and-off electronic impulses that constitute a computer program in operation—by means of a special translation program or *assembler*.

Assembly language is a very tedious and complex language to create programs with, since the computer must be instructed in exhaustive and unambiguous detail about where to find the data to operate on, how to operate upon them, and what to do with them once they are processed. And if any single symbol is out of place, the whole program will fail. Because the assembly language instructions correspond so closely to the electronic activities of the computer hardware, assembly language is called a low-level language, or one that, as some say, is "close to the machine."

Most programmers prefer to write their programs in a high-level language because it is more like English and is easier to use than the complex assembly language. When one learns enough BASIC to write programs on a computer, the BASIC interpreter built into the BASIC language program works as the program runs to convert each line of the program's instructions into machine language commands. However, BASIC programs are never as compact or as fast-running as code written by a programmer directly in assembly language.

The speed of execution of a program is particularly important in computer games, because people don't want to wait for three minutes to see if their shot hit or missed the alien invader. Graphics and animated figures are possible only when a program runs quickly. For these reasons, then, an assembly language expert like Bill Budge had an edge over other programmers when computer games came along.

But long before that time, when Bill was still learning assembly language programming in high school, he had the first "religious experience" of his programming career. His math teacher gave him a program for multiplying two numbers by repeatedly adding one of the numbers to itself and then stopping when the number of repetitions equaled the second number. This kind of instruction that starts the computer performing the same set of subinstructions over and over until a certain goal is accomplished is a basic programming technique known as "looping."

"I got real excited," Bill told me when he recalled that first insight, "because the whole idea of programming became clear to me when I saw what a loop could do. It was an incredibly exciting moment. I wrote down the lines of the program, then checked them to make sure they were right. All of a sudden, I saw what a loop really was for, why there could be such a thing as a loop, and how you could do a lot of things with the right kind of repeated sequences of simple instructions. By the end of high school I thought I was the world's greatest programmer."

But although he had far surpassed his teacher's ability to show him anything new, he was still a novice, and there was no hacker subculture of other high school–age software prodigies, such as there is today, to initiate him into the deeper mysteries of programming. He was virtually on his own, and when he was graduated from high school, he realized that spending so much time with his programs had locked him away from his peers. He went to the University of California at Santa Cruz as an English major, determined to expand his horizons beyond his obsession with programming virtuosity.

"I was fooling myself into believing that I didn't want to program computers as much as I did," he remembers. "I didn't want to be a nerd. I wanted a social life. I wanted to date. So I started acting cool. I wanted to be a writer. But I didn't want to write. Then it became clear that although writing was a struggle for me, programming was still a pleasure. So I transferred to the computer science program in Berkeley and concentrated on learning as much about computers and programming as I could."

The year that Bill went to Berkeley was 1975—a signal year in the history of microcomputers, since that was when the introduction of the MITS Altair brought programming out of the world of expensive mainframe computers and within the reach of hobbyists. Of course, Bill didn't have to build a microcomputer from a kit to program. He could program on the finest equipment available at Berkeley. He wasn't interested in kid stuff like microcomputers, and video games were still in their infancy then.

Instead, Bill wanted to create systems software and write compilers. It was the deep stuff of computerdom, and by now Bill was more interested in his career goals in the mainframe world than he was in the kind of intense emotional involvement that had gripped him at sixteen, when he first discovered the loop. Then, in 1977, as a graduate student in computer science at Berkeley, he had his second "religious experience" when his friend and fellow graduate student Andy

Hertzfeld showed him one of the earliest Apple computers. Bill still gets a wide-eyed look when he talks about it: "What I saw was the graphical bandwidth that was possible with the Apple. Like the loop, it opened a door onto a huge universe of possibilities."

"Bandwidth" is simply jargon for a measure of the amount of information than can be transferred between the computer and the display screen, and between the display screen and the eye of the person looking at it. Think of bandwidth as the width of a pipeline of information. Morse code can transmit only one bit of information at a time, so it has a narrow bandwidth. A television image can convey millions of bits of information in less than a second, so it has a very high bandwidth.

When it comes to computers, bandwidth is a very important measure of how interactive the device is and thus is a direct indicator of how interesting the programmer or user will find the device. We humans are very information-hungry creatures, particularly when it comes to visual information. It takes a lot of bandwidth to attract and hold our interest. Think about the first, simplest *Pong* games, with the ball bouncing back and forth, with some primitive sound effects. Then think about something like *Pac-Man*, with animated characters in color and high resolution, moving fairly quickly in a rich visual environment. Finally, think about a television show and a wide-screen movie image. It's pretty obvious that one's interest increases as bandwidth increases.

Bill got hooked on the Apple's bandwidth because it offered him something the mainframe computers he was using at Berkeley could not. Even though mainframes had vastly greater processing power than the first Apples, the way they communicated with the programmers was through a very low bandwidth device known as a terminal. Terminals allowed many people to share the services of a central computer—an arrangement known as time-sharing that was a revolutionary breakthrough in the early 1960s but that was old hat in computer terms by the late 1970s.

By entering commands on keyboards and receiving printouts through a typewriter-like device, programmers on time-sharing systems could run their programs and see the results. But they couldn't interact with the computer at the same communication rate that they used when they interacted with people. It's very much like trying to carry on a conversation by means of a teletype machine. And so, since most programmers want to have a conversation with a computer, their hunger for high bandwidth is understandable.

The nice thing about the Apple that Bill saw that day in 1977 was not that it had huge computing power, but that the power it did have was immediately available to the person using the computer, and the information that mediated the human–computer interaction was visible through the graphic display on the screen. That's what a personal computer is—a computer that is interactive enough, visible enough, and fast enough for one person to use. Bill was therefore so captivated by the Apple's interactive capability that he immediately sat down and wrote a *Pong*-like game for the Apple—his first microcomputer program.

To the faculty and the other students at Berkeley's computer science department, the Apple was an amusing toy, but certainly nothing for a sophisticated programmer to get serious about. Bill's friend Andy Hertzfeld tried to declare personal computers as his academic subinterest, and everybody gave him a hard time about it. At the time, computer scientists, programmers, and the computer industry all saw them as smaller and far less powerful computers with bad or nonexistent software. To some extent, those were valid criticisms—but computer people, of all the different technological specialists, ought to have known how quickly crude prototypes can evolve into sophisticated devices.

Not too long after he left graduate school, Hertzfeld joined the Apple Corporation at a very early stage in that institution's history and later became one of the most influential software people on the Macintosh team. Bill himself also worked for Apple at one time, but before that, while still a graduate student, he spent months just trying to buy an Apple at a discount. Computer science graduate students aren't wealthy people, unless they moonlight as professional programmers. By Christmas of 1978, in his second year of graduate school, he finally went as deeply into debt as he had ever been in his life and bought his own Apple at full price.

"I remember putting the whole machine back in the boxes every night after I used it, just to keep it as new as possible," he told me recently. It was an ironic reminiscence, considering the tens of thousands of dollars' worth of computer equipment and audio gear that surrounds him in his workplace–playroom now. All of the models of Apple computer are scattered around the room, although the one that appears to be used the most is the 1978 Apple II, now battered-looking and only partially operational. And there's what appears to be a coin-operated video game machine in the corner. It turns out to be a customized programming device sent him by Williams Electronics, the coin-op giant, who evidently hoped that Bill could be persuaded to write some coin-op games for them. (He couldn't.)

BASIC was the only high-level language that was available when Bill got his first Apple, but he quickly realized that he couldn't write anything interesting in BASIC. So he started writing in assembly language. With the speed and precision afforded by assembly language, Bill was able to approach a new level of high-resolution graphics—indeed, his programs became known for their "high-res" effects.

"In early 1979," Bill remembers, "everyone was discovering the tricks of microcomputer programming through trial and error. I'd turn on my machine and start fooling around with different locations in the memory, trying to figure out how to put dots on the screen and move them around fast."

Then, referring to Bob Bishop, the first person to sell a lot of Apple software and actually make a little money for his efforts, Bill said: "Nobody but Bob Bishop had ever written any high-res stuff. He was everyone's hero." "Everyone" consisted of the hard-core fanatic Apple programmers of that era. "When I first got my Apple, the first thing I did was to get a disk that had some Bob Bishop games.

"One of the games on the disk was called *Bomber*, a really famous game because it was in hi-res and had so much detailed animation. These tanks would go across the screen and you'd fly a bomber. When you released a bomb, it would make a parabolic curve as it fell, and if you made a hit the tank would blow up and pieces would fly up in the air and then settle to the ground. It was a whole new level of realism from bouncing square *Pong* balls around a screen.

"I wanted to make cartoons and games. That's what I thought was really neat about these new little computers that you could plug into your television. I thought that computers by themselves were a lot less interesting than computers combined with other things—like entertainment or education or art. Despite my specialization in microcomputer programming, I've always been interested in a lot of different subjects. The Apple looked like a great vehicle for turning my programming abilities to a much wider range of applications than just science or business programming."

And after a while, it also looked like a fun new way to pick up a few bucks on the side. At that time, Bill was making about $4000 a year as a teaching assistant—a stipend that paid for his tuition, but not much else. In the tradition of grad students everywhere, he was just getting by. Still, the prospect of making some money from his microcomputer dabbling wasn't his major motivation. At first, the primary motivation was the raw challenge of exploring and conquering the unknown. There were entire libraries full of programs for the bigger, older, more serious computers, but virtually nothing available for the Apple. Bill simply enjoyed poking around in the machine's memory and using assembly language programming to come up with new ways to move graphic objects around the screen.

"When I saw what you could do with a personal computer like the Apple, I was thrilled by the prospect of jamming on the computer, the way a jazz musician might jam on a piano. I've always been the kind of person who gets something kind of clunky working quickly, then spends more time fixing it and tuning it—as opposed to the type of person who breaks down the process into logical steps, then gets everything arranged mentally before trying to make it work. There are a lot of advantages to the more analytic mode, but I found that my seat-of-the-pants style was powerful and fast. Mostly, I found that it was the way I like to do things."

Then one day, later in 1979, Bill drove across the bridge from Berkeley and down the peninsula to Cupertino, where Apple's headquarters were located. He wrote four different *Pong*-like games, put them together with an intriguing little graphic leader, copied the program onto a diskette, and took the diskette with him. The people at Apple looked at his software, liked it, and told him they wanted to add it to the demonstration disk they included with every machine they sold. Nowadays, such offers are known as "bundling deals," and they can make programmers rich. Apple offered Bill a printer worth about $750 as payment for *Penny Arcade*, and he was happy to get it.

The main thing about programming microcomputers is that it's fun to do, but it's always nice to get paid as well. That's the way all great programmers start out—intrigued by the idea that they could earn money from such an enjoyable hobby. Six or seven years ago, however, it never really occurred to any of us just how lucrative programming could be. We learned eventually that we not only could make a living at it, but a very decent living at that.

At about the same time that I was beginning to consider having my first game published, Bill began to think about making his sideline into a full-time career: "Although it took me a month to write the first programs I sold, I knew that when I got up to speed I could create twenty of them a year. And that meant I could make around $20,000, which was a very decent wage compared to what I could have pulled down in a computer science department at a university or as a programmer for a mainframe computer company. So I started grinding out games."

Despite his "factory approach" to software production, the games that Bill started producing weren't bad. In fact, they were visibly superior to almost every other product on the market. They were just as visually intriguing as his first. He kept Apple enthusiasts supplied with new and exciting software, and these early games brought Bill up to speed on assembly language and game-programming techniques.

"My parents went to Hawaii that summer, and I had the whole house to myself," Bill recalls. "I wrote four programs in three months and took them to Hayden Publishing. They liked the programs, but they couldn't decide on the provisions of the contract quickly enough for me. Three months later I took the programs to a company called Softape. I wanted to sell them outright for $2000 each. They liked them but they didn't want to buy them. Then I met a fellow who wanted to sell them for me on a royalty basis. He was a sort of frontier ethic, software gold-rush kind of entrepreneur. He had what was then a new idea—he gave demonstration copies of my programs to the managers of computer stores. In Christmas of 1979, a year after I bought my Apple, he brought me my first royalty check—$6000 for my first month!"

That was more money than Bill made in two semesters as a graduate teaching assistant. If it kept coming in at that pace, it would be more than the head of the computer science department earned. It didn't go quite that fast, however. The first year that he devoted himself to turning out programs for a living, 1980, Bill made around $10,000 rather than the $20,000 he had hoped for at first. But the year after that, 1981, he made $80,000. And he was now making a name for himself in a field that was just beginning to blossom in the marketplace. Computers were selling faster and faster. And as the rate of computer sales increased, so did the sales of good programs. By 1982–83, Bill was making in the neighborhood of half a million dollars a year.

For a while, in 1980, Bill worked at Apple, along with his old friend Andy Hertzfeld. He became friendly with people like Wozniak and Jobs, who had been his heroes. The fun factor had jumped an order of magnitude, and the challenges were more intriguing every day. And financially, he was rocketing past what his computer science colleagues were making in academia and the mainframe world. But to Bill, programming offered more than just money and even more than sheer enjoyment. It also offered what he wanted most of all: glory.

He had seen what Jobs and Wozniak had done. He had seen what programmers like Bob Bishop and Paul Lutus had done. Like any other artist, he wanted a broader canvas, a more ambitious scope for his vision. He wanted to create *the* state-of-the-art program in the world of Apple software. He then stopped writing all of the short, sweet, throwaway games that had been his bread and butter, and he took a risk. And this was before he started making the big money. He spent several months working on one masterpiece, a best-selling program that lives in software legend under the name *Raster Blaster*.

As usual, Bill's idea was to take one of his personal interests and combine it with his programming skills to create something new. In this case, it was his interest in playing pinball. To most people, the old-fashioned electromechanical pinball games are the very antithesis of computer games. Pinball is very mechanical and physical, with steel balls and bumpers and lights and buzzers. Computer games are electronic and more perceptual than physical. Instead of steel balls, computers manipulate dots of light. But Bill realized that the ball, the flippers, the effect of gravity, the "bounciness" of the bumpers—all the essential elements of pinball— were, in principle, capable of being simulated by a computer program.

"I wanted to make one great video game," Bill told me when I asked if he consciously set out to create a best-seller. "The idea of creating a 'hit' in the commercial sense really wasn't part of the atmosphere back then. I realized that video games were getting kind of boring, from the point of view of the programmer, if not yet the consumer. I could crank them out and make a good living, but they weren't very satisfying. I started working on *Raster Blaster* when I was at Apple, in late 1980, and I finished it in March '81. When I realized how good it was, in comparison to everything else that was out there, I started thinking about marketing it myself."

Bill is actually a pretty modest guy, especially in comparison with some of the unabashed egotists that seem to abound in the software game. When he says that he realized how good it was, he is simply stating a fact. Everyone in the software industry realized that it was a significant programming breakthrough. Besides the idea of designing a computer version of a pinball game, Bill's creation included a lot of important innovations that inspired other programmers to try to top *Raster Blaster*. The game exhibited a graphic complexity that had not been seen before on a microcomputer (although arcade-type video games, with their dedicated graphics hardware, had attracted attention and money with dazzling graphics).

By April 1981, the software market was maturing rapidly. Bill had had a series of bad experiences with existing software publishers and wasn't happy with the contracts he was offered by various distributors and publishers for his products, so he decided to take matters into his own hands. He started a software publishing company—Budgeco, it was called—to market *Raster Blaster*, and his sister and brother-in-law set up an operation in their house, not too many blocks away from Bill's place in Piedmont. Bill happened to be correct in his initial estimation of *Raster Blaster*'s impact. It was the third program to (temporarily) dislodge *VisiCalc*—at that time, the all-time best-seller in microcomputer software history—from *Softalk*'s list of the top thirty Apple programs. (The other programs to temporarily outsell *VisiCalc* on the Apple were Tony Suzuki's *Alien Rain*, a Broderbund publication, and Nasir Gebelli's *Space Eggs*, a Sirius product.)

By the time *Raster Blaster* hit, Bill was more than a legend—he was a significant industry in himself. There were many more people buying programs, the price of the programs was going up, and so was the programmer's share. But running a publishing company turned out to be a drain on his creative time, so Budgeco eventually faded away. He started out publishing the Apple version of his next program but soon grew tired of worrying about marketing it and began shopping around for another publisher—one that would take him on his own terms.

That next program was, like *Raster Blaster*, a masterpiece. It was called *Pinball Construction Set*, a program generator in the guise of a game, and it turned out to be another watershed in the programming art, as well as another smash hit in the marketplace.

The origins of *Pinball Construction Set* are particularly interesting to me, because they involved a challenge that two of our programmers and I set for Bill one summer afternoon, and because they involved as well some obscure but important breakthroughs provided by others in various kinds of computer research. The use of program generators was not unique. But Bill's program generator also included graphic symbols known as icons, and graphic editors that enabled users to create new programs by manipulating those icons—a new kind of human–computer interaction that had been pioneered at high-technology thinktanks like Xerox Palo Alto Research Center and was included in Apple's new (and then-unreleased) machine, the Macintosh.

The general idea of graphics construction sets first emerged more than two decades ago with Ivan Sutherland's brilliant *Sketchpad* program. When Sutherland was a graduate student at MIT in the early 1960s, the standard way of seeing computer output was on teletype machines. *Sketchpad* was a program that enabled programmers to actually control the computer's operations by means of graphic symbols that were displayed on a television-like screen. By using a lightpen, the user/programmer could actually create different shapes on the screen, then manipulate the shapes by means of the computer's processor and store the end product in the computer's memory.

Innovations happen so fast in the software world and become standards so rapidly that the idea of creating graphics on a screen and storing them in a computer seems old hat to even the youngest computer user today. But in 1961, when *Sketchpad* was written, this idea was truly revolutionary. The idea of designing a graphic world inside a computer—the concept known as simulation—was another such breakthrough that is now commonplace. Several years after *Sketchpad*, a computer scientist and educational expert at M.I.T. by the name of Seymour Papert was experimenting with graphics and simulations and a new computer language called LOGO.

One of the key concepts in LOGO was that programming a computer doesn't have to be as esoteric and difficult as the first computers and the old-time programmers made it seem. The idea behind the LOGO project was to develop a new computer language—one that even children could quickly learn to use. LOGO starts novices on the path to programming not by having them type in unfamiliar commands but by introducing them to a means of controlling graphic displays known as turtle graphics. The turtle was originally a small turtle-shaped robot that crawled around the floor, drawing patterns on pieces of paper, but eventually it became an abstract turtle—a symbol on a computer screen.

Between the older ideas like Sutherland's *Sketchpad* and Papert's LOGO and the newer ideas like icons and program generators, the fundamental concepts of software construction sets had already existed for years when Bill Budge came along with *Pinball Construction Set.*

But although Bill's program generator was one of the best in the microcomputer world, it was not the first to be developed for that market. The previous summer, Broderbund had published a game called The Arcade Machine that enabled the user to create a variety of "shoot-'em-up games," admittedly an easier and less general task than constructing a variety of pinball games. And there was a famous piece of software called *The Last One* that was heavily advertised in 1981 as a generator so powerful that it would be the last program you would ever need to buy. Even before that, another, very sophisticated game generator was designed in 1978 by a game programmer at Atari named Warren Robinett. Robinett decided to do an animated version of the *Adventure* games that had originated on the mainframe computers at MIT and Stanford and had migrated, via the efforts of people like Scott Adams and me, to the microcomputer world. The original *Adventure* was strictly a text game with no graphics. In order to produce a version that had animated graphics, Robinett created a simple graphics editor that would allow the player to move through *Adventure*'s various caves while dragging various graphical objects along on the journey.

When Robinett left Atari, he teamed up with a couple of education experts to create a microworld simulation that took his simple graphics editor into the realm of true program generators. The much-acclaimed program *Rocky's Boots*, written by Robinett and Leslie Grimm, published after *Pinball Construction Set,* is a game that allows children to build various "machines" by putting together various graphical "parts." One very interesting aspect of this game is the fact that the machine parts are very advanced in that they are actually Boolean logic symbols, while the machines themselves are Boolean logic circuits. The child who uses the game ends up knowing how to design Boolean logic circuits—a skill that was formerly reserved for college mathematics majors or computer science students in graduate school!

With *Pinball Construction Set*, an even more advanced program generator entered the marketplace. In fact, when it was first released, it had an enormous impact on those who used it because it seemed to be more than just a great game. It looked and felt like a whole new way of using computers. I can remember the first time Bill talked about the idea of programming such a game. The topic came up on the day he, Nasir Gebelli, another set of programmer–entrepreneurs, and I met in Sacramento to talk about the prospect of merging our companies.

It was hardly the kind of giant merger discussion you read about in regard to the old-fashioned computer business, where phalanxes of three-piece-suited attorneys engage in marathon negotiations over hardwood conference tables. As I remember, we spent some time talking in a pizza joint in Sacramento. Nothing came of the merger discussion, but the same people ended up in a conversation at a barbecue I held at my house in San Rafael shortly thereafter. Chris Jochumson, who had created Brøderbund's *The Arcade Machine*, was there, and so was David Snider. David had written a best-selling pinball game that Brøderbund sold under the name *David's Midnight Magic*. The game was very complex, but it did not give users an option to create their own game from the elements provided.

David was of the opinion that a generalized pinball microcomputer construction set, one that could simulate a wide variety of pinball layouts, couldn't be created. What with the effect of simulated gravity, and the angles the ball would bounce at, and the effect of bumpers and flippers and obstacles, David felt that there were too many factors involved to generalize. But although David thought that a general pinball game would be too hard to write, Bill was convinced that it could be done. It took him longer than he thought it would take, but he was certainly right.

Like *Raster Blaster, Pinball Construction Set* simulates all the elements of an old-fashioned pinball game. But the new program allows players to make their own modifications on the basic game, and to create their own games. Previously, one had to dig into the program and modify the code to change a computer game. Bill made the modification process accessible to the nonprogrammer by providing a set of software "tools" that are displayed as icons—small symbolic graphics—on the screen. At the time Bill was developing this program, Andy Hertzfeld and other friends of Bill's at Apple were incorporating icons into the Macintosh.

If players want to pick up a bumper or a flipper, they use the joystick to move an icon that looks like a hand and touch it to the bumper or flipper. That icon is actually a tool that can pick up the bumper or flipper icon and places it where the game creator wants it to be. When the hand icon touches the flipper icon and moves it into position, part of the program's code tells the computer's memory that the flipper icon has been moved. By selecting different parts and putting them together in various combinations, the user/player/game builder can make an almost infinite variety of pinball games. Bill included another tool that allows users to magnify an area of the screen so that they can work on fine details.

Naturally, the program was another smash hit. It was also a sign of things to come. People who were knowledgeable about the evolution of software design began to point out that this program actually allowed the user to directly manipulate the computer's operations without using a programming language: When the little hand icon drags the little flipper icon over to a representation of a pinball game board, the same thing is accomplished as would normally take a programmer pages of programming code to do.

The idea of modifying a basic template is much more palatable to most people than the prospect of designing a game (or any other complex creation) from scratch. Software construction sets can give novice computer users their first taste of the kind of power exercised by people like Bill Budge. Instead of seeing computer programming as mysterious and difficult, people are beginning to perceive it as a skill that can be easily mastered and that gives them more control over what they can do with their computer.

Program generators like *Pinball Construction Set* have already spawned a whole new category of stand-alone programs and tools that are included within other programs. Brøderbund includes generator tools in several of its programs. *Lode Runner* and *Spare Change*, for example, are multi-level games that allow users to modify the program, thus creating their own variations once they have mastered the basic game. Other publishers are marketing programming generators in one guise or another—for learning how to read, write, and compose music, for steering a simulated Space Shuttle, and even for learning biochemistry and immunology.

As for Bill's decision regarding a publisher for *Pinball Construction Set*, certainly I strongly pitched the advantages of signing up with Brøderbund. Any software publisher in his right mind would give a great deal to have a Bill Budge on board. But at the same time, a group of ex-Apple people, headed by Trip Hawkins and backed by Steve Wozniak, had decided to form a new kind of software publishing company that would be modeled on record companies, and they strongly urged Bill to join them. In effect, they told him that the success of their venture, Electronic Arts, depended on his participation. They also offered him a substantial share of the company's ownership.

So Electronic Arts published *Pinball Construction Set* and started sending Bill out on tours to computer stores, printed up Bill Budge posters, and promoted him as the first software artist to become a pop star. It couldn't happen to a more deserving person, as far as I'm concerned. As far as Bill is concerned, his apprenticeship was shoot-'em-up games, he became a journeyman with *Raster Blaster*, and he just started his career as a master software craftsman with *Pinball Construction Set*. He and a lot of others, including me, think that the world has only begun to see the effects of his unique talents.

Bill's ambition for the near future is to create more tools that will enable other kinds of artists to do things in their own fields that they weren't able to do before Bill Budge made it possible. "I want to help create the language for a universal medium of knowledge. I want a filmmaker like George Lucas to use my tool to create films he couldn't have created without the program I plan to make for filmmakers. I want choreographers and playwrights and water polo players to use my tools."

What Bill is talking about, and what program generators demonstrate, is that programming is a metaphor for controlling information. The old metaphor involved complex codes, punch cards, and giant machines, and a newer metaphor involved strange new languages and smaller machines. The program generator is a different metaphor altogether, and Bill thinks that there are still newer and more powerful metaphors to be found beyond the program generator.

"Right now, I think theater is the best metaphor for programming," Bill claims. "That's what I'm trying to make concrete. Alan Kay, who is one of the original visionaries of personal computer software, says that programming is a process of choreographing multiple agents. I want to figure out a way for people to do that choreography by using skills they already possess."

I think Bill is trying to say that people understand theater far more easily than they understand mathematics. If programming arcana like procedure calls and data types, loops and stepped variables can be turned into analogies we already understand—like props and characters, scenes and sets—then the population of people who are able to understand how those elements are combined will be vastly expanded.

In the ancient days of computerdom, only the scientifically literate and the technologically obsessed were interested enough in programming to become good at it. Bill Budge is a significant member of a new generation of artists and craftsmen, thinkers and activists and dreamers—a generation that sees the advent of the computer as the opportunity to create a new level of human culture. I think something similar must have happened back when the new technology of the printing press created a large literate population and made it possible for artists to create sonnets, politicians to draft manifestoes, and scientists to write treatises.

I know a few young programmers, and they give me good reason to suspect that Bill Budge is just one of many software artists who will make themselves known in the next three, five, or ten years. But today's teenage programmers have at least one advantage over Bill: As a pioneer, he didn't have any role models himself, but the up-and-coming hackers of today and tomorrow have Bill Budge and his products to emulate.

John Draper, fanatic wizard in the programming language Forth, jackpot programmer–entrepreneur, and folk hero of those technological enthusiasts called phone phreaks, is known to most of the microcomputer world as "Cap'n Software." His involvement in the industry began in the myth-shrouded era of the homebrewers, but long before then, he and Wozniak were fellow technopranksters back when apples were still just small red fruit that grew on trees. He's cherished by many as a stubborn, independent, free spirit in a software market increasingly dominated by large teams of programmers. To others, however, "cherished" might not be the best word to describe their feelings about John Draper. Ask around the industry and you'll collect some strong and often less than favorable opinions when you mention his name.

Indeed, his reputation almost precedes him, for he is a man with a past—a past that involves one of the more notorious and romantic episodes from technological folklore of the 1970s.

This is one of the few profiles in this book that are not based on years of friendship or extensive personal interviews. Frankly, I'm a little wary of approaching John for a direct interview, especially after hearing what he did to a couple of journalists I know. There is apparently a kind of informal

Draper initiation ritual that all interviewers must survive before they get anything out of him. One of the journalists who suffered through a Draper interview agreed to describe the legendary ceremony, with the understanding that I wouldn't use his name.

"Fifteen minutes after I met John Draper," my journalist friend told me, "he ordered me to assume an anatomically questionable position."

What this friend meant was that Draper asked him if he wanted to "help out with some stretching exercises." That in turn meant that my friend had to take off his own shirt and shoes and get down on his hands and knees on the floor of John's apartment. Then John got on my friend's back, threw a full nelson, and barked orders into his ears. Such was a typical Draper interview, but it turns out that the Draper treatment is a form of amateur chiropractic. He has a bad back, and he actually does go through various calisthenics and contortions every day.

But nobody had fully explained this to my friend: "By the time it sank in that somebody who I had been warned was rather eccentric was taking it upon himself to debug my spine, I was duckwalking around the room, carrying out odd instructions barked into my ear by this big sweaty guy with an itchy beard. I knew that programmers can be weird, but it had never come to *this*." My friend survived the initiation, conducted his interview, but canceled his plans for a second conversation.

Draper is intimidating enough without direct physical contact. I've seen him at Computer Faires and trade conventions over the years, and I can vouch for the fact that his appearance alone can unnerve the unprepared: A gray-flecked tangle of dark hair and beard frame his famous gap-toothed grin; ice-blue eyes focus an inch and a half into your forehead when he talks to you. If you remember the face of Blackbeard the pirate or Long John Silver, and if you can imagine one of those fellows wearing slightly skewed eyeglasses, then you'll be able to recognize John Draper.

Then there's the matter of John's personal communication style. Expansive gestures often accompany his words. He has been known to raise his voice, which is pitched at a particularly piercing frequency range. He doesn't lack for strong opinions. And if anybody within 200 yards lights a cigarette, cigar, or pipe, watch out. He's allergic to tobacco smoke and is not too shy to say something about it.

Draper is definitely a graduate of the "take it apart and see how it works" school of computer wizardry, rather than the rarified heights of MIT's or Stanford's computer science department. But programming was really his second career. The escapades that brought him notoriety, if not financial rewards, took place long before the Altair era and involved the global telecommunications network rather than anything as simple as a personal computer.

Before he became reknowned as "Cap'n Software," the programmer of the late 1970s who was involved in one of the major software deals sin the history of the microcomputer software industry, Draper was known only as "Cap'n Crunch," techno-anarchist hero of an entire subsect of the technological underground: the phone phreaks. Although he had been a legend in phreak circles since the late 1960s, his saga as Cap'n Crunch wasn't told to a general audience until 1971, when a journalist named Ron Rosenbaum wrote an article for *Esquire* entitled "Secrets of the Little Blue Box." Rosenbaum described the antics of an electronic genius in California who performed strange and technically illegal pranks through which, by means of a device known as a "bluebox," he was able to gain access to the telephone system free of charge.

Years later, Draper still claims that his motives for his former activities were unjustly misunderstood. He's not an anarchist or a vandal, he has always maintained. He just likes to learn how complicated systems work and is driven to find out how to control the activities of these systems—whether they are electronic systems, software systems, or telephone systems. Unfortunately, in 1974, Federal judges didn't agree with John's interpretation of his motives, so Draper temporarily moved into Federal correctional facilities.

But long before that time, Cap'n Crunch was just one— albeit the most well known—of thousands of "phone phreaks" who for years conversed over their own clandestine communication system that just happened to make use of Ma Bell's own vast network. Their very existence stemmed from their urge to tinker, which was in turn stimulated by something as accessible, complex, mysterious, and vast as the telephone system. That they could even learn how that system worked came about as a result of their discovery of forbidden knowledge about a technical loophole in the telephone system's security. Nearly thirty years ago, AT&T made the long-term multibillion-dollar decision to base its long-distance switching system on a series of audible tones. These tones, which triggered various internal switching devices, were based on a series of specific frequencies. Unfortunately, an article in a technical journal divulged the frequencies of the control tones.

An unusual group of people, having read the article, began to take advantage of this technological vulnerability, apparently independently of one another—at first. A mutant variety of the kind of adolescent boy who is likely to fiddle with soldering irons and ham radio outfits, the first phone phreaks made clever use of tape recorders and electric organs to facilitate entry to the switching system. By knowing when and how to enter the right tone into their home telephones, these electronic trespassers were able to "phreak around" the network and to learn how it worked. Soon, those phreaks with electronics skills began building tone generators.

The person who is universally acknowledged to be the founding phreak, predating even Cap'n Crunch, was a blind young man with perfect pitch who *whistled* into the phone and thus gained access to virtually any telephone in the world, free of charge. Joe Engressia was his name. His dream in life was to work for Ma Bell. In fact, he liked to tell her about flaws in her system—a bit of outlaw gallantry that eventually led to his legal downfall. In fact, the first phone phreaks considered themselves to be harmless, and for the most part even helpful. They *liked* having the system function perfectly, and they liked to help the phone company fix any bugs they found. Many of them, curiously, were blind. The more aggressive phreaks, however, were bringing down the heat.

In the late 1960s, Cap'n Crunch himself got his name from a breakfast cereal that offered a toy whistle as a premium. The sound produced by the whistle was coincidentally close to a pure 2600 cycle tone, and as every phreak who ever thumbed a bluebox knows, 2600 cycles is the most important of the control tones needed to build one's own shadow network within the international switching system. When he was an Air Force electronic engineer stationed overseas, John Draper started using his whistle to talk to his friends back in the States, toll free. But free phone calls to friends weren't his biggest goals. He wanted to learn the ins and outs of the wonderfully complicated global switching system.

When he got out of the Air Force, the Cap'n got full-tilt into phreaking, driving around northern California in a van crammed with electronic equipment and performing late-night experiments from public telephone booths. He set up complex, satellite-linked, global communications circumnavigations in order to talk to himself from adjacent phone booths in remote areas. Or he would call public telephones in faraway places. What's happening at the American Embassy in Moscow? Who's passing by a phone booth in London? What's the weather like in Uruguay? The object was not to make free phone calls. The goal was to play the communications network like a musical instrument, to reprogram it as if it were a giant computer that he could command from any telephone.

After the *Esquire* article came out in 1971, Draper got a message through the phreak underground that two young fellows from Silicon Valley wanted to meet him. Crunch knew how to put the right electronic components together to make a bluebox. Steve Wozniak and Steve Jobs were interested in building their own blueboxes and maybe making a few dollars by selling them to students. Ever the advocate of a free exchange of technical information, Crunch told the two would-be entrepreneurs the technical details they were seeking. Shortly thereafter, the two Steves were holding "bluebox parties" in Berkeley dormitories and selling their elegantly home-built blueboxes for $60 apiece.

In 1974, Cap'n Crunch was busted twice. The first time landed him in a Federal penitentiary in Allentown, Pennsylvania, for six months. His second conviction for wire fraud landed him for several years in Lompoc, another Federal pen, located in California. It was in Lompoc that a Mafia-connected inmate tried to bribe John to divulge the secrets of bluebox construction, then, failing that, to extort them from him. Draper refused to divulge what he knew, and the other inmate broke Draper's back—hence his ongoing interest in chiropractic exercises. While serving his second term he became eligible for the prison's work-furlough program, which enabled him to learn programming and try to find programming jobs.

Draper and Wozniak continued their friendship, although the Cap'n's relationship with Jobs was not as close. When Apple was barely out of the garage stage of its operations, Draper became one of its early employees. One of his jobs was to design a telephone device for the Apple. The telephone board Draper designed had very sophisticated properties—*too* sophisticated for Jobs's tastes, because Draper had included features that phone phreaks might find very useful. They were no longer having fun and making a few extra bucks selling blueboxes to undergraduates. They were trying to build a legitimate company. Draper was fired. But not before he used the prototype phone board for one last, massive prank.

Draper was looking for WATS extender numbers—codes that allowed people in a particular area to gain access to free long-distance lines for major companies. Phone phreaks like to use these numbers to help them set up some of their pranks. The codes were four-digit numbers, which meant that he would have to dial up to 10,000 numbers if he were to find these codes by brute force. But Draper wired up an early Apple computer to his prototype phone board and programmed it to dial 5000 calls a night and automatically record which attempts led to legitimate WATS connections. The city of Mountain View, California, where Draper was living at the time, has determined that Draper was responsible for more than 50 percent of the calls originating from that city during the period his experiment was in operation.

Draper had dabbled in programming for years—after all, phreaking is a way of programming the communication network—but it wasn't until he was on a work-furlough leave from his second prison term that he started to seriously teach himself Forth. Forth is a peculiar programming language in that it uses "grammatical" structures different from those of other languages. Because Forth consists of programmer-defined "words" that can be combined into customized programs, it enables programmers to work in a highly individual manner. Because of the fanatic devotion that some programmers tend to develop for Forth, one of the clichés in the software industry is that "Forth isn't a language—it's a religion."

Because of his self-taught, freewheeling style, John's method of programming had several advantages and disadvantages when it came to the world of microcomputer software. While he was at Apple, and afterward, he developed a reputation for writing very concise code, which meant that he could produce an applications program—like a word processor, for example—that could fit into the limited memory of one of the early personal computers. He could also work very fast and accomplish a great deal during prolonged programming binges that sometimes took several days. His style was also vulnerable to criticism on some counts, however. Instead of revising his whole system to fix an error, he might create a "patch"—additional code that doesn't eliminate the problematic feature of the program but rather bypasses certain annoying results.

In the late '70s, John decided to design a word-processing program for microcomputers. Text editing and word processing were already catching on, but such programs then in use in offices were too large and cumbersome to shoehorn into an Apple. So John created *EasyWriter*. But by this time, he was *persona non grata* around Apple, and even though he maintained his friendship with Wozniak, his program was rejected by the corporation. Eventually, in 1978, Apple decided to support a word-processing package called *Apple Writer*, created by that other eccentric character, Paul Lutus.

After Apple turned down *EasyWriter*, Draper found a partner, Matthew McIntosh, who was able to handle his mercurial mood changes and bizarre work habits. He and McIntosh set up a booth at an early West Coast Computer Faire, and when Adam Osborne came around, they asked him how they might go about selling their new *EasyWriter* package. Osborne was a well-known author and computer-book publisher at the time—although he had yet to start the innovative and ill-fated Osborne Computer Company—and they were eager to get advice from someone of his caliber. Osborne suggested that they visit another booth where a young fellow was promoting a primitive database manager and whose start-up software publishing company was called Information Unlimited Software. Draper and McIntosh took Osborne's advice and went to the IUS booth, where they found a transplanted midwesterner in his early twenties, an aggressive and confident entrepreneur by the name of Bill Baker.

From the moment Draper first talked to Baker about *EasyWriter*, the destiny of Cap'n Software became more of an entrepreneur's story than a programmer's tale. That story will be continued in the next chapter. Suffice it to say now that when Baker happened onto one of the juiciest deals in microcomputer history, Draper became one of the first microcomputer programmers to make a lot of money in a very short time.

5

Legendary Entrepreneurs

If you were casting a movie about the software industry, Bill Baker is the last person you would pick to play the man who made money for John Draper. John is anarchic, hirsute, and profane. Bill is conservative, button-down, and reverent. But between them, John Draper and Bill Baker pulled off one of the greatest deals of the software gold rush. Their story became the prototype for all the other brilliant-programmer-meets-marketing-genius scenarios of that era.

When they met at the Computer Faire, Draper was finishing a work-furlough program from his wire-fraud sentence and struggling to make ends meet as a programmer. Baker was a twenty-three-year-old entrepreneur, trying to sell enough software to fly home to Indianapolis. Several years after they met, Draper was driving a new Mercedes and spending much of his time on his Hawaiian ranch, while Baker was moving into a mansion next door to George Lucas's Skywalker Ranch in northern California.

Baker started Information Unlimited Software when he was a twenty-one-year-old business student in Indiana. At first, the business was nothing more than an official-looking letter-head that Bill used to obtain discounts on microcomputer hardware. Like so many others, including me, he had never thought of computers as anything more than a hobby. It took him a while to realize that they could offer him a full-time, and very lucrative, career.

Years later, sitting by the pool of his new Marin County estate—the kind where one drives in through high iron gates and follows a quarter-mile-long driveway to get to a garage— the then twenty-seven-year-old multimillionaire recently recalled that before his senior year in college he was far more interested in profit and loss statements than computer languages. He was a business major, not a computer scientist.

"At the university," he remembered, "computers were expensive machines that a bunch of guys in white coats used behind locked doors. The computer center was a high-tech kind of place with special raised floors and air-conditioning, and hardly anybody was allowed to touch or look at whatever was in the middle of it all."

Like many others in the microcomputer industry, Bill had been a ham radio operator in his youth. But he had been less interested in the technology behind these radios than in the communications that they provided—learning Morse code and making contact with other voices in other parts of the world. Then, in his senior year of college, he met somebody who had built a small computer from a kit. It was strictly Altair-era stuff—a wire-wrapped collection of circuit boards that had no chassis and that was hooked up to a keyboard salvaged from some ancient teletype machine. Bill was fascinated with the idea that he could actually afford to build his own computer, so he looked into it as a hobby.

It was 1976, when groups of homebrewers across the country were meeting to talk about Altairs, IMSAIs, Cromemcos and all the other esoterica associated with homemade computers. Through a local computer club, Baker met two fellows who were about to open the first computer store in Indianapolis. He was their first customer.

"I sold my ham radio station to buy my first computer kit, toward the end of 1976," Bill remembered, eight years and tens of millions of dollars later. It was one of the first post-Altair computers—the Polymorphic 88. "The thing looked like a toaster or some other kitchen appliance," he added. "It was a bright orange box, and the only thing on the front was an on-off switch and a reset button. I decided to get it instead of the IMSAI because the IMSAI front panel had a bunch of lights and knobs and flipper switches and looked very technical."

In no time at all, Bill was soldering components and trying to learn something about programming from the very minimal documentation that came with the machine. When he finished his senior year, Bill's parents asked him what he wanted as a graduation present. He remembered an ad he had seen in a hobbyist publication. "I subscribed to the only computer magazine I could find back then—*Interface Age*—and there was an ad for a computer show that featured a seminar in assembly language programming. I didn't know what that meant, but I knew it had something to do with microcomputers, so I told my parents that what I really wanted was to go to that seminar."

The seminar was held in New Jersey, and Bill took his first airplane ride to get there. In fact, it was the first airplane ride anybody in his family had ever taken. At the programming course, Bill met a fellow by the name of Lyall Morill who had also put together his own computer kit. But Lyall was quite a bit more technically knowledgeable than Bill; he was, in fact, an MIT graduate. His father had left him very wealthy, so he was just having fun with his new hobby. He had even written a little program for his own use, and Bill asked to take a look at it.

In 1977, if you wanted software for a device like the Poly 88, you created it yourself. Bill had been fooling around with programs to calculate business formulas like depreciation, or compound interest. Morill's program, on the other hand, would be even more useful in that, unlike Bill's own programs, it could actually keep track of the data from these calculations. It was in fact a primitive database management system, and Bill liked it so much that he talked Morill into letting him sell the program, which Bill named *Whatsit?* Why, if you went to a whole lot of trouble, you could use your 4 K home computer as an electronic telephone book! Just the kind of thing homebrewers would go for. The agreement Bill and Morill drew up gave the programmer royalties for each copy Bill managed to sell.

Bill's company was already in existence when he saw *Whatsit?* He had set up the company when he wrote letters to different hobbyist computer manufacturers, asking for discounts on their hardware. His father had helped him name his new venture one morning at breakfast, when he asked Bill what the program did, and Bill replied that it stored a lot of information. When his father asked him how much information it could hold, Bill replied that as long as he kept buying tapes or floppy disks, the amount of information he could put into the database was unlimited. So his father suggested "Information Unlimited" as a name for the company.

The version of the program that Lyall had shown Bill needed to be improved in order to make it useful to anyone but hard-core programmers. Morill finished such improvements on Christmas Eve, 1977. It ended up as a collection of related programs for the Northstar, Sol, and other hobbyist computers. Morill then wrote up a manual to accompany the program, and Bill arranged for it to be printed. He then took the big step of flying out to San Francisco for the second West Coast Computer Faire, in the spring of 1978. The only two software publishers at that event were Information Unlimited and another outfit called Structured Systems Group. Bill's only goal was to sell enough software to pay for his ticket home. He ended accomplishing far more than that.

"I put on my salesman hat"—Bill actually says things like that—"and shocked myself by selling over $25,000 worth of programs at that show. And that's when I knew it was more than a hobby." Thereafter, thousands of copies of the programs sold, to the astonishment of the programmer and the entrepreneur. Bill then started looking for other promising products.

A year later, at the third West Coast Computer Faire, the product ended up coming to him—via a crazy-looking programmer with an untamed beard, a gap-toothed grin, and piercing blue eyes. John Draper was as wild and woolly as ever, but now he had a more conventional-looking (and acting) partner—Matthew McIntosh. Together, they were trying to find a publisher for Draper's new program, a word processor for the Apple.

The program still needed some finishing touches, but for the time being, John needed money to live on and a printer for his computer. When Adam Osborne came by their booth, John and Matthew asked him for advice. This brought them to the IUS booth, and when Bill Baker took a look at *EasyWriter*, he agreed to pay Draper and McIntosh an advance for it.

While Draper was finishing the program in California, Baker was in Indianapolis taking care of IUS business. But even though his company was profitable, Bill wasn't ready to stake his future on it, and as a result, for added security, he took a job with a bank. Then the bank relocated him to San Francisco at about the time Draper completed *EasyWriter*. The program then started selling even better than *Whatsit?* It was at that time that Bill quit his job and finally took the plunge into full-time publishing.

By then, IUS was based in California. Baker's next project, a mail-merge program for *EasyWriter* called *Easy-Mailer* (a means of printing mailing lists), brought him into contact with Dan Remer, another person who was to have a profound effect on his destiny as an entrepreneur. Because he thought he could save money on the *EasyMailer* documentation if it could be typeset directly from computer disks, Bill started looking for someone who had a typesetting machine and also knew something about computers. Dan Remer was just that person. Not only did he have a typesetting business in Berkeley, but having done a fair amount of business for microcomputer companies, he was also very knowledgeable about computers.

During the time they were figuring out a way to link the computer and the typesetter, Bill and Dan became friends. Then, in 1981, Bill was visited by some serious-looking strangers in dark-blue business suits. They were from IBM, and although they couldn't say anything definite or specific, they indicated that they might possibly be interested in talking to Bill about something they could only be vague about at present. So Bill, smelling the deal of a lifetime, "put on his sales hat" and gave these somber visitors a heavy-duty pitch about what a significant company IUS was going to be some-day. When they came back a week later and told Bill it was time to set up a meeting, he went to Dan for advice.

Bill told Dan that because he was getting involved in what looked like some kind of huge business deal, he needed a lawyer, adding: "I don't like lawyers in the first place and don't know one I could trust." Bill recalls that Dan grinned and said: "How much do you dislike lawyers?" It turned out that Dan himself had a law degree and had passed the bar, even though he didn't practice. Nevertheless, he agreed to represent Bill in the IBM negotiations, and a week later they were told to show up at a room in a hotel on the Berkeley Marina. The room had been rented under a phony name—only the first of a series of strict military-like security measures that IBM insisted upon. In the room were nine heavyweight negotiators in dark-blue suits, white shirts, and dark-blue ties. Facing them were the twenty-four-year-old software publisher and his twenty-six-year-old counsel.

Dan still remembers the way it started: "I had written up a little nondisclosure agreement and passed it around." This was a pretty audacious gambit—a nondisclosure agreement is the legal document one makes people sign if one plans to show them a secret prototype or reveal proprietary information. The agreement threatens them with all kinds of penalties if they leak what is revealed to them. Naturally, the IBM representatives did not even glance at Dan's little agreement. Instead, IBM's attorney presented Bill and Dan with a considerably thicker document which said, in effect, that everything IBM told IUS was a secret but that anything IUS told IBM was not. Period. Of course, the boys signed.

The IBM representatives began discussing a secret project and referred to it by using a code name. This is a common practice in the hardware side of the computer industry whenever very important new technologies are concerned. A different code name is used with every group of negotiators, and that way the source of any leaks can be traced. In any case, IBM's secret project was a desktop computer that, when announced, would revolutionize the personal computer industry. It was the IBM PC. In the meantime, IBM wanted to license or purchase an IBM-compatible version of *EasyWriter* so that PC customers would have a word-processing program right away.

A proposition like that is an entrepreneur's dream, of course. IBM doesn't do things on a small scale, financially or otherwise. Even a considerably discounted royalty can add up to a lot of bucks when the number of projected sales is in the hundreds of thousands. And for the initial period at least, there wouldn't be any competition from other software publishers—IBM was offering IUS an exclusive and critically important six-months-to-one year jump on the prospective market for PC software.

They went back and forth on the royalty negotiations. IBM wanted to put a cap on royalties and specify a maximum figure that IUS would be paid. But Bill and Dan didn't want to make a concession that could cost them a fortune if the new machine sold as well as they suspected it would. Then IBM's main negotiator asked them how much money they wanted to sell the program outright.

"Bill and I went out on the marina and took our calculators with us," Dan recalls, "and we walked up and down the pier, but we couldn't ever get a realistic grip on the numbers because they were all too big, so we picked one out of a hat." They walked back into the negotiations and said: "Five million dollars."

After an appropriately dramatic silence, IBM's main negotiator finally spoke: "We only want to buy the *program*, not your *company*." And that is about as close to humor as anybody gets in a meeting like that.

They finally settled on a royalty arrangement, and afterward Bill went out to start John Draper working on the program's conversion immediately. There was a very limited amount of time to translate the Apple-based program to a form that could be used on the IBM machine.

Draper was famous for burning out other programmers— because of the intensity of his programming demands and the raw force of his personality. But Larry Weiss, who worked for IUS, turned out to be one of the few people on Earth capable of working with Draper for lengths of time. Larry and John were sequestered in an apartment in the Bay Area with a prototype PC—a machine with absolutely no identifying names or numbers. They were still working on the program conversion when IBM announced the PC in August 1981. By October, when the machine was shipped, there were still a few bugs in the software, but IBM insisted on going ahead with publication anyway.

Not that there was anything terribly wrong with the program. IBM itself officially notified Baker that the program had been tested and was judged ready to ship. And when IBM speaks, people listen. And so, even with its few bugs, the program was published. When the reviews of the program began to come in, they weren't exactly raves. Still, not even bad critical reviews could put a dent in the phenomenal sales of the only word-processing program available for the most successful product introduction in microcomputer history.

IUS upgraded the program as soon as it could, and *EasyWriter* continued to be very successful—which made IUS a cash rich enterprise and John Draper much wealthier than he had been in his Cap'n Crunch days. In the meantime, Bill and Dan signed up new authors. Theirs was no longer a one- or two-product company. With IBM entering the market, games weren't the only thing people were buying. *VisiCalc* was no longer the only program a businessperson might want to use. Business software had now come to the microcomputer market in a big way, and accounting packages, general ledger and accounts receivable programs, order entry, and inventory programs were going to be the best-sellers of the next few years. By 1983, IUS was ranked number 16 by *Publishers Weekly*—tied with such software publishers as Epyx, Perfect Software, Softword Systems, and Spinnaker, all of which had an estimated $10 million in sales that year.

Also in 1983, a mainframe-oriented company, Computer Associates, approached Bill. Would he be interested in selling his company? Bill still had primary ownership of IUS. The IBM deal had brought in so much operating capital that IUS had never been forced to give up controlling stock to venture capitalists. A deal with Computer Associates would therefore bring Bill a great deal of money. In the ensuing negotiations, he, Dan, and a broker who specialized in acquisitions arranged a sale of IUS that would be worth more than $10 million to Baker, depending on how well his products sold after Computer Associates acquired them.

After the sale, Bill stayed on with Computer Associates and drew a big salary, as well as stock options, on top of his original deal. He was now in charge of new product acquisitions for Computer Associates. But being an employee, after building a company from scratch and selling it for $10 million, didn't hold Baker's interest for long, so he quit. In the course of his job, he had looked at a lot of graphics packages, most of which were pretty bad. He talked about this situation with Dan, and they agreed that with the right programmer they could probably do a better job than most of the graphics software developers that were then making good money.

Baker believed that graphics would become increasingly important in the home computer market because, as he puts it: "People communicate with each other visually, and computers aren't going to be usable to the majority of the population until the quality of computer graphics increases." With that in mind, Bill and Dan started looking for their next entrepreneurial frontier. Before long, they found it in the form of a small startup software company called Island Graphics, owned by Steven Dompier, who had been one of the founding members of the Homebrew Computer Club.

Island Graphics was already turning out some excellent computer graphics packages. So in 1984, instead of buying a big yacht and sailing off into the sunset, Bill and Dan bought into the company—just before its fortunes, like those of many other software companies that year, sailed right into the teeth of a major upheaval that stemmed from the sudden and sharp decline in the market demand for software—the "shakeout," as it came to be called. As of this writing, Dan Remer is running the company, although Baker retains his interest.

One of Baker's favorite lines is from a Kenny Rogers song: "You've got to know when to hold 'em, know when to fold 'em." One year after he sold IUS, it looked as if he had chosen exactly the right time to fold 'em, given the grim year that 1984 turned out to be. And whether or not Island Graphics survives the long-term effects of 1984's shakeout and becomes the same kind of success IUS was, Baker is financially secure—and the IUS–IBM deal is firmly established in industry legend.

Not all business-oriented software publishers fared as well as Baker's, however. Another entrepreneurial partnership, whose efforts predated Baker's and ultimately created a substantial portion of the business software market, went from a meteoric industry leader to a troubled survivor in a few tumultuous years. The stormy relationship between Visi-Corp, the marketing company founded by Dan Fylstra and Peter Jennings, and Software Arts, the software development company started by Bob Frankston and Dan Bricklin, the creators of *VisiCalc*, was one of the grimmer, more ironic tales of the early software entrepreneurs.

In 1978, the Radio Shack salesman who sold me my first personal computer told me about a Boston-based company called Personal Software that was selling a TRS–80 program that could actually play chess. This was a very exciting prospect. Game software—or any software, for that matter—wasn't abundant in 1978. I was having fun writing my own games, but a microcomputer version of a chess-playing program was far beyond my level of programming ability.

I was living in Maine at the time, but as my parents lived in Boston then, I made an effort to locate the chess software the next time I visited my family. When I called Personal Software's number, which the computer salesman had given me, the person who answered confirmed that the company indeed sold a program called *MicroChess*. But when I went over to their address in Allston, a Boston suburb, and knocked on the door, they didn't want to let me in. The fellow who answered the door explained that they were strictly a mail-order company and weren't allowed to sell through the door. But like any self-respecting computer enthusiast, I persisted in waving a $20 bill until he let me in.

The company headquarters weren't exactly in a luxuriously appointed office. At that time, Personal Software was housed in the living room of an apartment. There were two tables on which were three different computers—a Commodore PET, an Apple, and a TRS-80. All were hooked up to tape recorders that were duplicating programs onto cassettes directly from the computers. The only other items in the room were a couple of unmade beds on either side of the computer tables, a few packing crates and cardboard boxes stacked in a corner, and a large bowl of peanuts. I didn't know it at the time, but that room housed the beginnings of a famous software publishing bonanza.

Peter Jennings was the author of that chess program I was so anxious to find. He and a Harvard Business School student by the name of Dan Fylstra had formed Personal Software to market *MicroChess*, along with a few other game programs, via advertisements in hobbyist magazines. Not long after I stumbled into their operation, Fylstra got together with another student at the Business School, Dan Bricklin, who, with his own partner, Bob Frankston, had started a company, Software Arts, and had just created a prototype of the electronic spreadsheet program that was to become famous as *VisiCalc*. In a meeting that took place in a local Chinese restaurant, Software Arts agreed to license Personal Software to market a more highly developed *VisiCalc*. That agreement between the two companies turned out to be the basis of a far more fertile and, eventually, tempestuous marriage than any of them could have initially suspected.

During that meeting in late 1978, the two companies agreed that the more polished version of *VisiCalc* would be Apple-compatible, would have menus to assist the unexperienced computer user, would recalculate the spreadsheet in fewer than ten seconds, and would fit in the 16 K memory that the Apple (and other personal computers) had at that time. But when they brought the polished version around for preview demonstrations, their first audiences weren't terribly impressed. Bricklin and Fylstra's professors at Harvard knew all about mainframe versions of electronic spreadsheets and couldn't see the use of this "toy" version. Ironically, the other group that couldn't at first figure out a use for the thing consisted of the folks at Apple.

Two months before the program was released, however, one person who had seen it in action was enthusiastic. He happened to be the right person. Ben Rosen, a renowned microcomputer-industry analyst and venture capitalist, wrote in his respected (and expensive) newsletter that it was "hard to imagine any serious user of a personal computer not owning—and frequently using—*VisiCalc*." In the same article, he articulated a prediction that was to become an endlessly quoted cliché—that "software will soon become the tail that wags the dog" of the microcomputer industry.

By the time the program was ready for market in 1979, $100,000 of the revenues from *MicroChess* had been invested in the program, while Bricklin and Frankston had committed all their own resources to the gamble. Everyone involved with it was convinced that the program would sell quickly as soon as businesspeople understood what it could do. The sales figures soon confirmed their beliefs—more than 150,000 copies were sold in the first year the program was available. Ultimately, the program was to sell more than 700,000 copies, which made it the second-best-selling software product in history, surpassed only by *WordStar's* estimated one million copies.

The *VisiCalc* partners seemed to have a marriage made in heaven—Software Arts' software was revolutionary, and so was Personal Software's approach to the business of marketing it. Before *VisiCalc* came along, software had been strictly a cottage industry. VisiCorp brought in modern mass-marketing techniques: While other publishers were still selling their product packaged in plastic bags with photocopied documentation, Personal Software, which was later renamed VisiCorp, was packaging *VisiCalc* in a brown and gold binder and providing with it documentation that was actually typeset and illustrated.

Rosen's famous remark about the tail wagging the dog turned out to be accurate, judging by the claims made by computer dealers who said all the businessmen who were buying Apples did so because they wanted to use *VisiCalc*. When the sales of its machines shot up with the sales of *VisiCalc*, Apple itself changed its mind about whether anybody would find this program useful. By legitimizing what had heretofore been largely a hacker's tool or a teenager's game machine, all those business-suited buyers of *VisiCalc* broadened the mainstream market for personal computers in the early 1980s.

Shortly after *VisiCalc* sales skyrocketed, VisiCorp stopped publishing games altogether. Fylstra and Jennings turned their full attention to what was to become known as the "office productivity" market. They bought two programs called *VisiTrend* and *VisiPlot* for more than $1 million, from an author named Mitch Kapor, who was later to parley that stake into the even richer Lotus Corporation. In the meantime, it looked like VisiCorp had another winner.

For the next few years, the money kept flooding in. VisiCorp moved to California and started a small army of programmers working on an even more grandiose scheme that was to be known as *VisiOn*. Software Arts stayed in Wellesley, Massachusetts, and Bricklin and Frankston hired some people to start working on both an upgraded version of *VisiCalc* as well as a follow-up to it. Frankston and Bricklin, the originators of the program, now were personally worth tens of millions of dollars apiece, while VisiCorp, as marketer of the program, had become a power to be reckoned with in the software world. In fact, at COMDEX and National Computer Conference—the huge trade shows in Las Vegas and Atlanta that were the business software community's equivalent of the West Coast Computer Faire—Fylstra was treated with the deference reserved for only the youngest, richest, and savviest entrepreneurs.

Then, sometime around late 1982 and into 1983, the fortunes of both companies took a sudden turn for the worse. One of the biggest problems centered on VisiCorp's much-ballyhooed *VisiOn* system. It was billed as the slickest thing since microchips and involved extravagant roadshow demos and much commotion at trade shows. It was a scheme to use a very complex program to integrate different software functions into a single "environment." Unfortunately, development of the *VisiOn* project stretched on far beyond the announced release date.

This delay sparked rumors in the industry which suggested that the software was running on a powerful minicomputer but resisted attempts to be fit into a microcomputer's limited memory. The company's investment of resources and reputation in the scheme was staggering, but the software was still nowhere to be seen. Ironically, in 1983, ex–VisiCorp author Mitch Kapor's Lotus Corporation came out with software similar to that conceived for *VisiOn*. Called *1-2-3*, it too was an integrated package that offered a spreadsheet, a business graphics program, and a database all in one. The package made hundreds of millions of dollars in sales. *VisiOn*, however, barely sputtered out of production. Although the program was eventually released, it sold at only a fraction of its original price. Eventually, the whole project was sold to Control Data Corporation.

In the meantime, Software Arts finished its long-awaited *TK!-Solver*, the successor to *VisiCalc*. But unfortunately, few people in the business world understood what to do with *TK!-Solver*, an equation-based program more suited to those with scientific or mathematical training, and although it didn't fail, it certainly wasn't the hit everybody was expecting.

One of the major factors contributing to VisiCorp's problems was that by 1982, the company in general and *VisiCalc* in particular had competition. Microsoft's *Multiplan*, designed for the newest generations of powerful personal computers, was a "second-generation spreadsheet" that offered more power and greater speed. There seemed to be two or three new *Calc*s on the market with every passing week. By the time the advanced version of *VisiCalc* came along in the fall of 1982, later than VisiCorp had expected, the competition had become almost overwhelming.

Software gets old fast if it isn't upgraded, and the nerve-wracking wait for the *VisiCalc* upgrade was a key contributing factor to the nasty legal conflict that erupted between Software Arts and VisiCorp. Sales of *VisiCalc* dropped sharply in the summer of 1983. In October 1983, VisiCorp filed suit against Software Arts for $60 million, claiming that

Software Arts had failed to adequately support *VisiCalc* with a timely upgrade. In November, Software Arts countersued VisiCorp for $87 million, claiming that VisiCorp wasn't marketing *VisiCalc* adequately.

In the middle of their suit, as they were trading nasty innuendoes in the press, both companies were hit by the 1984 shakeout. Both companies underwent what is euphemistically known as a "reduction in force"—massive layoffs. In mid-September 1984, they reached an out-of-court settlement that involved a simple agreement whereby VisiCorp would pay Software Arts the $500,000 in royalties that it had been withholding since the beginning of the lawsuit. The overall result of their conflict, however, was enormously damaging to both companies. While neither had to pay out the millions of dollars it had originally sued for, they nevertheless expended so much to fight each other that they were severely wounded at a time when they needed all their strength to fight the forces of the marketplace instead.

Adventure International is one of the very few software publishing houses that succeeded primarily on the strength of the software written by their founders. Microsoft was founded on the language interpreters created by Gates and Allen, but its biggest successes—*MS-DOS*, the operating system for the IBM PC, *Multiplan*, the "second-generation spreadsheet," and *Flight Simulator*—were all written by other programmers. Most of the other software houses are run by people who are businessmen first and (perhaps) programmers second. Scott Adams, on the other hand, minored in business in college, but his major and his first love was computer science. He not only produced the first several programs sold by Adventure International, but nine of them were among the best-sellers that AI's catalogue, which in time included more than 150 titles, promoted.

Scott is a tall, goateed, curly-haired fellow in his early thirties. His wife, Alexis, is distinctly shorter and more heavy-set. They make an odd couple as they stand together in their ever-changing supermarket-like booths at trade shows.

But they have also been among the most dynamic and—in keeping with their company's name—the most adventurous entrepreneurs in the software industry. It was, after all, Scott and Alexis who took a chance and published my first simulation game in 1979. In so doing they helped to launch me in the software business by demonstrating that it was actually possible for me to make a living as a programmer. I would have been shocked to know it at the time, but I later learned that I was their first outside author.

By the time I got in touch with him, Scott had been involved in the microcomputer revolution for quite some time. In 1969, he started attending the Florida Institute of Technology. The school is located near Cape Canaveral and is, predictably, oriented to the latest technology. Scott went to the school's computer center, looking for part-time work to help cover the costs of his education. His first job was putting shipping labels on the computer center's newsletter, but he soon learned how to program as well, and three years later he had advanced so far that he was programming the school's financial software in exchange for his tuition.

Perhaps a restless nature and a nose for adventure are prerequisites for entrepreneurial success. Just as I had broken up my college years by wandering off to Africa in search of adventure, Scott left school after three years for a stint in the South Atlantic, working for RCA on tiny Ascension Island, down near Antarctica.

I know several programmers who either learned how to program in the first place or honed the skills they already had when circumstances removed them from the distractions of ordinary life. One of Brøderbund's star programmers, Chris Jochumson, learned how to program when the Army stationed him on the top of a lonely Korean mountain, where his sole responsibility was to keep the communications gear operational. Scott Adams, down on that bleak island, developed his programming skill while analyzing the radar signatures of spacecraft during his work shifts and playing space games on the same radar scope during his off hours.

Scott then went back to school to get his degree. Afterwards, he returned to RCA for a stint in Antigua and later moved to Orlando, Florida, where he found a job making digital telephone switches. When hobbyist microcomputers arrived on the scene, Scott was immediately intrigued. He purchased a computer for $750 from a computer manufacturer called Sphere. In fact, Scott Adams was Sphere's first customer.

Adams even wrote a game for the Sphere, but just as he submitted the game to Programma, a Los Angeles software publisher, Sphere folded, along with its software market. Adams was far from discouraged, however. He went out and purchased another microcomputer, and this time he made a more fortunate selection. He bought the same machine I had—the Radio Shack TRS-80 Model 1.

There was a mainframe computer in the office where Scott worked at the time, and he often used it to play the famous Crowther and Woods game *Adventure*. But when he tried to get his friends in to play this game that could keep him absorbed for hours at a time, weeks on end, he found that his friends didn't qualify for security badges and were therefore denied access to the computer. So in 1978 he resolved to write a version of *Adventure* that would run on his microcomputer. Everyone told him it was impossible to shoehorn that big mainframe-originated program into the tiny memory space of his TRS-80.

Scott managed to complete his microcomputer version of *Adventure Land* despite the opinions of skeptics. His wife didn't enjoy computer widowhood, however. At one point she became so furious at his abandonment of her that she took all his program cassettes and put them into the oven. Fortunately, she neglected to turn the oven on.

When his program was finished, Scott showed it to his local computer users' group, which he had founded in 1977. They loved it and suggested that he sell it. The problem was that TRS-80s were sold only in Radio Shack stores, and those stores did their buying through corporate headquarters in Fort Worth, Texas. Unfortunately, one of the things corporate headquarters wasn't buying back then was third-party software. It wasn't handing out lists of stores, like Apple did, either. So there weren't many publishers selling TRS-80 software with any success. Scott and Alexis decided to start their own company.

Adventure International, they called it, thinking that they would sell adventure games around the world as the microcomputer revolution swept the globe. But their only sales success at the beginning came through users' groups like the one Scott had started, and through magazine ads. Still, those sales were more than respectable, given that Scott and Alexis not only published the first microcomputer adventure game, but theirs was also one of the first software mail-order businesses in existence. And I can personally testify to its success. My royalty checks from Scott and Alexis were always much greater than those that came from anyone else. It was obvious, to me at least, that they were doing something right.

To expand their business, they started going to trade shows in all parts of the world. Alexis told me that in one year alone they went to thirty-eight shows. The Adventure International booths were very different from most other booths at these shows. Most companies came to trot out their new products and show off their technology. But Scott and Alexis came to *sell*, and they set up their booths like a supermarket, with row after row of products on display and cash registers at the two exits. Alexis told me that they made more than $30,000 at one of these early shows. The booth decor was usually a take-off on the latest adventure game theme. One year it looked like a gigantic South Pacific grass hut. The next year it was a medieval castle.

Scott and Alexis helped me in more than one way when I started my software career. After Alexis called me to say that she and Scott wanted my permission to ship copies of my *Galactic Empire* tape, the fact soon dawned on all three of us that publishing programs was a lot harder than we had assumed. That early *Empire* tape was, as it turned out, riddled with bugs—hidden mistakes in the program that would cause it to work incorrectly or to stop working under certain circumstances. Certainly, before mailing the tape I had gotten the program to function in the first place, but just because a program will start working on a computer is no guarantee that it won't stop working when a bug comes up later on. In any case, when I sent *Galactic Empire* to Adventure International, I was unaware that the program had any bugs in it and remained so until the complaints about it started coming in from customers.

We eventually put out twenty-three versions of the program. Scott was incredibly patient with me and understood about debugging from his own experience. And our market was very understanding and patient as well. Our customers were mostly hobbyists, and since the programs were written in BASIC, a simple language that many of them knew, many of the hobbyists probably regarded the bugs as personal challenges. I must have received 200 letters over the next two years, suggesting fixes for and enhancements to the program.

While I was debugging *Galactic Empire* and programming the next installments in the *Galactic Saga* series, Scott and Alexis were becoming major publishers in the home computer market. Virtually the only channel available for TRS–80 programmers, they started acquiring more products. They purchased entire lines of TRS–80 software from companies that had discovered how hard it was to find end users. Scott and Alexis didn't have any trouble finding customers, however. By mid-1983 they had more than 100,000 names on their mailing list and were mailing quarterly catalogues to every one of those names.

The company had indeed grown rapidly since its inception in 1978. In October 1979, when Adventure International moved to a shopping mall, the Adamses opened a retail computer store in the storefront part and ran the software company out of the back. The store prospered, and they opened another one. The Scott Adams Computers retail chain was born. Plans were laid for seven stores, all to be located in central Florida.

Scott and Alexis didn't stop there. Having attended a lot of trade shows, they had seen how incredibly profitable some of those shows could be for the organizers. So they set up a Computer Expo Division of their empire and successfully produced a number of regional computer shows.

They tried everything, and for a while everything seemed to work for them. But changes were taking place in the marketplace, gradually at first, that would take their toll on the company. The rise of computer-store chains made mail-order less interesting to many computer owners, and it also took a lot of business away from Tandy, the owner of Radio Shack. Most computer stores were stocking Apples and, when they became available, IBM PCs. These were not Scott's market for software—he and Alexis had never made the impact on the Apple market that they had made on the TRS–80 market, even though they eventually created Apple and IBM versions of most of their products.

Another change was beginning to have a significant impact on Scott and many other software publishers that had been oriented to the home computer market. Having originally been made up almost entirely of hobbyists and game players, the home computer market was becoming more business- and applications-oriented by the early 1980s, and games were becoming a much smaller piece of the software pie. Although Scott and Alexis set up a business products division in 1983, the company's name remained associated with games, and it was hard to get an audience for AI's business programs, given the awesome competition that AI faced in that market—particularly in the strong IBM and Apple markets.

But the biggest problem Scott and Alexis faced was the rise of distributors such as Softsel. This was an ironic circumstance, considering the fact that Softsel started out as a regional distributorship for Adventure International. When it became national, Softsel, like other nationwide distributors, culled the products of hundreds of suppliers, cherry-picking a tiny portion for active sales. Broad-based lines like Adventure International's may have been too diffuse to fare well under such a distribution system. Their hits were lost in the list of more than 150 programs in their catalogue. It was hard for distributors to know what to do with Adventure International.

Adventure International's biggest asset has always been Scott Adams's formidable programming talent. But as his company grew, Adams was increasingly drawn into the day-to-day operations of the business. His plans for a new adventure program generator with far more capability than past such generators fell further and further behind schedule. Soon, the ads he had taken for the product were no more than faint memories in the minds of a few of the old-time aficionados.

Many founders of entrepreneurial ventures find themselves in the kind of fix that confronted Scott Adams. There are only two ways out of this dilemma. Either the entrepreneur brings in professional management to run the business and goes back to spending his time developing new products, or (and this is far less likely to succeed) one *becomes* professional management and contracts for product development. Successful companies like Microsoft chose the former route. Brøderbund has tried the far-riskier latter route. Scott and Alexis appear to have opted for the latter route too.

As of early 1985, Adventure International seems to have put all of its chips on one major outside relationship with the Marvel Comics Group. AI's plan appears to be to develop programs using the well-known Marvel characters. It remains to be seen whether or not the software AI is developing for these licensed characters will catapult it from its present obscurity back into the ranks of profitable publishers.

Adventure International's former regional distributor, Ken Williams (founder of Sierra On-Line), sold his inventory and receivables to Bob Leff in 1980. Shortly after that, Leff found a partner, Dave Wagman, and they turned their company, Softsel, into the world's largest distributor of microcomputer software. In June 1984, Softsel had 330 employees and was closing the books on $150 million in sales. Bob, who only recently turned thirty, and Dave, who is only a few years older, moved more smoothly and with less help from their origins as programmers than any of the rest of us. Indeed, I was surprised to learn that they are both accomplished programmers. Bob in particular has always appeared to be the quintessential businessman. Yet it has become clear over time that Softsel's success has been due far less to their experience or business training than to their intelligence and capacity for extraordinarily hard work.

I first heard of Bob Leff and Dave Wagman from a computer-store manager in Illinois during my first (and only) sales trek across the country in August 1980. The store manager told me that although Leff and Wagman's company, then called Robwin, had started distributing to his store only very recently, he already knew that the company was just what computer dealers needed. Robwin had a reputation for fast delivery and good service. I later heard the same thing from a dealer in Connecticut, who gave me his business card and scribbled the name R. Sherwin Leff on the back.

After I got back to Oregon, Gary and I frequently talked about distributors. The industry clearly needed them—it just didn't make sense for stores to call every supplier for goods. The problem was that we, the suppliers, didn't see how we could afford distributors. We sold everything to dealers at 50 percent off list price (usually $11 to $14), and our manufacturing and royalty costs were $7 to $10. There just wasn't room in our budget for the 15 percent that a distributor would need.

The only way we would be able to afford to do it would be to cut back the dealer margin by ten points, and that seemed like a fairly hostile thing for a small software company like ours to do to its customers. Still, we couldn't see any other solution. Stores were proliferating, and we couldn't afford to track down and service every account personally and at the same time try to run our company and come up with new products. Distributors were clearly the wave of the future. More and more of the stores that Gary called were recommending that we sell to Robwin, to whom they were starting to turn for their purchasing. The dealers had some of the same problems we had—they couldn't afford to keep track of every new software publisher, especially in those early days when a new one appeared every week.

In November 1980, Gary called Robwin and talked with Leff, who was friendly and outgoing. He was twenty-six at the time, which was even younger than we were. (I was thirty-two, and Gary was twenty-eight.) No matter when we called, he was always there to talk to us. We had no idea that he was also operating out of his house. We thought he just worked all the time. We liked that. We liked Wagman as well. Both he and Bob were professional and pleasant, and we worked out the details of our business relationship with them very quickly and easily.

Robwin is one of three entities (the other two are *Softalk* magazine and Star Craft of Japan) that Gary and I credit as most responsible for ensuring Broderbund's survival in our early days. Bob and Dave gave us a tremendous lift right at the end of our first year. We had just received an unfinished version of a terrific new game from Star Craft called *Apple Galaxian*. Bob wanted to send 400 copies of the game to dealers along with his new catalogue to encourage the dealers to buy from Robwin. We agreed to provide the demonstration disks at our cost, but we worried about being able to handle the orders. Broderbund still didn't have much money in the bank.

Bob was talking about getting orders of five to ten copies of *Apple Galaxian* from at least 50 percent of the stores on the list, which amounted to two or three thousand disks. We couldn't afford to supply them. "How much money do you need?" he asked. We told him that we were going to be at least $5000 short, and a day later we received a check from Robwin for $5000. We spent every penny of it on floppy disks. If Bob Leff said he was going to sell at least 2000 disks, we had no doubt whatever that he was going to sell them.

Minoru Nakazawa, the president of Star Craft, came over from Japan with the finished master disk, and we worked in shifts through the night for a week to duplicate those 2000 disks. Nakazawa slept on the living room couch while Gary or I duplicated disks, two at a time, on the kitchen table. Gary worked in the early evening, I took over in the late evening, and Nakazawa started working at three in the morning. When I finished my shift, I went into the living room and tapped Nakazawa on the shoulder. He would awaken abruptly and immediately sit up, talking as though he had never been asleep. It would take him a few moments each time to realize that he was speaking in Japanese.

December 1980 was a truly phenomenal month. In retrospect, it is clear that it was a breakthrough for the company.

Our sales more than quintupled, from $10,000 in November to $55,000 the following month, and the level of monthly sales never went below that from then on—in fact, monthly revenues kept growing. We were grateful to Robwin for its assistance. But it wasn't until later that we realized that its $5000 loan to us represented a significant portion of Robwin's liquid assets. In fact, technically speaking, Robwin didn't have any cash assets at all. The money it had loaned us came directly out of its cash flow. But we shipped the products to Robwin right away, and it sold our products (and everyone else's) COD, which brought in money quickly enough to cover the loan.

Robwin was a contraction of Leff's first and middle names—Robert and Sherwin—and it was begun, sometime before Dave Wagman came into the picture, as a corporate shell that Bob had set up for a previous entrepreneurial fling. He had gotten into software distribution in a funny way. At the beginning of 1980, Bob was a product manager at Informatics, a mainframe computer software firm. He was twenty-six, had received his masters in computer science at the State University of New York in Albany, and was on a relatively common corporate track for men of his age and background. He's a fairly striking person in both his appearance and his manner. He has a dark complexion, dense, curly hair, and a heavy beard and mustache. Although generally pleasant, he does have a temper, as well as a sharp, incisive manner, and he seldom gives the impression of uncertainty.

One of Leff's programmers at Informatics prior to 1980 had been a high-energy kid who was even younger than Leff and who was always moonlighting three or four jobs in addition to his regular one. The kid's name was Ken Williams, and he and his wife, Roberta, had fallen in love with adventure games. As a result, Roberta even started to write one on her own, while Ken tracked down Scott Adams at the 1980 West Coast Computer Faire to strike a deal for exclusive distribution of Scott Adams adventure games in southern California.

But Ken and Roberta soon decided that they liked writing and selling their own adventure games better than selling someone else's, and when they decided to move to the Sierra foothills to run their newly founded software publishing company (then called On-Line Systems) in the kind of setting they liked best, they sold some of their assets to raise money for the move. Ken offered Bob Leff all of the assets of his little regional distributorship for about $1300. At the time, Bob felt that none of the distributors who were then selling to computer stores was effective at distributing software, and so he eagerly accepted Ken's small franchise.

Ken and Roberta went off to Coarsegold, California, and turned On-Line Systems into one of the most exciting home computer software publishers, and Bob Leff started to sell their products. Ken also directed other new software companies in Leff's direction. Soon Bob found himself swamped—he was now moonlighting at Robwin and working days for Informatics. And so in the summer of 1980 he began looking for a partner. When he started working for Transaction Technology, a CitiBank subsidiary, he met Dave Wagman. A TTI manager like Bob, Dave was, if anything, even more enthusiastic than Leff about the possibilities of software distribution. The two seemed to complement each other.

Dave is a softer, gentler soul than Bob. Lighter in complexion and beardless, he has far less appetite than Bob for the rough and tumble of business. He prefers to deal with more abstract systems. Nevertheless, he is an effective public speaker with an informal, candid style and a vision of the software industry's potential that was every bit as clear and far-sighted as Bob's. Still, Bob is a little more hot-headed. Although he is considerate in speech under normal circumstances, many people in the industry have been subjected to one of his wrathful episodes. He is the first person who ever hung up a telephone on me in the middle of a conversation. His saving grace is an ability to see himself and those around him in proper perspective—a trait that is very disarming and that has always led me to wonder whether his occasional outbursts are simply negotiating ploys, consciously inflicted for a calculated effect.

When Leff first valued Robwin at $20,000 and offered Dave a 50 percent interest in it for $10,000, Wagman didn't even flinch. This was serious money for a young man of about twenty-eight who was just starting his career, but he nevertheless agreed to the deal. Both men had high hopes for the industry and supreme confidence in their own abilities. They seemed undaunted by the fact that in July 1980, Robwin was more or less broke, and the $10,000 contributed by Wagman constituted the entirety of the company's working capital.

The two were able to stretch that money by mixing Robwin business with TTI business. TTI flies its managers around the country fairly regularly, and so whenever either Bob or Dave went off on a business trip for TTI, they added a third city to the trip and stopped in on all the computer stores they could reach. They had only just begun this practice at the time I drove across the country, and it was simply a coincidence that I hit upon two of the stores that Bob or Dave had called upon during one of their "triangular" trips during the summer. I got the impression that they were all over the country. They weren't nationwide yet, but it wasn't long until they were.

By the end of the year, both of them were working full time at Robwin. In January 1981 they hired their first full-time employee, and changed the company name to Softsel. They then embarked on a course of absolutely prodigious growth. Within nine months they had thirty employees and twice had to find new, larger facilities. By their first anniversary, they were *the* microcomputer software distributor in the country.

They did it, I'm convinced, by working harder and smarter than anyone else. Gary and I showed up at their Los Angeles office twice in 1981, once at 1:00 A.M. on a Friday and once at 11:30 P.M. on a Sunday. Both times we arrived unannounced, and both times Bob and Dave were there, working with a few of their staff.

Hard work is a big part of their story, but it isn't all there is to tell. They also figured out what services were critical to their dealers and tried to provide them. Same-day shipment was one of their early selling points. At that time, stores were desperate to get products quickly so that they could sell them quickly and keep their own inventories as low as possible. Later, as the market matured, returns of products became a major issue, and Softsel, with its huge inventory of suppliers, was able to replace a dealer's slow-moving products with the latest hit products. In addition, Dave Wagman wrote a computer program in 1981 that gave each dealer a quarterly inventory analysis and profit report on all products. It not only proved to be a valuable tool to the dealers, but it also helped them order more intelligently and lowered the risks to Softsel of having to take back unsold products.

Although Softsel later dabbled in distribution to mass-merchandisers, it focused most of its energy on providing services to the retail computer stores. And so, as the stores changed, Softsel changed as well. Its original line of largely hobbyist-oriented, mostly entertainment products became more and more heavily skewed toward business products as the business market mushroomed. In 1982, 70 percent of Softsel's sales consisted of entertainment products (games). By early 1984 only 12 percent of Softsel's sales were of entertainment products. These weren't the only changes. The company developed a management infrastructure and took in venture financing. A small partnership had become a large corporation. They toyed with the idea of going public and then retreated when the market for computer-related stocks took a nosedive.

Softsel has become a big business. Typically, entrepreneurs don't do too well in big businesses, even in ones they have founded. It seems to take one kind of person to build an enterprise from the ground up, and an entirely different kind of person to manage a business with annual revenues over $100 million. I wondered from time to time how Bob and Dave were handling the astonishing growth of their company, in view of the changing marketplace.

I got a chance to talk with Leff about this question in May of 1984, the year of the big shakeout. We had been to Sierra On-Line's fourth-anniversary party the night before. A lot of the "old people," as Bob called them, had come to the party, and we compared notes about them. Many of those people's companies had been hit by the shakeout and had not survived, and Bob was clearly uncomfortable at the way some people blamed an unjust world for their failures. "The big guys moved in and took over," someone had said. Bob's reaction was a little puritanical. "This is silly," he said to me the following day. He pointed out that people have different levels of business ability and this shakeout was only to be expected. People with lots of ability were going to prosper, but a lot of the rest wouldn't. The old "survival of the fittest" rule was now applying to the software industry.

I wasn't surprised to see Leff's show of self-confidence about Softsel's own ability not only to survive but also to prosper in the stakeout. What did surprise me was realizing that, underneath the bravado, he still obviously thinks of himself as an amateur who has to work smarter and harder than anybody else just to compete. Deep down, he is just as unsure about his ability to run a really big company as I am about mine. But it's a part of him that hardly ever shows.

Bob Leff and Dave Wagman both have clear memories of where they were four years ago. All the momentous changes that have taken place in their lives have happened too quickly, too recently, to have acquired an aura of permanence yet. As a result, they share with some people in the software industry a feeling of vulnerability. Everything could go away as quickly as it came. In the beginning, we all had been a little group of entrepreneurs going out into the wide world together. But later each company evolved its own separate strategy for survival, and Softsel in particular moved along a separate path and now must exist in a world that contains very few of those cottage entrepreneurs but a lot of very tough, very established professional businesses. There is a great deal of nostalgia for the early days. At the same time, however, no one really wants to go back.

6

The Brotherhood

One small group of entrepreneurs, most of them oriented toward products and services for the Apple computer, became particularly good friends of ours. For most of us in this group, our home ground was the West Coast and, more often than not, California. We shared common experiences as our companies grew, and we tended to view one another as co-explorers of uncharted waters rather than as deadly competitors. We traded information relatively freely because that was the way it was in the hobbyist days and because we had no other benchmarks by which to measure our progress. And if we exaggerated our business performance to the outside world at times, we were more candid with one another, since we knew that important decisions would be based on the information we shared.

In May 1980, four months after we had started Brøderbund, our monthly sales had declined from a high of around $900 to zero. We made all of our sales by calling stores on the telephone, but three of the four products in our line worked only on the Radio Shack TRS-80 computers, and there weren't a lot of stores other than Radio Shack stores that carried TRS software. Radio Shack itself wasn't entirely helpful to us either—it wouldn't give us a list of all its stores. As a result we had to locate outlets by looking at the ads in computer magazines and copying the names of new franchises off the backs of the Radio Shack inserts in the Sunday *Oregonian*. This was not an enormously effective technique.

Since we didn't have to worry about customers calling us, we spent a couple of hours each afternoon playing basketball down at the Eugene YMCA. It seems incredible to me today that we had that kind of free time then. Today, each day is a nonstop schedule of telephone calls, meetings, conferences, conventions—and I haven't played basketball more than twice in the past twelve months.

But back then, when we weren't shooting baskets or combing through newspaper advertisements, we were programming. And in June, when we started trying to convert the three *Galactic Saga* programs to run on the Apple computer, we finally had lots to do. In the meantime Apple had provided us with a bonanza and had given us something of inestimable value—a list of all the stores in the country that sold its computers. At last we knew exactly where to sell our products. What we didn't know was how we were going to reach those stores without having any money in the first place. We were financially strapped. We had spent every penny I had saved and were heavily drawn on both my VISA and Master-Charge cards. Telephone sales weren't working very well. And our relatives couldn't afford to loan us any more money.

It was one of those desperate times when one relies on old contacts and friends. In this case our salvation began with several women from Gary's Swedish basketball team. Several of them were going to be in San Francisco at the end of June and wanted to see him. They wanted to know if he could come down to the Bay Area for a few days. We just didn't have the money to send him. So one of Gary's friends from the Swedish days bought him a plane ticket. One way—Eugene to San Francisco. It was up to Gary to figure out how to get back. He assumed that he would hitchhike.

Getting back was easier than he anticipated. Gary saw his friends. He also sold close to $3000 worth of software to computer stores. Most of it consisted of the *Galactic Empire* and *Galactic Trader* programs we had just converted from TRS-80 to Apple format.

During this trip, Gary got over to Sacramento, where he made a call on the local Computerland store. The store owner was Terry Bradley, and the manager was Jerry Jewell. They had just started a company called Sirius Software. Ken Williams, co-owner of the newly founded On-Line Systems, had just been to the store the day Gary visited, trying to sell his first programs. As it turned out, Sirius and On-Line were soon to become our most formidable competitors.

But at the time, what most interested Gary during this visit to Sacramento was hearing Jerry Jewell talk about a couple who had just left the store before Gary arrived. That couple also had a software company, and like Brøderbund, it was based in Eugene. Jerry said they had been showing their wares, and to him it seemed like weird stuff.

It *was* weird stuff. Their software had names like *The Creativity Life Dynamic* and *The Life Conditioning Dynamic*. Gary didn't know what to make of it, and neither did I when he told me about it. But we were eager to make the acquaintance of anyone who knew anything about this strange new world of software into which we were venturing, and the idea that there was another software company in Eugene, Oregon, piqued our curiosity even more. Eugene is a beautiful place, in a fertile river valley between snow-capped mountains, surrounded by rolling pasture lands and forests. It also has a rich cultural life provided by the presence of the University of Oregon and a goodly number of artists, writers, and other creative people who like to live far away from the asphalt jungles. It is an exceptionally pleasant place to live, but in 1980 it wasn't exactly a hotbed of software entrepreneurs. So when Gary returned from California we made an attempt to contact the couple Jerry Jewell had spoken about.

We ended up having to contact them by mail because that was the only way to get hold of them. They were not listed in any phone book. It turned out that they didn't even have a phone. Their business operated solely out of a post office box— a fact we learned about after we saw a magazine ad for their company, Avant Garde Creations. So we dropped them a card and shortly afterward got a response.

The couple was Mary Carol Smith and her programming partner, Don Jones. Unlike most other entrepreneurs who were starting software companies at that time, they didn't get into the business to get rich, or because they loved programming. Instead, they had a cause that was not immediately connected to personal computers. They are true believers, out to change the world, and they see the microcomputer as a tool that will help people to take control of their own lives. Software was merely a medium for the promulgation of information about their idiosyncratic utopia.

The primary purpose of Avant Garde Creations, as I understood it after the first few times it was explained to me, was to effect positive changes in the world by helping people look at their lives in new ways. And the purpose of much of the software was to provide a tool for this kind of personal transformation process. Much of their work always has had too much jargon in it for my taste, but then again, one develops a high tolerance for jargon if one is in the software business for very long.

You have to remember that the Carlstons are more Protestant than Transformationalist, and we come from the Midwest, not the West Coast. I had my fun with "Galactic Saga," which was an unabashed fantasy world, and then we had some serious fun when Brøderbund got started. But neither Gary nor I entertained the notion that we were engaged in any kind of quasi-religious quest that would change the world. Still, microcomputer software is a very ecumenical religion in and of itself, embracing both the straightest mainframe Cobol-heads and the most wild-eyed raving Forth hackers.

Mary Carol is fond of saying, "You have to be where you're at before you can get anywhere." Nowadays, with the rise of a whole category of adult self-help and psychologically oriented software, the program titles and personal philosophy of Avant Garde Creations might not sound too odd for a software publisher. But back in 1980 when spreadsheets and word processors were still pretty exotic stuff to most people, it was definitely unusual to hear about software that was supposed to have some effect on your state of mind.

Frankly, we wondered where they found enough buyers to keep their company afloat. We knew that thousands of people were playing games and keeping track of their accounts receivable on their Apples, but it seemed unlikely that very many folks were undergoing self-analysis via floppy disk. Nevertheless, Avant Garde Creations has managed well. Although it is hardly a Microsoft or an Apple, it is the very stereotype of the neo-utopian fringe software company that cropped up in the boomtimes of the early 1980s. It is one of the few of those conceptual wildcatting ventures that survived the 1983–84 shakeout. And Don and Mary Carol are two of the very rarest of the old utopian fringe who managed to prosper as well as survive.

After we first met Mary Carol and Don, Gary and I saw them frequently for at least a year, during which time we would have regular "show and tell" sessions about our products. We liked one another, but despite the fact that we eventually became their friends and were their only colleagues within several hundred miles, Don and Mary Carol refused to tell us where they lived. All we knew was that they were located "outside Eugene," which could have meant a suburban house, a small farm, a trailer park, or a deep-forest cabin.

Still, even if they didn't want to show us their location, they certainly had no qualms about showing us their software, and they were always eager to share their ideas. They told us they were running a kind of human potential workshop, which to my limited experience sounded quite a bit like est or Lifespring or the other personal growth workshops that were popular in the 1970s. They also told us that they had been book publishers before they got into software and had produced books that, like many of their programs, were about their vision of social and personal transformation. These even included some children's books that were a bit bizarre for our tastes. I remember one of them, entitled *The Magic Carpet and the Brick Wall,*—in which the young protagonist of the story is violently beaten by his father—that struck me as utterly blood-curdling and probably quite terrifying to young children.

They knew we thought they were a little weird, and we suspected that they thought we were more than a little square. And all things considered, we probably found them a lot more interesting than they found us. Mary Carol is a dynamic and very savvy businessperson, and I wouldn't have been surprised if I had met her in a position of responsibility at Apple, Microsoft, or IBM instead of at a small, slightly strange software shop somewhere outside Eugene. Don Jones—or as he was calling himself some time later, Don Fudge—has an engaging, earnest manner, a head full of ideas, and a somewhat mysterious past. We knew that he was from Indiana, went to school in Pennsylvania, was a Vietnam veteran, and refused to allow himself to be photographed—and that both he and Mary Carol had lived in a totally self-sufficient commune in the backwoods of northern California in the late 1960s.

From the start, they were very helpful to us, even though we didn't profess even to understand, much less agree with, whatever point their more esoteric software was attempting to make. They were capable of producing more mainstream software, however. They even gave us copies of their programs that had nothing to do with transformation and everything to do with bringing in some income—a mailing list program, some nice utilities for doing graphics routines—little pieces of programs that could come in handy when you are designing a computer game.

While Brøderbund was just getting on its legs, Avant Garde was building a network of people for itself. Some of those people were from the same unusual social-ideological scene, and some of them were programmers. Don and Mary Carol established their own corner of the software subculture, and somehow all those retailers, wholesalers, programmers, and salespeople that Don and Mary Carol cultivated in the early years have helped carry them through times that have seen many other companies go under or merge with larger outfits.

When we first met them during those early years, Don

had a very intriguing ideological bias regarding software marketing, especially considering that Avant Garde Creations was a struggling start-up company. In 1980, he firmly believed that no commercial software package should cost more than $9.95. Like a lot of the true believers in the early 1980s, Don was convinced that our market would grow from 100,000 enthusiasts to 100 million product-hungry consumers in a matter of a few years.

Another one of Don's ideas—and we always teased him about this—was his predilection for conspiracy theories. I have noticed that there is a significant minority of the general population who think like Don in some ways—people who are very susceptible to theories that the whole world is secretly manipulated by other people whom none of us know or understand. He thought that the 55-miles-per-hour speed limit was a conspiracy, for example, but I never did discover who was conspiring against whom.

In one interesting episode involving Don and Bill Budge, Don called Bill to find out how his 3-D graphics package worked. "It's a conspiracy," Don fumed when he told me that Budge wouldn't divulge his trade secrets. "Bill Budge won't tell the secret because he's trying to lock it all up. His 3-D graphics package is copy-protected." This was a pretty typical hacker's reaction. Programmers, in the days before programming became such a valuable proprietary exercise, were used to sharing information freely with one another. Don was outraged that the graphics utility was copy-protected; this, he felt, kept useful knowledge about the tool from other programmers.

In fact, Bill had nothing to do with the copy-protection scheme. It was his publisher's idea, but by the time Don found out about this (if ever) he was firmly entrenched in his conspiracy hypothesis. Don cooked up a pretty silly-sounding scheme whereby he would figure out what Bill was allegedly trying to prevent him from knowing. Then he was going to write a program called "Hi-Res Secrets," put a picture of a sexy woman on the cover, rename himself Don Fudge, and make the subtitle: "If you can't Budge it, Fudge It." The funniest part of the story is that he actually came up with the product, actually put the sexy picture on the cover, and even adopted Fudge as his last name. He got a lot of flack, though, so he took the woman off the cover. The program ended up selling a respectable number of copies—certainly a lot more than the Creative Life Transformation stuff.

Brøderbund left Eugene in August 1981. Avant Garde Creations, however, stayed "somewhere outside Eugene" until its customer base expanded and it began to see some money coming in. At that time, Mary Carol and Don had to face the same growing pains that were confronting all of us. They finally moved into Eugene. They expanded to a staff of four. By 1983, the staff had grown to twenty-four, but the corporate headquarters—although it was in Eugene rather than in the woods somewhere and had a real address as well as a post office box—was still characteristically unorthodox: Their last Eugene headquarters was in a typically professional, handsome wood-paneled office building—with a fairly large river flowing where the foundation should have been. To get from the parking lot to the glass-fronted lobby of the main building, people had to cross a bridge at the third-story level.

But because of the downturn in the house construction trade, Eugene was in a depressed state economically when they moved into town. As a result, these ex-communards from the backwoods, purveyors of transformational software, had all of a sudden become respectable members of the community—employers of twenty-four taxpayers.

I remember one peculiar episode before they became quite so respectable. It was before they had much income from their products and couldn't afford to go to a trade show in Boston—a place where small software companies stand to make a decent amount of sales. Mary Carol asked us if they could put some of their software on exhibit at our booth. We said "sure" and thought nothing of it. That sense of community was always a big part of the fun of trying to publish software in the early days of the industry, before the shirts and ties and armies of accountants joined the fray. So we agreed, and we put up some new Avant Garde programs in our booth.

My father—a Presbyterian minister, mind you—was manning the Brøderbund booth at that Boston show, blissfully unaware of what was going on around him. Among the Avant Garde packages, it happened, was one of their little social experiments—a very explicit software version of a sex manual. The first thing that happened to Dad was that a nine-year-old Brøderbund enthusiast rushed over to the booth and said "Brøderbund's my favorite company; what's *that?*" pointing, of course, to the sex manual.

"Well, that's not us, that's something from Avant Garde," my dad replied.

"Okay, I'll take it," said the kid.

And of course, an hour later a furious father came stomping up with the nine-year-old young man and said to the person at the Brøderbund booth: "He says he bought this from *you.*" Except, by this time, the person in charge was not my father, but my mother. And she said: "Oh, we're just selling those for some friends." Then the father told my mother about the contents of the program, and she was properly mortified.

"We were just doing it for some friends," she repeated, rather weakly, refunding their money.

"Some fine friends you have," rejoined the irate father.

When I related the story to Mary Carol, she said, "You know, the world is like that. You try to give out some good information to people and they just can't take it." And that fit right into one of Don's major premises—that people are against you because they won't accept the perfectly valid information you offer.

Eventually, Avant Garde became profitable enough to attract venture capital. It started taking money from David Silver, a venture capitalist, in 1983. He had to provide progressively more money to keep the company going through the lean times of 1984, which meant that he gained a controlling interest, and eventually he bought out Don and Mary Carol's share of the company. Don and Mary Carol stayed in Eugene, and in 1985 they started a new software company named Abracadata; once again, they started operating their business from a post office box. Tom Measday, an old friend of David Silver's (and a former vice president of sales and marketing for Brøderbund), became president of Avant Garde.

In 1984, Avant Garde announced its intention to acquire Human Engineered Software, one of the largest software companies. (We'll hear more about HES when we look at the shakeout of 1984.) Although the HES acquisition may fall apart in bankruptcy court, in January 1985, Tom Measday announced his intention to buy another *dozen* software companies within the year. He sent out 200 inquiries to companies, asking if they were interested in being acquired. In February 1985, it looked as if our old neighbors would become our new neighbors, because Measday announced plans to move Avant Garde to San Rafael.

Measday's decision to relocate Avant Garde may have stemmed from a realization that the company had been too geographically removed from the California action for too many years. Don and Mary Carol never joined in the California social activities during which people from various software companies got to know one another. Perhaps Measday thought it would be beneficial for the company if it played a more prominent role in the California software scene. As for myself, I remember, when Broderbund was still a newcomer to the industry in 1980, feeling very much like an outsider. I felt this particularly at the West Coast Computer Faire that year when I watched people who were obviously old friends greet one another. After all, not only had nobody heard of us— we didn't know terribly much about computers either!

In addition, everything about the industry was changing daily and becoming more complex. We soon discovered that. In May, Gary and I had an argument over a prospective $8000 order that I muffed from a company called Automated Simulations. The company had wanted to distribute our products and had asked for a 60 percent discount from list price. I had answered truthfully that our largest discount was 50 percent, so they refused to order. Gary felt that I had mishandled it. We badly needed the money. Why not offer a little extra incentive? We called back, but the order never materialized.

Automated Simulations eventually decided that it didn't want to be a distributor of other people's products after all.

The incident pointed up one of the problems we were having: We simply didn't know anything about retailing. If you had said the words "pricing structure" to me in early 1980, all you would have received in return would have been a blank look. We didn't really know the difference between a manufacturer and a distributor or a publisher. To us, everybody did everything. Our first catalogue included items from other software companies like Adventure International, Stoneware, and Softape. We bought as low as we could and sold as high as we could. And often we bought higher than we could sell.

But there were two people who didn't have this lack of know-how. They were businessmen, and they knew all about esoterica like discounts and volume purchase arrangements. They were Terry Bradley, the owner of Computerland of Sacramento, and Jerry Jewell, his manager, and they had everything it took to start a software company except one all-important item—software to sell. And in the spring of 1980, that vital ingredient was about to walk in their front door.

When a programmer named Nasir Gebelli, an undergraduate from the University of California at Davis, walked into that Computerland store one spring day, he carried a diskette in his briefcase. Some graphic utility subroutines he had programmed for the Apple computer were recorded on the diskette-programs that made it possible to draw simple patterns on the Apple screen. They were called "utilities" because other programmers could use them to construct their own graphics programs. Since "amateur programmer" was synonymous with "Apple owner" in 1980, as Gebelli pointed out, there was a healthy market for programmers' utilities. What Gebelli neglected to mention to Bradley and Jewell was that he had owned his own Apple for only forty-five days. Needless to say, he liked to program fast.

At the time, Terry Bradley, a retired Air Force colonel, and Jerry Jewell, a Vietnam vet and a programmer himself, were leading relatively quiet lives running their Computerland franchise. They didn't know it then, but their lives shifted into overdrive the moment they booted up Gebelli's program. A year later, Gebelli had earned more than a quarter of a million dollars in royalties from a string of hit Apple programs, while Bradley and Jewell found themselves in charge of a multimillion-dollar software company—Sirius Software.

The rise and fall of Sirius Software was perhaps the most spectacular but far from the only instance of the rags-to-riches-to-rags scenario. The convolutions of Gebelli's, Bradley's, and Jewell's fates reflected not only the results of their decisions but the larger currents of the economy as well. The abrupt transition from a small community of homebrew computer enthusiasts to serious business and the equally rapid transition from gold rush to shakeout had dire financial consequences for and, in some cases, violent psychological effects upon the lives of many people involved in microcomputer software from the late 1970s through the early 1980s.

Within three years of the day he met his soon-to-be partners, Gebelli went from undergraduate to superstar programmer to the owner of his own software company to obscurity. Sirius Software quickly grew from a small business to a position at the head of the Apple entertainment software market in the early 1980s. But I believe Jewell and Bradley, like Gebelli, made a series of errors that turned out to be fatal when the software market turned from a gold rush to a more normal competitive business: They never diversified beyond their original inventory of strictly entertainment software; because of their need to expand, they put out some software of inferior quality; they jumped into the Atari VCS market at exactly the wrong time; and they committed themselves to the wrong machines and wrong distribution channels.

All they knew at the beginning was that Gebelli seemed pretty sure of himself. When Bradley first saw Gebelli's program, he said it was "okay" and asked to keep the diskette for a day or two. Nasir came back three days later and said, with characteristic immodesty, "what do you think of it *now?*" knowing undoubtedly that if they knew anything about Apple software they were bound to be impressed. Jewell offered to help turn Gebelli's utilities into a package they could sell to the nonprogrammers who were buying Apples by the thousands. *E-Z Draw* was their first program.

Bradley and Jewell didn't have to wait very long for their one-man program factory to come up with a successor. It was a home computer game that had the same kind of high-resolution, flicker-free animation that only the hugely popular arcade games had heretofore been able to offer to the video game industry's huge, audiovisually sophisticated market of thirteen-year-olds with quarters in their pockets.

In 1980 and 1981, the whole world was paying puzzled and envious attention to the sudden, strange, and lucrative mushrooming of the video game industry. What was the power of this entrancing new technology out of Silicon Valley and Japan that was shaking so much wealth from the world's all-but-zombified youth? The financial giants turned their eyes toward this promising new expansion of the consumer electronic market. But software wizards of the microcomputer realm knew that with the introduction of more sophisticated microcircuitry into inexpensive computers equipped with high-speed disk drives, rather than with the slower cassettes, the future lay in bringing high-performance graphics to the personal computer market.

The home software industry evolved from the perceptually hypnotic, apparently addictive, unbelievably lucrative video arcade games like *Pong* (the grandaddy), *Space Invaders* (the original "shoot-'em-up"), *Galaxians*, and *Pac-Man*, the most successful of all. For a period lasting a little less than three years, video addicts from Tokyo to Peoria fed enough quarters (or 100-yen pieces) into the arcade versions to add up to several billions of dollars annually. *Pac-Man* alone brought in more than a billion dollars in its first year. The successful transfer of even a fraction of this new source of wealth from the video game market to home computer versions would be a tremendous boost to the infant microcomputer industry.

But bringing arcade-style graphics to 1980-era microcomputer screens was no mean feat. The trick lay in the software. How could a programmer use the limited visual-display capabilities of the relatively small-memory Apple to duplicate the effects that were accomplished in arcade games by big screens and special microchips dedicated strictly to graphics functions? Enter Nasir Gebelli and his new-found representatives.

With *Both Barrels, Cyber Strike, Star Cruiser*, and other fast-action, high-resolution computer games, Gebelli started to build his reputation as one of the fastest, most graphically sophisticated programmers in the world. To a microcomputing audience that had grown from a few dozen technically sophisticated hobbyists to thousands of people—many of whom knew very little about computing before they met their first arcade game—the fact that computers could be used to create visual effects was very important. The early hackers of the 1960s might have reveled in technical complexities of how the computer worked, but the microcomputer generation of the 1980s wanted to *experience* something, to *see* something that could compare to 70-millimeter Technicolor movies and optically dazzling video games. Gebelli's shoot-'em-ups were colorful, animated, not terribly imaginative after a while, but wildly successful while the winning streak lasted.

As a measure of how astonishingly successful Nasir was, keep in mind that most programmers took anywhere from six months to two years to program a video game. Nasir finished nine in the space of a single year, and *all* of them made it onto *Softalk*'s Top Thirty chart. He was innovative and bold, but compared with some who came after him, he wasn't the world's most elegant programmer. He did find ways to create programs fast, however, and in the hot market of 1980 and 1981, that was a real advantage.

Bradley and Jewell weren't afraid of innovation, either. They took the software world by storm. Back when Broderbund's total annual sales were around $100,000, Sirius sold a million dollars' worth of software to Apple. Then the company went on, long before most of us could afford such stuff, to put its software into really slick packaging. Sirius bought eight pages of advertising in *Softalk*. Nasir was turning out a program every six weeks, and every one was a smash hit. The programming was quick and dirty, and the material rewards came thick and fast. Nasir bought a very fancy sports car, bought a beautiful house with all the accoutrements, and married a beautiful blonde.

But Nasir wasn't happy with the structure of Sirius—he felt that he as one of the three people who started the company, deserved some equity. Sirius was developing a stable of young programmers, based on the profits provided by Gebelli's programming *blitzkrieg* of 1980–81. By 1982, feeling that he was entitled to something more than a royalty arrangement, Gebelli and Phil Knopp, general manager at Sirius, left to start Gebelli Software. They moved into relatively luxurious offices with beautiful furniture, a state-of-the-art photocopying machine, and a former quick-and-dirty programming hotshot who was now a full-time businessman and no longer had time to program. Nasir was always thinking big. But the industry was changing, and a dazzling new generation of software hotshots had appeared from nowhere, just as he had walked into that computer store not so long before. Broderbund's importation of Japanese products, for example, created some stiff competition; Tony Suzuki's *Alien Rain* ruined the sales of Gebelli's *Star Cruiser*.

Gebelli Software sputtered and died within a year of its founding. One of the mixed blessings associated with setting up your own business is that there is no longer anyone to tell you whether your behavior is proper or improper. Although this liberation from the constraints of ordinary workaday life is emotionally very satisfying, it can permit one to drift away from conventionally acceptable behavior. A venture investor told me that she once set up an appointment to visit Gebelli Software at 8:30 one morning. She was there on time, but the company's doors were locked. The first employees didn't show up until 9:30, and the principals of the company weren't there until 10:00.

Never mind that they had probably worked late into the night, or that this was their ordinary way of doing business. The investor was not impressed and predicted that few others in the "real world" would be eager to work with a company that kept such nonstandard hours. I couldn't help but think back to Brøderbund's bucolic early months and our two-hour afternoon basketball games. But we had given that up long before we started making appointments with venture capitalists. When the world of software hobbyists became the software industry, however, some people were unwilling to abandon their unconventional lifestyles simply because the conventional business world expected it. A few of those companies succeeded despite their principals' nonconformity; many did not.

Sirius lasted a bit longer than Gebelli Software. Its young programmers, attracted by the legends of six-figure royalties, turned out *Beer Run*, *Jellyfish*, *The Earth Dies Screaming*, and a dozen others. But although the products were hot, many of them were shallow and failed to sustain their hold on the market of increasingly sophisticated Apple users. Then, at the end of 1982, Sirius decided to jump into the Atari video game market. It had seen the huge profits companies like Activision had rolled up and decided that it was time to play for bigger stakes. They joined up with 20th Century-Fox Video Games, attracted by that company's marketing clout among mass merchandisers, and for more than a year Sirius's programmers worked on virtually nothing but video games. Unfortunately, it was the wrong year to work on video games. As we shall see when we examine the causes of the software shakeout, the collapse of the Atari game cartridge market caught many people unprepared.

Brøderbund didn't have a better vision of the future than Sirius did. Atari, one of the most spectacular success stories in history, didn't seem to be heading for a fall. We managed to avoid trouble simply because we didn't have the technical ability to figure out how to program the Atari VCS, or at least we didn't back then. It was a very tightly guarded secret. The Sirius people offered to give us the technology, but only if we published through them, which we didn't want to do.

We became better acquainted with the people at Sirius and other software companies (especially Sierra On-Line) at the shows and at a series of parties and activities that we shared. At shows we would rush over to one another's booths on set-up day to see who was putting on the most impressive display and who had the most interesting new products. If one of the others had outdone us, we would feel chagrined, but it wasn't the kind of cutthroat competition that was happening in the hardware realm. One would hardly expect to see IBM and Apple planning parties together.

There truly was a sense of brotherhood among the California game companies, but that didn't mean we always shared our trade secrets with one another. Sirius, as the "leading company," seldom shared information with the rest of us, although we socialized together. The Sirius people saw us as competition, and they wanted to win. Brøderbund's relationship with Ken and Roberta Williams, however, extended much further. Although we wouldn't have expected anyone to give us information that had been obtained at great cost, like the secrets of the Atari video game machine, we helped one another when we could.

Ken and Roberta Williams's company—On-Line Systems, or, as it was called later, Sierra On-Line—constitutes its own software empire up there in the gold rush country of the Sierra foothills. Ken Williams himself is a major part of anybody's history of the software industry. He has cooked up and implemented more ideas over the past four years than anyone else in the industry, and, as an innovator, he has no match.

Ken is a big, amiable, slightly sloppy-looking man with a congenial twinkle in his blue eyes. His wife and business partner, Roberta, is tiny in comparison with him, and in contrast to his aggressive and outgoing style she has to push through her natural shyness in order to speak out on matters she feels are important. She has strong opinions and is less carefree than Ken. Theirs is a combination that works—she channels his raw energy and focuses his creative ambitions. Although Ken is the programming talent in the family, they might never have started their own business if Roberta hadn't taken the initiative to create their first product.

Without Roberta acting as a rudder, Ken would probably be over his head in projects, instead of just up to his neck. A short list of his achievements—and attempted achievements—is startling. He started the distribution company that later turned into Softsel, the world's largest distributor of computer software. He and Roberta added the first graphics to adventure games and co-founded On-Line Systems. He co-founded one of the first mail-order businesses, Calsoft. He co-founded one of the earliest magazines, *Softline*. He wrote one of the first game generators that could be used by a nonprogrammer. He was one of the very first publishers to take in venture capital to accelerate the growth of his business. And he got into licensing deals long before most of the other cottage publishers dreamed that such marketing activities could be within their financial reach.

As an example of his continual exploration of new possibilities, one day in 1982 Ken called me and said that he had a proposition for me to consider. How would I like to form a company with him to put computers and computer software into hotel rooms? He had done a lot of thinking about it and suggested that we meet in Los Angeles to try to whip the idea into shape.

So I flew down to L.A. while Ken and Roberta drove down from their Sierra foothills headquarters in their big pickup. They were buying a motorboat and were planning to haul it back home the next day. We all went to a steak house and talked about the plan. What emerged was a blueprint for an intriguing new business that might permit us to profile our software products for a lot of bored travelers. However, the whole idea depended on finding the right person to run the business. Ken clearly didn't have the time, and neither did I. When we were unable to find the right manager for the business, we let it drop, but the episode gave me a sense of the way Ken's creative mind works. He not only comes up with an extraordinary number of ideas, but he pushes and prods them along until a lot of them come to fruition.

But our discussion in L.A. wasn't the first time we had talked about joining forces. In the summer of 1981, Ken extended invitations to about fifty people—including Gary, me, and our sister Cathy—in the microcomputer industry to join him on a whitewater rafting trip down the Stanislaus

River, a beautiful, exciting, Sierra riverway that would be buried forever by a new dam only a few months after our trip. That trip was the first time I had spent any time with Ken or Roberta other than at a trade show, and it was a pleasure to see them away from the competitive pressure. Of course, it was impossible for fifty computerists to go anywhere without talking shop, and the river guides frequently had to shout at us: "Hey, *forget computers*. Look around you!"

The river guides had a point. The river was extraordinarily beautiful. We had water fights. We swam and ate and spent our time in honest sunlight—a refreshing change from being squirreled away in musty offices or basking in the midnight glow of computer screens. Ken rode down some of the rapids while standing on the bow of his raft and holding the bowline like a pair of reins. At other times we all swam through the rapids, shrieking like kids in the ice-cold water. And in the evening when everyone gathered around the campfire, Ken and I wandered off and speculated about whether or not we should merge our two companies.

It was good fun. What was more important to us than the possibility of an actual merger was our willingness to consider it in the first place. In effect, the merger discussions were a way of saying to each other: "I like you and respect your business and your abilities." We also shared a desire to be important, and if merging our companies could make us important in the eyes of the world, that might be reason to at least consider it. The merger never happened because of geography (we didn't want to move to the Sierra foothills and they didn't want to move to San Rafael) and because there were no real benefits to such a measure (our companies were too similar).

The competitive sides of our personalities were never too deeply submerged either. On the second day of the trip, we came to a place in the river where the water was deep and smooth, and cliffs rose up above the river banks. Ken hollered: "Stop the boats! We're going to go up there and jump off," and he went tearing up the cliff. Lots of people followed and started jumping into the river from the cliff. But when I got to the top, Ken and Roberta were still standing there, looking down.

Ken came over to me and said: "I've made a big mistake. How would you like to do me a favor, Doug? Why don't we walk down to the boat? If you go with me, nobody will think anything of it."

"We can jump off this. It's not so bad," I replied.

"Why don't you take a look," he said.

It did seem like a long way down, but everyone else was jumping off and surviving. By this time my sister Cathy had joined us. Cathy is not very afraid of water—when we were growing up in Iowa, she was voted outstanding swimmer in the state two years running. Furthermore, she is nine years younger than I am and was then still too young to have any sense of her own mortality. She was clearly ready to jump off the cliff.

I said to Ken, "Well, Cathy will take one of your hands and I'll take the other, and I'll grab Roberta's hand and we'll jump off together. What do you think?" "Okay," he said. We linked hands and headed for the cliff's edge until Ken put on the brakes. "I'll do it next time," he said.

So Cathy and I jumped off. It was fun but not so much fun that we wanted to try it again, so we didn't go back up. Eventually everybody jumped, but Ken and Roberta climbed back down. Ken said, "I think my reach exceeded my grasp. I pushed myself a little further than I was ready to handle." It was rude to leave them up there like that. But it is a fair analogy to our business relationship. We are friends, but the competitive spirit is never too far away. I doubt that any of us would do anything that would harm any of the others, since their opinions of us are important. But we all like to win, and if the other falters, we aren't likely to wait too long for him to catch up.

In the business arena, when Ken and Roberta came out with their low-priced word-processing program, *Homeword*, he called us to bet that it would displace Broderbund's word-processing program, *Bank Street Writer*, on the charts. In fact, our vice president of sales and marketing at that time,

Tom Measday (who is now president of Avant Garde), bet Ken $500 and lost it three weeks later when *Bank Street Writer* temporarily fell to the number two position behind *Homeword* on the Softsel chart.

But if Ken and Roberta weren't gamblers at heart, there never would have been an On-Line Systems in the first place. They would still be in the San Fernando Valley, living off Ken's earnings as a programmer, instead of residing in a mansion in the Sierra foothills, running their own software empire.

Ken was twenty-five and Roberta was twenty-six when they founded their company in 1980. They had married shortly after high school and had had the first of two children less than a year later; Ken went to a computer-programming school, found that he had a talent for it, and worked his way up through a series of programming jobs. By the late 1970s they were living in a tract house in the suburbs of Los Angeles. Roberta took care of their two sons, and Ken worked as a programmer.

Ken couldn't have cared less about tiny hobbyist computers like the Altair. The company he worked for until 1979, Informatics, was the largest mainframe software company in the world. There, Ken had developed a reputation as a real wizard. Ken could debug huge programs, create new programming languages, or learn how to program a new language in a matter of days.

But Ken didn't like working under anyone else. He quit Informatics in 1979 and became an independent software consultant, pulling in a very respectable $30,000 a year. Then Larry, Ken's younger brother, bought an Apple and showed it to Ken. Compared with the truly powerful computers Ken was accustomed to programming, this was a pathetically puny toy. But fooling around with the machine's limited capabilities was strangely addictive, and without really knowing why he was doing it, Ken bought his own Apple in January 1980. At the time, the $2000 he put out for the machine was a significant investment—close to every penny he had saved. Roberta was less than ecstatic. She suggested to Ken that he ought to spend some of his time thinking of a way to make some money with his new toy.

But while Ken was cooking up a scheme to create a FORTRAN compiler for the Apple, Roberta was doing her own kind of computational exploring. They had a terminal at home that was connected, via telephone lines, to a mainframe belonging to one of Ken's clients. Ken had introduced his wife to a mainframe version of *Adventure*, and Roberta had quickly become addicted to it. She spent night after night working her way through the maze of caverns, drawing huge maps, and collecting clues. When she had used up all of the *Adventure*-type games available for the Apple (mostly Scott Adams creations) she was sorely disappointed. She started daydreaming about a truly challenging adventure game. Then she started planning one.

Roberta spent weeks plotting and planning. She had an idea about a game-puzzle-mystery that took place in a big house, full of mysterious locked rooms and secret passageways. She created plots and characters and mapped out the connections between the rooms. Of course, she had no idea how to turn her maps, character sketches, and plots into the kind of programming code that would make her adventure come alive on the Apple. She talked to Ken about doing the programming, but he was skeptical about her idea. He had a lot of other irons in the fire and didn't think that working on an adventure game was likely to be worth his time.

He soon changed his mind when Roberta came up with an idea for a unique feature: Why not put some graphics on the screen to accompany the game's text? Roberta had no idea whether or not it was even possible to put pictures on computer screens, but Ken looked into it and found a piece of hardware that would enable her to sketch a few primitive scenes to accompany her text. Ken started working with Apple assembly language. Within a month he had found a way to put the whole game and seventy illustrations on a floppy disk. It occurred to them that there might be a market for this game.

When, in early 1980, they had a demonstrable product,

Ken took it to Dave Gordon of Programma, then the largest publisher of Apple software. Gordon claimed that he'd be able to sell at least 500 copies of the game each month and offered Ken a 25 percent royalty on a $12 wholesale price. Ken and Roberta decided that they would try to sell it themselves. If they couldn't do any better than $3 per copy, then they could always go back to Programma. The Williamses took their program—*Mystery House*—to a few retail outlets around Los Angeles. Adventure games were enormously popular, and when the retailers saw the high-resolution graphics they were immediately enthusiastic. It looked as if they might actually make some money on this program.

By this time, Ken already had a company. He had called it On-Line Systems, thinking no doubt of the grand systems and applications programs he would be creating. It was a strange name, however, for a game company. They bought a box of one hundred blank disks and paid $200 for an ad in the May 1980 issue of a magazine called *MICRO*. Like Ed Roberts and the first Altair orders, they were totally unprepared for the flood of phone orders for *Mystery House* that started the day the magazine hit the stands. They made $11,000 that first month, $20,000 the next month, and by July their revenues were up to $30,000—about what Ken had been making in a year as a consultant!

Ken had taken on another programming job while Roberta copied disks, put them into plastic bags, and sent them out via U.P.S. At night, Roberta started working on an even more ambitious adventure game. A few months into the enterprise it became clear that On-Line Systems would require more than part-time attention, and so Ken quit what would be his last job to devote his energies full time to the business. They then packed up the kids, the Apple, and the disks and headed for a cabin in the Sierra foothills, where they proceeded to live out a fantasy they had of living in the country while making a fortune. They finished a second game, *The Wizard and the Princess*, which had considerably better pictures, and it was even more successful.

They opened a small office in the town of Coarsegold, not far from Yosemite, in December 1980. They hired their first employee to help out around the office. Two weeks later they hired someone to help their first employee, and a week later they had to hire someone to help their help's help. Money was pouring in at an astounding rate. Here they were, in their mid-twenties, living out their fantasies—raising their children in the beautiful Sierra foothills, creating their own software in a cabin they had bought with their first few months' profit, and expanding their cottage industry to the point where it was the largest single employer in the country.

On-Line was probably much more profitable than Sirius or Brøderbund in 1981 because Ken and Roberta had written their best-selling programs themselves and didn't, therefore, have the huge royalty expenses that the rest of us had to pay. Over at Sirius, Nasir was getting 35 percent of the receipts off the top. Brøderbund was paying anything from 20 to 45 percent. But eventually Ken became so involved in the business that he had less and less time for programming, and so he ended up having to pay royalties too. And as he did, he watched his profitability shrink.

In a lot of ways Ken and Roberta treated On-Line more as an extension of their personal lives than as a business back then. In those early years, they still paid for everything out of the same checkbook—floppy disks, shoes for the kids, royalties, groceries—you name it, it all came out of the same place. That may account for why their reaction was stronger than ours would have been to the decline in profits occasioned by their increasing royalty costs. Ken wouldn't stand for it, in fact, and he told me what he was going to do about it.

He planned to build an all-employee, wage-earning programming force that he could train and control so he wouldn't have to give up all those percentages that were escaping through royalties. He figured that there were a lot of programmers out there, mostly young, who would jump at a chance to live in California, right next to Yosemite National Park, where Ken could provide them with housing and vehicles, take them water-skiing every Wednesday, provide for their earthly needs like food and clean laundry, and cut them loose to program nonstop. And he had every reason to believe the plan would work. He was enough of a programming wizard to win the respect of any young hacker, and he and Roberta had created a lifestyle and self-contained community that would be tremendously appealing to young programmers who were tired of being loners and outcasts.

But I had my reservations about Ken's plan, and I told him so. It seemed a little too paternalistic to me. I have always believed that it is impossible to mass produce creativity, and that's what it seemed to me that Ken was proposing. But Ken argued that, in fact, he was creating the perfect creative work environment.

As it happened, Ken's scheme didn't work smoothly. By 1982, when On-Line had become Sierra On-Line, press stories about young programmer–millionaires were popping up all the time in magazines like *Time* and *Newsweek*, and all the programmers understood that the way to achieve such status was through the mysterious financial device known as royalties. As a result, it proved very hard to hire competent hackers on a wage basis. And Ken and Roberta had to keep paying royalties anyway, even as increasingly large portions of their sales receipts went into marketing expenses and licensing activities. They still have some programmers. They lost many, and Ken is now programming again himself.

Even though Ken and Roberta had their problems with programmers, they did manage to run their company as a kind of extended family. They had a lot of fun, especially in the early days. Some describe their outfit as a summer camp in the woods. What is clear is that it very much reflects the personalities and temperaments of Ken and Roberta Williams.

Although Roberta is far less gregarious and outgoing than Ken, she has a very strong personality. Ken tends to see the best in everybody and look for the upside potential of every deal. I think that Roberta, however, is the practical one of the pair, and the less adventurous. Once in a while, though, the pair decides to take action that seems foolhardy at first, and when they do, it is often because Roberta is standing up for a principle.

For instance, there was the time Ken and Roberta decided to take on Atari. Understand—this was not the small-scale, entrepreneurial Atari of Nolan Bushnell's era, but the corporate giant of the early Warner days, with an income that was still in the black by hundreds of millions of dollars.

Ken and Roberta's conflict with Atari started because of a dispute over Atari's billion-dollar baby—*Pac-Man*. In our early years, Brøderbund and On-Line both marketed products that turned out to be *Pac-Man* derivatives. In fact, our product, *Snoggle*, came from Japan and was originally named *Apple Puckman*. But that was before *Pac-Man* had been introduced into the U.S. market, so we thought that our product was original. When Atari came out with its home version of *Pac-Man*, however it was clearly the same game. Atari demanded that Brøderbund remove *Apple Puckman* from the market, and we complied. Ken and Roberta had a game called *Gobbler*. It was similar to *Pac-Man* in many respects, but it was not identical. When Atari came down on them and demanded that they withdraw the product from the market, Ken and Roberta got their backs up and decided to fight. They didn't like the way big companies like Atari pushed people around.

So Ken hired a lawyer who managed to get the case tried locally. (Remember, On-Line was a prominent employer in the small Sierra foothill towns of Oakhurst and Coarsegold.) And Ken cleaned Atari's clock. Most of us in the industry, including Ken, felt that the On-Line product was a rip, and my reading of several prominent cases in other jurisdictions reinforces that feeling. When Ken and I talked about it, he even worried that it could set a precedent favorable to those who might pirate *his* software. But Atari obviously mishandled the case. Its lawyers came in and tried to browbeat a local judge, implying that the case was beyond his competence. But Atari was never known for its common sense or humility. That's why I think it must have been Roberta who prodded Ken into taking on Atari. I can just hear her saying to him: "You know we can't let them push us around. We can't have that. You have to do something about it."

All in all, Ken's plans always seemed grander than ours. He was ready and willing to move into the fast track while we were still worrying about whether or not to start shrink-wrapping Brøderbund's products. And he started playing for very high stakes in 1982, beginning with his first round of venture capital money. Ken wanted to be the biggest and best software publisher, and he didn't think he could do it unless he became involved with professionals who knew more than he did about "going public" and high finance.

Jackie Morby is an investor for a Boston company called TA Associates, and in the spring of 1982 she was familiarizing herself with the home software industry. Gary and I met her for the first time at a Chinese restaurant near the San Francisco airport, and she listened as we told her our story and then talked about the other companies in our industry. She is a very friendly, direct woman. We immediately felt comfortable with her, and she was very patient as she explained to us what venture investors were and how they worked.

And so we were a little miffed when she let us know that TA had invested in Sierra On-Line instead of in our company (even though we had not yet decided that we even wanted any such investment). Although she said that the investment didn't rule out further talks with us about investing in Broderbund, we assumed that she was only being polite. After all, if she had an interest in On-Line, what would be the point of investing in Brøderbund?

We couldn't really fault her decision, though. After all, On-Line was a much bigger company than ours (at that time, we had about twenty-five employees; they had about fifty, as I recall). Most important, Ken knew more about computers than we did. Gary and I had started out as hobbyists, whereas Ken had been a hotshot at Informatics and a highly paid software consultant before he and Roberta started On-Line.

He was fluent in assembly language and familiar with all the arcana of programming. In fact, after his years as a mainframe software wizard, game programming for microcomputers was fairly elementary stuff. And he seemed to be the perfect businessman, too. He is an action-oriented person. He sometimes gets ahead of himself, but I think most effective entrepreneurs prefer action to inaction any day. He'd rather do a dozen things and have eleven of them bomb than be careful and avoid mistakes but miss the one real opportunity among the dozen attempts. Overall, he and his company were probably better investment material for TA Associates than we were at the time.

Ken is always flying off to New York and Boca Raton and other venues far from our insular little world in Silicon Valley and Software county, with plans to cut one big deal or another. I remember one such deal, also in 1982, that Ken told me about. He had just come back from New York, where the had obtained his first license and secured the rights to the latest Muppets movie, *The Dark Crystal*, which he thought had the potential to be a blockbuster film, à la *Star Wars*. If the film turned out to be as successful as he suspected it would, he told me, he was sure that an enormous number of people would run out to buy On-Line's latest adventure game, which was also named *The Dark Crystal*. The sales potential for this project, he assured me, went far beyond the 20,000 units that most well-received software products could be expected to sell. As it turned out, both the movie and the software were only moderately successful.

But it was the 1982 IBM deal that left me wondering if we'd ever catch up with Ken. He had figured that IBM was bound to come out with more and more low-end computers (that means low-priced) like the PC. And he figured that IBM would have to deal with somebody who knew how to provide software for the home, since it certainly didn't have any experience in that area. So he went down to IBM headquarters in Boca Raton "for a week," he told me. He made it sound as if he actually sat on the doorstep until the IBM people finally relented and granted him an audience. But he was rather mysterious about whom he met with and whether or not he actually had an official audience.

What had he discovered? IBM has such an enormous influence on any field it enters that it was natural for me to be both curious and apprehensive about whatever plans they might have in the home computer field. But Ken couldn't tell me a thing. In fact, he couldn't even tell me that he had actually ever met with anyone at IBM, because of nondisclosure documents that he had been required to sign. Instead, he told me to watch the newspapers and pay attention to the industry rumors. All he would say about On-Line's new project was that it was going to be big—very big.

The project was the PCjr—or, as it was first called, the Peanut—and it turned out to be not so very big after all. It was one of the very rare instances where IBM made a big entry into a new marketplace and bombed. But Ken was in there, all right. When the PCjr came rolling off the assembly lines, there was lots of On-Line software ready to go along with it. And if the PCjr had done well at first, On-Line would have prospered along with it. But the initial public reaction, considering everybody's high expectations, was close to disastrous. A year after its less-than-spectacular introduction, the PCjr was redesigned and its price slashed. But even radical surgery failed to resuscitate the project, and IBM ended up doing something it rarely does—admit a mistake. In March 1985, IBM announced that it was going to cease manufacturing the PCjr.

Ken is not easily taken aback, however. He is a gambler by nature and prefers to risk everything for a potentially great reward than to settle for something less. If settling for something less were his way of doing business, he'd still be working for somebody else at a salary of $30,000 or $40,000 a year. And so, even as he was directing a large part of his company's programming resources to the PCjr project in 1982 and '83, he was continuing his involvement in other potentially risky ventures and in particular, pursuing his interest in licenses.

Ken explained this interest to me once. More and more people were purchasing software through mass-merchandisers, he said. These outlets don't have highly informed sales staffs, so customers have to decide on their own what to buy. Since very few of these customers read computer magazines, they will base their decisions on the packaging. If the program looks interesting or familiar, they will be drawn to it.

That's what licensing is about: If you are a software publisher, you buy the right to use some famous character or name on a product as a means of drawing the consumer's interest to that product. Licenses can be very expensive—

Atari is rumored to have spent more than $20 million for the right to use names and characters from the movie *E.T.* on some of its software. Ken didn't pay that much initially. In fact, he had obtained the license for the arcade game *Frogger* for less than $50,000 in royalty guarantees. But he had to pay more for the next ones.

The first was his deal with Sydney Development Corporation to create a series of programs based on the characters from the comic strips *B.C.* and *The Wizard of Id.* Ken didn't say exactly what the deal was, but he did say that he had to commit to more than a million dollars in royalties, which means that you have to pay the royalties by a particular guarantee date whether or not you've sold that many copies of the product. In Ken's case, he said he'd owe $1 million in royalties by 1987. And having done that once, it wasn't so hard to do it a second time. When Texas Instruments, which had licensed Disney characters for a series of educational programs, bailed out of the microcomputer business, it no longer had an interest in its Disney license and just wanted to get out from under its commitments to Disney.

Ken badly wanted the Disney license. It fit right in with where he was headed—into educational software. Disney had just the clean-cut family image that would do well in that market. The license required multimillion-dollar payments to Disney—but not before 1987. Ken figured that he'd either be broke or able to pay them off easily by then. So he cut a deal and designed a whole line of educational software around the Disney characters.

Whether or not these licenses pay off, they are in keeping with the nature of the Brotherhood's most flamboyant pair of characters. Ken and Roberta have always been as unconventional and fun-loving in their personal lives as they have been bold and innovative in their business. They have been known to hop onto a private plane and fly hundreds of miles, just to come by Brøderbund's San Rafael offices and say hello. They like to charter raft trips, take their whole programming staff water-skiing, buy boats, build houses, and throw parties. No longer living in a cabin, they now own an enormous new home, and when I visited them in May 1984, on the occasion of On-Line's fourth anniversary, I found out that their home is as much a living fantasy as is their business empire.

The house is a 10,000-square-foot palatial country estate, situated on five and a half acres in a crook of the Fresno River, about a half hour's drive from the southern entrance to Yosemite. The house is built around a huge central room, an oversize racquetball court. Outside, acres of lush green lawn are watered twice a day by an automatic sprinkler system. An automatic security camera guards the gate, and the driveway is always filled with their favorite toys—cars, jeeps, pickups, snowmobiles, boats on trailers.

In many ways, the house is still an embodiment of Ken and Roberta's old fantasy of running a software empire in the countryside. Flanking the carved front door are stained-glass images of the fantastic characters from *The Dark Crystal*. The kitchen is filled with automatic devices—toasters that pop out of the wall, food processors that emerge from the counter. A mammoth playroom above the racquetball court sports a huge wetbar across one end of the room and arcade video game machines lining two entire walls. Most of the rooms are beautifully rustic, with rough-cut beams, spiral staircases, and large stone fireplaces all over the place.

Ken and Roberta want it all, and they want at least some of it right now. They are able to live the style they live because they were able to persuade their investors to buy more than half a million dollars' worth of "old stock" in On-Line, which means that part of the invested funds went straight to Ken and Roberta rather than into the company. It's not likely that having the house of their dreams will dull their competitive urges, however. Ken and Roberta have always wanted more, and I imagine that they always will.

At least as far as Gary and I are concerned, the informal association of friends we called the Brotherhood also included people who were instrumental in helping us get Brøderbund off the ground. Among those people were Al and Margot Tommervik of *Softalk* magazine. *Softalk* was born in Los

Angeles on September 12, 1980, roughly six months after Gary and I started Brøderbund. Al Tommervik, a thin, pipe-smoking man, was a copy editor at *Variety* magazine. He has a long red beard and almost equally long red hair. Margot, even thinner than Al, has long, straight brown hair that emphasizes the angularity of her features; she had held a wide variety of jobs, but in 1980 she was working as a free-lance writer. She was also an inveterate game player, and earlier that year she had won $15,000 on the television show "Password."

One of the things that Al and Margot decided to buy with Margot's winnings was a computer, and they settled on an Apple. Although they were not particularly technically in-clined, they fell deeply in love with their machine and were soon scouring the landscape for software. Then Margot saw Ken and Roberta Williams's first adventure game, *Mystery House*, in a store, and she bought it immediately. By this time, On-Line Systems was sponsoring a contest that offered a prize to the first person who could solve the game. Margot couldn't resist a challenge like that, and she worked full time on the game until she had solved it. Her solution won, and when she and Al started *Softalk*, they decided to include a contest of some sort in every issue. It was one of the most popular parts of the magazine.

Softalk, or rather a prototype of it, was in fact already in existence before Margot and Al got involved with it. It was initially just an in-house newsletter for a small software pub-lisher, called *Softape*, which published a variety of Apple software on cassette tapes. Virtually everyone who had an Apple in early 1980 had at least one or two of Softape's pro-grams. As for their in-house newsletter, the Softape people at one point were looking for someone to manage it. They hired Margot, who was a natural for the job, and who was by this time totally enthralled with computers. But Margot had even bigger plans for the newsletter than just to manage it—she wanted to go national with it, to take the newsletter and turn it into a full-scale magazine that every Apple owner in the country would read.

Margot was ambitious, but she wasn't a mercenary in

terms of dollars and cents; her motivations were more evange-listic than financial. She's always been one of the most gregar-ious, community-minded members of all the microcomputer enthusiasts I've known. Perhaps one of the reasons behind her ambition was a hope that the magazine would bring her into closer touch with the growing group of like-minded people who owned Apples and played with them, often to the exclusion of all other activities.

So Al and Margot, a couple of the Softape people, and an investor named John Haller formed Softalk Publishing, Inc. *Softalk* magazine was intended to be distributed free to all owners of Apple computers; revenues were to come from advertising. In fact, Al and Margot tried to persuade Apple to include a copy with each computer it shipped. Apple considered the offer but finally turned it down. Apple said it didn't want to offend other magazines.

The articles on Apple programming, the mail column (which often pointed out program "bugs"), excellent software reviews—features that are now mandatory in any self-respecting computer magazine—these were some of Al and Margot's pioneering features. But *Softalk*'s most influential contribution to Appledom was its best-seller list, first published in the second issue. *Softalk* polled stores (representing approximately 15 percent of all sales of Apple computers) and asked them which software products were selling well. It then published a list of the top thirty programs, along with a short piece describing the companies and the people behind them.

The first list was a hodgepodge of now long-vanished organizations and current powerhouses. Some continue to exist but under new names. Personal Software became VisiCorp. Automated Simulations (one of my favorite names) became Epyx. On-Line Systems became Sierra On-Line. Synergistic is now a software development house; California Pacific and Creative Computing Software are both gone. The second number on the list shows the relative strength of the products (*e.g.*, a title with a 40 rating sold half as many units as a product rated 80). Here's what the first list looked like:

The Top Thirty, October 1980

1. 94.06 *VisiCalc*, Personal Software
2. 87.50 *Flight Simulator*, Sublogic
3. 79.06 *Bill Budge's Space Album*, California Pacific
4. 62.50 *Sargon II*, Hayden
5. 61.56 *Odyssey*, Synergistic Software
6. 60.62 *Adventure*, Microsoft
7. 56.25 *Hi-Res Adventure: Mystery House*, On-Line Systems
8. 51.25 *Typing Tutor*, Microsoft
9. 46.26 *Temple of Apshai*, Automated Simulations
10. 44.38 *Bill Budge's Trilogy*, California Pacific
11. 44.06 *Morloc's Tower*, Automated simulations
12. 43.44 *Head On*, California Pacific
13. 43.13 *Rescue at Rigel*, Automated Simulations
14. 41.88 *Datestones of Ryn*, Automated Simulations
15. 41.88 *CCA Data Management System*, Personal Software
16. 40.31 *Super Invader*, Creative Computing Software
17. 37.81 *Wilderness Campaign*, Synergistic Software
18. 37.50 *Bill Budge's 3-D Graphics System*, California Pacific
19. 36.25 *EasyWriter*, Information Unlimited
20. 33.75 *Asteroids in Space*, Quality Software
21. 33.44 *Computer Bismark*, Strategic Simulations
22. 31.88 *Apple Writer*, Apple Computer
      31.88 *Gammon Gambler*, Personal Software
24. 31.25 Scott Adams's *Adventures*, Creative Computing Software and Adventure International
25. 29.69 *Computer Ambush*, Strategic Simulations
26. 28.44 *Tuesday Night Football*, Shoestring Software
27. 24.06 *Apple-Doc*, Southwestern Data Systems
28. 24.06 *Tranquility Base*, Stoneware
29. 22.50 *The Controller*, Apple Computer
30. 22.50 *Apple Plot*, Apple Computer

Permission to reprint granted by Margot Comstock, *Softalk* Magazine.

The list was extremely useful to everyone in the software industry. For Gary and me, it was particularly so. It told us a lot that we needed to know about the market—how we were doing *vis-à-vis* everyone else, what kinds of products were selling, and how many units we should be able to sell. It was noteworthy, for example, that only five of the thirty top-selling programs could be considered business-oriented. The major market was oriented toward games. Even Personal Software, the marketers of *VisiCalc*, had a game program on the chart. It was equally noteworthy that lots of little publishers were outselling Apple with many of their products. Clearly the market was open to new products. That gave us hope.

But the Tommerviks gave us more than hope—they gave us an opportunity to get into the market. We had sent them copies of our games to review for their October 1980 issue. Shortly after that issue came out, our phone in Eugene started ringing. Dealer after dealer called to say that they had heard about our product line from the Tommerviks and would like to place an order. The afternoon basketball games disappeared. Our list of active customers tripled in a month, and most of these new customers claimed to have heard about us from Al or Margot.

In addition to running a magazine that kept people informed about what was happening in the market, the Tommerviks brought many of the game publishers together on a social basis. Since Al and Margot talked daily with people all over the country, they were better informed than any of us, and they came to know all of us with their frequent calls inquiring about new products and plans. They usually hosted a dinner bash at some restaurant during each of the major trade shows. Some of those dinners were quite memorable.

There was the evening that about thirty of the attendees/exhibitors at the 1982 San Francisco Computer Faire descended on Alioto's, a well-known and perpetually crowded restaurant on Fisherman's Wharf. One of our number, a new employee at Apple whom we shall call George, betrayed his New York origins when he took charge of the negotiations with the maitre d'. Upon being told that there would be a forty-five-minute wait, George beckoned the man over to the side, slipped a bill into his hand (we learned later that it was a ten—the man was as cheap as he was brassy!), and, as he gripped the maitre d's hand with both of his, said in a loud voice that he was sure that the wait could be shorter than that.

The maitre d' eyed George stonily and turned away. Kurt Wohlner, art director at *Softalk*, turned to me and said, "I have a bad feeling about this. Why don't we go somewhere else?" So a group of about ten of us split off and went over to a nearby restaurant where we were quickly seated and enjoyed a delicious dinner. Back at Alioto's, a miserable group of dead-tired Computer Faire attendees waited more than two hours for a table. They looked pretty glum the next morning.

But that was nothing compared with the 1984 Computer Faire debacle. This time I had better leave the restaurant nameless. About fifty of us headed off for drinks and dinner after an exhausting, exciting day at the Faire. Margot, as usual, led the way. It wasn't easy to find a restaurant that would handle that many people on short notice, but Margot managed to find one down on the waterfront. The drinks were good and in plentiful supply. But I don't think that anyone noticed until around 10 o'clock that the food service was pretty slow. Then, around 10:30, there was a lot of rushing to and fro in the vicinity of the kitchen. The food was on the way, we were reassured, but some of our spies were dubious. One claimed to have looked into the kitchen and said he saw the food covered with white foam. He hypothesized that there had been a kitchen fire and proposed that the management didn't want to admit it for fear of losing the customers.

In fact, the management did admit it, but not until after midnight, by which time the whole group was pretty pickled. Only utter exhaustion kept us from getting ugly. Most of us slunk away hungry. A few brave souls found a twenty-four-hour pizza parlor and buried their miseries in sausage and pepperoni.

Those two dinners were the exceptions, however. Most of them were tremendous fun. Even the disasters seem to knit us closer together. As the Apple market gradually became more "button-down," and the hobbyists who had once dominated it became less significant to the dealers and distributors, the magazine that spoke to the hobbyist in all of us became the focal point about which the social part of our business lives revolved.

The Tommerviks started other magazines for the IBM PC and the Macintosh. But these never achieved the status of *Softalk*. The Tommerviks were perfectly in tune with the spirit of the home Apple purchaser—I don't think that they ever developed the same rapport with those other groups of users. In many ways, they were also the social center of the group of software publishers who were most closely associated with Apple computers and game programs. Like many others in the microcomputer industry, the Tommerviks' lives and business changed drastically after the IBM PC's entrance changed the nature of the industry.

Margot Tommervik was especially close to the people at Penguin Software, and so even though they were located in Illinois instead of in California, they joined with the rest of us in many of our activities and became an important part of the Brotherhood's small group of friends.

Indeed, while most of the cottage software companies are located on the West Coast, there were other pockets of intense activity scattered across the country. Adventure International, one of the first software publishers for the home market, is in Florida. Sir-Tech is in New York. MicroLab is located in Illinois. Several of the successful computer magazines were located in the East, and most of them spawned further computer activity in their areas.

One of the real hotbeds of interest in microcomputers was New Hampshire. Magazines such as *Byte, Microcomputer, 80 Micro,* and *Softside* originated there. *Softside* was one of the many enterprises of an entrepreneur from Milford, New Hampshire, named Robert Robitaille, whose other ventures include a mail-order computer sales company called Hardside and a software company called The Software Exchange.

In fact, The Software Exchange was one of the three companies (the others were Adventure International and Cybernautics) to which I submitted my first marketable program, *Galactic Empire*, for publication. I received respectable royalty checks from The Software Exchange for a couple of years. They stopped then, except for one more or less random check nine months later, and I assumed that the company was no longer in business.

The magazine *Softside*, however, became the spawning ground for Penguin Software, which was founded in the summer of 1981 by Mark Pelczarski. Long before doing that, Mark had been a math and computer science teacher at a high school in De Kalb, Illinois. That was where he met his future wife, Cheryl, as well as Mark and Trish Glenn, all of whom later became partial owners of Penguin Software. Pelczarski is an engaging fellow with tousled brown hair and a mustache who looks most comfortable in jeans and T-shirt. He also knows a lot about computers—he had majored in computer science at the University of Illinois. Two months after he bought his Apple in the fall of 1979, he published his first program—a graphics utility called *Magic Paintbrush* that allowed one to draw in colors on the Apple's screen.

Although he had little background in writing, Mark's interest in and knowledge of microcomputers landed him the job of editor at *Softside* just about the time Gary and I were starting Broderbund. He and Cheryl stayed in New Hampshire only about nine months before moving back to Geneva, Illinois, to form a software cooperative. Micro Co-op was intended to be a resource that would inform its members about the best software available on the market and help them acquire it for the lowest possible price. The Co-op grew to more than 3000 members, and Mark sold it in 1982.

While at *Softside*, Mark had made the acquaintance of Dave Albert, who eventually succeeded him as *Softside*'s editor. Dave, unlike Mark, was a writer. A journalism major at the University of Iowa, Dave met his wife, Mary, when they both worked for the school newspaper, *The Daily Iowan*. When Mark decided to form Penguin Software in 1981, he turned to his former *Softside* comrade, and Dave and Mary moved to Illinois to join him. It turned out to be an effective partnership. Their different backgrounds and skills fit together well. Mark was looking for someone with all-around ability, and a chief editor at a magazine has many of the same responsibilities as a software publisher. Dave and Mary got 10 percent of Penguin's stock.

Penguin's first products were graphics tools and animation tools for nonprogrammers as well as programmers, and graphic adventure games. Their products have always been oriented almost exclusively to the Apple II (and now Macintosh) markets. Mark has always subscribed to the "hacker ethic"—low-priced software, tools for programmers, and no copy-protection on software intended for programmers—an attitude that helped attract creative programmers to Penguin from the start.

Mark, Dave, and Mary have a lot in common. One of the traits they all share is a love of play. Mark's extensive collection of penguin figures has always been in evidence around the office, which has always been located in a house rather than in an office or an industrial building. They still spend a lot of time playing and are not above venturing into the Illinois winter to make penguin sounds and throw snowballs at one another. Their love of games brought them into contact with that inveterate game player Margot Tommervik, who quickly became a friend and introduced the Penguin crew to the Broderbund family.

The whimsical nature of their company reflects the management's playful nature. We always liked to have them around—Dave, Mary, and Mark could always be counted on for a good game of pickup basketball (Broderbund has always kept a hoop on the premises, at least since we moved to California). And when Broderbunders traveled East they could be sure of a warm reception in Geneva. We wished only that they were closer so that we could see more of them all.

But there was a competitive spirit that lay beneath the surface of our friendships, and it started to show itself in 1984 as the emotional bonds that held us together were seriously challenged by the pressures of an increasingly competitive market. One incident that occurred at the Summer Consumer Electronics Show exemplified this business-related strain on our personal relationships.

Mark and I had talked, as so many of us had, about merging our companies. Nothing came of it, but he had shared with me some of his product plans for the coming years. When he came by our booth at the Consumer Electronics Show, he saw three programs that struck him as being uncomfortably similar to products that he had discussed with me. He was terribly upset and told me so. I was upset, too. After all, we had exchanged information with people for years, just to avoid this kind of conflict. I was absolutely convinced that we had not stolen any ideas. How could he even think that we would do something like that?

Mark and I made up, and we're still friends, but the fact that such a disagreement could take place at all underscored the fact that an erosion of trust had taken place. By 1984, home software was a different market and a different business from what it had been only a few years before. Where previously there had been enough business for everybody, now there was talk of a software glut, of a shakeout in the offing. The camaraderie of the early days suffered as people's businesses and careers became endangered. Still, in the midst of all the hue and cry about a shakeout, Mark was sending me his dealer lists, and Ken Williams was swapping financial records with us.

The business was changing, and as always it was changing with a rapidity that took one's breath away. The laid-back atmosphere that the hobbyists had enjoyed and had propagated through their cottage industries was being swept away. And if you had to point a finger at the company most responsible for ushering in the change, you'd be pointing at IBM.

THE SOFTWARE INDUSTRY IN THE 1980s

7

Enter IBM

It's tempting to say that the microcomputer industry grew up very suddenly on August 12, 1981, the day IBM announced its entry into the personal computer market. Although the advent and rapid growth of Apple, Commodore, and Atari had transformed the personal computer business from a small group of hobbyists into a robust and growing industry, the fact remained that the words *computer* and *IBM* were synonymous in the minds of millions of people—particularly people in the business community. There is a lot of money to be made in games and entertainment, but the business of America, is, after all, business.

IBM had never shown much interest in personal computers. Their customers were Fortune 500 corporations, not teenage hackers, and their products were multimillion-dollar mainframes, not microcomputers. But the extraordinary success of Apple was not lost on the corporate planners at "Big Blue," as IBM is known in the computer industry. Its decision to enter the personal computer game legitimized personal computers in the minds of the business community.

The immediate effect of IBM's entry on home-oriented software companies like Brøderbund, Sirius, and Sierra On-Line was far less traumatic than the fall of Atari a year later. But the impact of the announcement on the public was undeniable: Personal computers were no longer toys. They were on their way to becoming office machines and even household appliances. To the people who bought automobiles and stereos, typewriters and copying machines, these small computers that had been heretofore perceived as nothing more than glorified video game machines now had something to do with real business. After all, International Business Machines itself was building them.

Even Apple, which had been the dominant force in the personal computer industry before IBM put its awesome resources into motion, welcomed the entry. At least it *said* it did. Apple bought a full-page ad in the *Wall Street Journal* that said: "Welcome, IBM. . . . Welcome to the most exciting and important marketplace since the computer revolution began 35 years ago. . . ." The official statement from Apple was that IBM's millions of dollars' worth of publicity would induce many more people to buy personal computers—and some of those people would buy Apples instead of IBMs.

Apple was right about one thing—people began buying IBM PCs. IBM shipped 13,000 PCs between August and December of 1981. Within two years, it would sell more than half a million more. The majority of these machines were destined for offices and small businesses; the home computer market was still dominated by Apple and Commodore. But the words *IBM compatible* had added a whole new dimension to the microcomputer industry.

You don't have to spend much time around a computer-related business in order to realize that an unprecedented amount of marketing clout looms behind the legend of IBM supremacy. In the mainframe world, the principal contenders in the computer industry (Honeywell, Control Data, Burroughs, Wang, Data General, Digital Equipment, and Sperry) are known as "IBM and the seven dwarfs." In the microcomputer hardware arena, IBM's entry was a distinct turning point. The age of the hardware wildcatter was coming to an end, and the software wars had already begun. Despite Apple's publicly proclaimed optimism, it was in a fight for its life.

Apple's chairman and co-founder, Steve Jobs, the business-oriented member of the original Jobs–Wozniak partnership, had long been aware that Apple's day of reckoning would come when the giant awakened. Jobs has been known to say that for years he knew Apple had to run as quickly as possible to get through "a gate that was rapidly closing." The impenetrable barrier that Jobs claimed to foresee descending upon manufacturers of personal computers was the day of IBM's inevitable entry into the market.

What Apple in particular had feared the most was the circumstance that was least likely—the slim chance that IBM would do something technologically bold that would capture everyone's imagination in one stroke. As it turned out, Apple had nothing to fear in that regard. Old homebrewers knew instantly that there was nothing particularly advanced about the IBM PC, technically speaking, from its choice of microprocessor chip to the way the screen looked to the way the keys were laid out on the keyboard.

The most dangerous part of the PC's design, as far as the independents were concerned, was not how advanced it was technically, but the fact that it was an "open" design that directly encouraged third-party vendors to create their own compatible hardware devices and software.

A computer doesn't do any good unless there is software available so that people can use the computer to perform tasks. And you can't create software for a computer unless you know some things about the computer itself—like the kind of chip it uses and the instruction set built into that chip (the language the chip uses to receive data and execute commands). Nor can you build a device like a new kind of screen or keyboard or joystick that plugs into a particular computer without knowing some things about the hardware of that computer in order to accommodate your device to it. And because every different computer has unique hardware and software characteristics, every vendor has to make many different versions of each computer accessory and software product.

Electronics and computer manufacturers often make their technical specifications freely available in order to encourage this third-party market. But all along, one hallmark of IBM's approach to mainframe technology was that

IBM used hardware that only IBM could obtain, or it kept software secrets very close to the vest. This is known as having a "closed" system, and it is one of the reasons IBM dominates the seven dwarfs and has regularly obliterated even savvy challengers like RCA, General Electric, and Xerox in the mainframe market. For the PC, however, IBM reversed itself. That was the brilliant surprise—the PC had an open system because IBM was out to establish itself as a standard in the personal computer market.

IBM's entry might not have been traumatic for home-computer-oriented companies. But it was cause for great turbulence in the "business productivity" software market—a category that was nonexistent until *WordStar* and *VisiCalc* came along. In addition to contracting for Bill Baker and John Draper's *EasyWriter*, IBM also commissioned its own version of *VisiCalc*—the program that had made Apple a serious contender with businesspeople. IBM spreadsheets, word-processing systems, and database management systems proliferated like wild. An even larger-scale software battle was looming, however, in the area of systems software—the programs that ordinary computer users rarely know anything about but can't do without.

At the heart of this battle—which pitted Gates and Allen's Microsoft against another pioneering, and equally powerful, software company, Digital Research—was the IBM PC's *operating system*. In general, an operating system is a program that, however complicated it is in and of itself, is designed to make life less complicated for the person using a computer. The heart (or, more accurately, the central nervous system) of every microcomputer is its microprocessor, where calculations, data processing, and logical operations take place. But it takes more than a microprocessor to make a microcomputer—just as a human being needs more than a nervous system in order to function effectively.

There has to be a way to feed data to the microprocessor (input devices) and a way to get the processed information back out again (output devices). The microprocessor also needs to be connected both to a short-term memory (RAM) and a secondary memory (disk or tape). And even if you assemble all the right hardware components and plug them together in the correct configuration, you are still going to need a special kind of software to enable all these elements to work together. And that is where the operating system comes in handy.

An operating system is, in effect, a "master control program" that can communicate with the microprocessor. Once an operating system is loaded into a computer's main memory (RAM), it serves as a kind of translator and traffic controller to coordinate all the different components of the computer system. This program also reads from, sends information to, and records the information to the disk drive, the keyboard, the display screen, and so on, all of which is called collectively Input/Output—I/O for short.

The operating system performs valuable services for the person who uses the computer by working behind the scenes to turn a dormant microprocessor into a real working computer. When a person sits down at a keyboard and types in a series of letters, the operating system oversees the series of electronic events that turn those keystrokes into letters displayed on a screen and into commands to be executed by the computer. A number of "utility programs" are included in the operating system, and these subprograms enable the human user to transfer file from a disk to main (RAM) memory or write a file onto the disk from memory, to print, copy, or delete a file, and to see the contents of a file displayed on the screen.

One other aspect of operating systems makes them strategically important to the software business. These master control programs also mediate the activities of *application programs* like word processors, spreadsheets, database management systems, games—any packaged program for the computer. As it would be far too much work for applications programs to handle all the details of transferring data from memory to disk to keyboard to screen, the programs contain instead portions that communicate with the operating system, which, in turn, performs these "housekeeping" duties.

Although there may be a dozen different application programs available for a particular computer, there are usually only a few operating systems. Naturally, if a software company sells one operating system when every computer of a certain manufacturer is sold, then that company is going to make a lot of money. That's why the battle to produce the most widely used operating system for IBM's personal computer had such a major impact on the two software companies involved—Digital Research, which turned out to be the loser in this battle, and Microsoft, which emerged as a dominant force in the microcomputer software industry.

To understand how and why Microsoft emerged victorious in its competition with Digital Research, it is necessary to know something about the way each company evolved. When Microsoft was introduced in this story, it was in reference to the pioneering days of the Altair. But Gates and Allen, despite their early fame among homebrewers and continued success in turning microcomputer software into a business rather than a hobby, were far from the only software experts who existed in the Altair days. And MITS wasn't the only pioneering company whose former employees or associates went on to launch their own software empires. Gary Kildall, before he founded Digital Research, was building microcomputers back in the days when Intel, the inventor of the microprocessor, was still trying to figure out what to do with this new chip. In fact, Kildall created a microcomputer operating system nearly two years before the first Altair existed.

Kildall was an accomplished programmer. In the early 1970s he was a computer science professor at the Naval Postgraduate School in Pacific Grove, California—an idyllic little coast town two hours from Silicon Valley. Kildall was one of the few people in the "real" computer world who had been drawn to the newly available 4004 chip. Legend has it that in 1972 he responded to a note on a bulletin board that said: "Microcomputer—$25." It wasn't a computer, of course, but the 4004. Kildall was fascinated and went as far as writing an IBM mainframe program that emulated the 4004's instruction set. But only Intel then had the equipment for connecting his mainframe language to an actual chip. So he started visiting the microprocessor development laboratory at Intel and soon procured a contract to produce a microprocessor version of one of the mainframe languages, known as PL/I. It was in his attempt to shoehorn the complex language into the limited memory capacity of the 4004 that Kildall first started creating the rudiments of a microprocessor operating system.

Operating systems on mainframes were massive projects that often took dozens of programmers several years to write. These huge programs also used far more computer resources than a tiny microprocessor could ever provide. So Kildall set out to produce a very simple, extremely compact control program. As microprocessor capabilities expanded with every new chip to hit the market, his program expanded to take advantage of those capabilities. Eventually, his creation evolved into the operating system he called *Control Program for Microcomputers*—CP/M for short. Intel wasn't in the software business, so it had no objections when Kildall decided to market his operating system.

Kildall and a hardware-oriented friend in San Francisco actually built their own homebrew microcomputer more than a year prior to the Altair announcement. When MITS proved that there was a growing market for hobbyist microcomputers, Kildall turned his microcomputer programming efforts into one of those whimsically named companies that proliferated in the 1975–77 era—*Intergalactic Digital Research.*

In 1977, when software publishing became less of a hobby and more of a business, the "Intergalactic" part of the name was dropped. But Kildall refused to move his operation to Silicon Valley—Digital Research remained in Pacific Grove. Kildall's wife, Dorothy McEwen, took over running the company while Kildall concentrated on programming, and in 1977 they negotiated their first big contract for CP/M. One of MITS' early rivals, the IMSAI Corporation, sent its marketing director, Seymour Rubinstein (who later founded Micro-Pro), to negotiate with Digital Research. IMSAI paid $25,000 for an IMSAI version of the operating system.

Without getting into more technical detail about how microchips operate, it can be said that CP/M dominated the market for operating systems when the successors to the early Intel chips began to be used for nonhobbyist computers (the successors to the Altair, which didn't require assembly of electronic components or extensive knowledge of computer hardware). Almost all of the computers based on the highly popular Z–80 chips used CP/M, and it looked like Digital Research had a virtual monopoly on microcomputer operating systems—until IBM and Microsoft came along.

The dramatic change in fortunes for both Microsoft and Digital Research began in July 1980, when Bill Gates received a call from someone at IBM who wanted to make an appointment to talk with him. "Fine," Gates replied. Did IBM want to set up a meeting the following week? "No," the IBM representative said—they wanted to fly up from Boca Raton, Florida, that afternoon. That put the young software entrepreneur in a difficult position, as he had a conflicting appointment already set up. Gates made the fateful decision to call Ray Kassar, CEO of Atari, to change their appointment. It took a lot of nerve to postpone a meeting with Ray Kassar himself. But if anything was bigger than a potential deal with Atari, it was a potential deal with IBM.

Gates and Allen called in reinforcements in the person of Steve Ballmer, whom Gates had known from Harvard. Ballmer had marketing experience and a business education. The three of them put their heads together and decided that IBM was undoubtedly getting ready to make its long-awaited entry into the personal computer market, and that in all likelihood it wanted to negotiate a deal with Microsoft for microcomputer software.

Sure enough, the IBM technical representatives asked a lot of questions about microcomputers—after the company's legal people made the Microsoft group sign their famed nondisclosure agreements—but they never actually came out and told Microsoft what they were up to. At least not at the first meeting.

A month later, IBM showed up again. This time it had an even heftier nondisclosure agreement. But it also had something to disclose—its plans to develop a personal computer. Gates wasn't terribly pleased with IBM's initial design for its machine. He thought that IBM would be making a big mistake if it used the kind of 8-bit microprocessor chips that were then dominating the personal computer industry. He felt that

Microsoft would be able to provide far superior software if IBM chose to use a 16-bit chip instead. It was an amazing scene. Here was this young fellow, a college dropout in his early twenties, telling IBM how to go about designing a computer. Even more amazing was the fact that IBM listened.

When IBM told Microsoft that it had decided on the 8086 chip—which is something of a halfway step toward a 16-bit processor, as Gates had suggested—Paul Allen talked to someone he knew who had already created an operating system for that very chip. The colleague was Tim Patterson of Seattle Computer Products. Gates, Allen, and Ballmer proposed to Patterson that Microsoft adapt Patterson's existing program for use with the PC. They didn't have any time to waste, according to the tight production schedule laid out by IBM, and it would take far less time to modify an existing operating system than to create one from scratch. Patterson went along with the proposal, and Gates and Allen flew to Boca Raton to talk to IBM about their plan.

The young hotshots from Bellevue, Washington, were questioned closely by IBM's technical experts, and by the end of the day it became clear that IBM was taken with the program and with Gates and Allen's presentation of it. But they had another advantage going for them, aside from their technical expertise and business acumen: an unexpected personal contact with John Opel, IBM's new chairman. At lunchtime, Phil Estridge, IBM's project manager for the PC operation, told Gates that Opel had asked if Microsoft was "Mary Gates's boy's company." It turned out that Bill's mother had served with Opel on the board of directors of the United Way.

In November 1980, Microsoft signed a contract with IBM. Never eager to put all its eggs into the same basket, however, IBM had contracted with Digital Research, which had been working on an 8086 version of CP/M. But from the first day, PC–DOS, Microsoft's operating system for the IBM PC (later joined by MS–DOS, a version for "IBM-compatible" machines), outsold CP/M by a wide margin. Microsoft's operating system was ready before Digital Research's and was therefore "bundled" (sold along with the hardware). It didn't take long before "IBM compatible"—the magic words of the early 1980s—was nearly synonymous with "MS-DOS compatible." By 1983, Microsoft was very close to knocking off Micropro for the number one position among microcomputer software companies. Digital Research was number four. But by 1984, Microsoft was almost at the top of the chart, soon to overtake MicroPro for the number one slot, while Digital was sinking.

Ex-homebrewers, computer science professors, game companies-turned-business software companies, and software entrepreneurs weren't the only people to try and cash in on this market that IBM had so vastly enlarged. Increasingly, people who had big money to play with were considering the possibility of starting their own companies from scratch to capitalize on this lucrative market. Those people were none other than the venture capitalists.

Enter the Venture Capitalists

At the beginning, the microcomputer industry was not only ignored by corporate America—it was totally unknown to the financial powers-that-be. But when teenagers began to build hundred-million-dollar companies in five years or so, the folks who were on the lookout for high-risk, high-gain investments began to get into the game. One of the earliest success stories was that of venture capitalist Arthur Rock, whose initial $75,000 investment in Apple Computer made him millions. It wasn't long before such "vee-cees," as they are sometimes called, turned their attention to software. Their sudden interest changed the industry: Most of the software companies that survived the 1984 shakeout (and several that didn't) either had started with venture capital money or had taken venture capital investors on board.

Venture capital is not a new phenomenon—people who like to gamble on infant companies have always been attracted to new technologies. But the Tax Reform Acts of 1978 and 1981 made the institution a great deal more appealing to professional investors who were looking for tax breaks with fantastic upside potential.

The 1981 Act reduced the tax on long-term capital gains to a maximum of 40 percent of one's ordinary tax rate. This is an extraordinary tax break, especially when you are talking about millions of dollars. Traditionally, most investors received long-term capital gains treatment by investing in the stock market. But the stock market didn't perform very well in the 1970s. Financiers started looking for alternatives.

One alternative was to invest in venture capital funds. These funds are usually placed in small companies in very promising industries—companies such as those in high-technology industries, including aerospace, electronics, and computers. Typically, the fund investor identifies a company that is still small and strapped for cash as a likely comer and invests venture money that would enable the ambitious entre-preneur to expand his or her business. Ultimately, the fund would want to sell its interest and realize its gain, so venture capitalists try to ensure that they either sell their investments to a larger company or "go public" by offering their stock on the public market. Ideally, this is done once the company has passed through its most rapid growth.

If the company prospers, it is possible for a fund to reap ten or even one hundred times its original investment in just a few years. It is equally possible, however, that the company will falter somewhere along the way, in which case the fund might well lose every penny of its original investment. The real trick for an investor is to be smart enough and connected enough to the grapevine to be able to spot likely successes early enough to maximize his or her return.

It isn't an easy business, and it never was. Good venture capitalists have to be able to separate form from substance. In the software game, where the product is not only intangible but unreadable to all but experts, this is especially true. Moreover, because they are generally too busy running their businesses, many of the most successful software entrepre-neurs never have the time or interest to put together profes-sional, polished business plans for an investor's consideration. It is left to the venture investor to determine which young entrepreneur's dream is likely to grow into an empire and which is likely to wither and die with most of the other start-up companies.

But most venture capitalists don't want people to come to them with plans anyway. They find it far more profitable to identify on their own the companies that they think would make good investments and then talk the owner of the company into taking the investment money. But in persuading the often reluctant entrepreneur to take the money, they also have to persuade him that his company's current value is far lower than he may believe. No investment is a good one if the price isn't right. The investor says he has one million dollars to invest. The entrepreneur says he has part of a company to sell. The key question is: How big a piece of the company's future is worth a million dollars right now?

If they find the company early enough and are willing to spend enough, venture investors sometimes end up with a controlling interest in the company. When this happens, venture investors often decide that the company would be better off if the entrepreneur yielded the operational power over his or her company to a professional manager. In return, the entrepreneur receives a greater yield on the percentage of stock he or she still owns.

These deals aren't particularly easy to figure out while they are happening, although brilliant investments and foolish decisions are abundantly clear in retrospect. What can sometimes complicate or even impede an investment arrangement in the first place, however, is the entrepreneur who suffers from a disease known as "entrepreneur's syndrome." This heady mix of boundless expectations and lack of restraints upon personal authority can lead to arrogance, which manifests itself in an inability either to delegate responsibility or to part with any portion of the ownership of one's company. The first manifestation can destroy the management of small companies; the second can destroy the same company's ability to become properly capitalized.

The best venture capitalists are true entrepreneurs in their own right. A mystique has grown up around successful investors like Don Valentine, Bill Hambrecht, and Ben Rosen, for it is no mean feat to pick the few winners from the thousands of ambitious men and women trying to bootstrap their kitchen-table operation into the next industrial giant. The best investors attract the most money to their funds, and this in turn leads (at least potentially) to the greatest investment profits. But the market became pretty crowded when software was hot, and then the venture capitalists deserted the field in droves when the shakeout began. Those venture capitalists who remain interested in software all seem to be chasing the same deals.

One of the great dangers in this investment game is that later-stage investors will buy into the company at a high price that reflects the fierce competition among the venture firms for good placement of their funds. Earlier investors will use these artificially high later prices to calculate growth in value of their own investments. These growth figures will be used, in turn, to attract further investors into their venture funds. But the price that a venture fund is willing to pay for a pre-public high-tech investment may actually be higher than the public, without such constraints upon its investment opportunities, would be willing to pay—the public may take the option of safer, lower growth investments such as bonds or mutual funds, while venture investors can't go these safer routes. If that's the case, the investors may be talking only with one another, and sooner or later the bubble may burst.

It is important to understand that venture capitalists don't typically pay the existing owners for their piece of the company. What they are doing is putting money into the company itself by financing the firms' expansion. The entrepreneur and the investor are in the same boat because their stock will be worthless unless the company becomes profitable enough, fast enough.

Existing companies that have managed to grow on their own often refuse venture money unless they are in bad financial trouble. It is relatively expensive money—but it must be remembered that no banker in his right mind will lend money on anything as speculative as a new program that might or might not be next year's best-seller. In effect, selling shares in exchange for investment capital is like paying a bank 100 percent annual interest on a loan. But many people who have good ideas and good management skills need venture money just to get started in business, and investments in these start-up companies have provided some of the most impressive returns for the venture community.

Start-ups are the riskiest of the risky investments, however. The investor is putting money into an organization that doesn't even exist yet or that at most exists in name only. It doesn't have products, management, or sales, and it may never have them. Still, if the people with this venture start-up proposal are the right people, and if their analysis of a market opportunity is correct, then the risk may be worthwhile.

Some of the software industry's most visible and successful companies are venture start-ups. In each case, a strong management team developed a plan based upon exploitation of a market opportunity that was being ignored by existing companies. Although these companies differ in most respects, Lotus and Electronic Arts both possess aggressive management groups who believe they have the key to certain markets and who have been able to persuade some very tough-minded investors to see those markets the same way.

The origins of the most phenomenally successful product introduction in the history of microcomputer software can be traced back to a microcomputer users' group in Cambridge, Massachusetts, and to a program that was written in 1978 as a favor to an MIT student. The ultimate product of that chain of events was *1-2-3*, which was introduced at COMDEX, a huge computer trade show, in the fall of 1982 and officially released in January 1983. In the few days that the show was open, more than a million dollars' worth of advance orders were written. By April 1983, the program reached the top of Softsel's chart. By the beginning of 1984, *1-2-3* was outselling the next best-selling program by a factor of more than two to one.

Mitch Kapor, co-author of *1-2-3*, was more than yet another under-thirty millionaire programmer. His company, Lotus, was the envy of other software designers and the object of outright awe in the venture capital community. And his program *1-2-3*, an "integrated package" that combined several different office-related functions in the same program, was the first sophisticated program of its kind to be successfully released into the market. It set a new standard in business software, triggering an avalanche of integrated packages like it. In the meantime, Lotus's venture backers, primarily Ben Rosen and his partner, L. J. Sevin, made a killing of legendary proportions. And it wasn't even Kapor's *first* million-dollar program.

The story of Kapor's route to his software jackpot was as full of unpredictable twists as any other microcomputer entrepreneur's, and his employment history is probably as eclectic as anybody's, except perhaps Paul Lutus's. Kapor had been an authentic mathematics prodigy who discovered and published a new method of calculating square roots while he was still in high school. He entered Yale at a tender age as a mathematics major in 1967, but, as many others of his generation were discovering in those turbulent years, Mitch was finding that a conventional course for his life didn't particularly appeal to him. He had already been a math prodigy. He wanted to try something else.

He found that he was spending more and more time at the campus radio station, and when he left Yale he took a job at a Hartford, Connecticut, radio station as a disk jockey. Then he went to Europe to study Transcendental Meditation for a year. After he returned to the United States, he became a full-time meditation teacher in Boston. Then he quit and went back to college, where he picked up a master's degree in psychology. The first job of his new career was as a mental-health aide at a psychiatric hospital, where he found out that "the best contribution I could make to the mental-health field was to leave it."

By 1977, Mitch Kapor, still in his twenties, discovered yet another enthusiastically embraced avocation to add to his apparently aimless career trajectory. First it was mathematics. Then it was radio and T.M. and psychology. This time, the object of his fascination was the same seductive object that had hooked so many of us—the TRS-80 Model 1. Six months later he bought an Apple. The day after he bought it, he returned to the store to ask a few questions about his new machine, and, never known for his lack of self-confidence, he managed to talk his way into a job as an Apple programmer.

In the store at the same time as Kapor was a businessman who was purchasing an Apple. From the questions the man was asking, Kapor could tell that he was a novice. It turned out that the fellow needed some custom programming done for his Apple. Having been an Apple owner for all of twenty-four hours, Kapor decided that he was an expert and took the job for $5 an hour. He turned out to be good enough at BASIC to learn programming on the job.

Programming was an enjoyable vocation, so he started looking around for other jobs as a programmer. But at that time there were only twenty or thirty other Apple owners in the Boston area. He looked for a users' group as a way of meeting potential clients. When he couldn't find any group in existence, he contacted another Apple owner, who got hold of a couple others. The first Boston-area users' group meeting was held in Kapor's living room and was attended by seven people. Inauspicious as that beginning may have seemed, the earliest contacts Mitch Kapor made with other Boston-area hobbyists put him in touch with two people who would have an enormous influence on his destiny—Ben Rosen and Robert Frankston.

Back in 1977, users' groups were the primary channel for distributing software, much of which was created by hobbyists and distributed for free as "public domain" programs. Kapor started collecting early Apple public-domain software and trading programs with other users' group librarians. At about this time, he met a graduate student at M.I.T., Eric Rosenfeld, who was finishing a research project that required a large amount of the university's computer time to perform statistical analyses of his research data. Upon hearing Rosenfeld explain how the analysis worked, Kapor offered to write him a program that would do something similar to what M.I.T.'s mainframe statistics programs did, except his version could run on an Apple instead of on one of the expensive time-sharing computers.

Kapor's effort to write a statistics package in BASIC led to the program he named *Tiny Troll*. The program accomplished the statistical work Rosenfeld needed for his project, and once they saw how much time it saved, they realized that other scientists and students could probably use it, too. Kapor looked at Rosenfeld and said the words that have launched so many of us in the unpredictable game of software publishing: "You know, I bet people would pay money for this."

With Rosenfeld handling much of the design and Kapor coding the program in BASIC, they created, in 1978, a new version of the original program that would do simple graphics and primitive text editing as well as statistical analysis. In some ways, then, *Tiny Troll* was a prototype of the much more sophisticated integrated software Kapor was to produce years later. Kapor's informal distribution of the program through his users' group led him to meet several people who would later play important roles in his career. Among the people who purchased *Tiny Troll* was Ben Rosen, who called Kapor for explanations of how different features of the program worked. Another person Kapor met through his users' group was a programmer named Bob Frankston.

Frankston, who was at that time co-developing *VisiCalc*, mentioned to Kapor that his publisher, Personal Software, was looking for new products. Peter Jennings met with Kapor, and in 1979 Personal Software contracted with Kapor and Rosenfeld to produce two new programs based on *Tiny Troll*, incorporating Dan Fylstra's suggestions for additions and changes. The new programs were to be known as *Visi-Trend* and *VisiPlot*. When the prototypes were finished, Personal Software offered Kapor a full-time job as new products manager and offered stock options as inducement for him to relocate to California with the company. Kapor accepted, and he signed an employment contract in March 1980.

It was a great time to have stock options in Personal Software. *VisiCalc* was racking up astonishing sales. But Kapor's involvement in the company kept him from completing the final versions of *VisiTrend* and *VisiPlot*. Ever the gambler, he traded back his valuable stock options in exchange for release from his employment contract. He moved back to Cambridge and ended up borrowing money to live on while he finished the programs. When the programs hit the market in April 1981, his gamble turned out to have been a shrewd one. With his 1979 contract guaranteeing a 33 percent royalty, Kapor collected almost half a million dollars in royalties in one six-month period after the software came out.

By 1982, Personal Software had changed its name to Visi-Corp, and 33 percent royalty contracts were things of the past. Fifteen and 20 and 25 percent royalties were more common. With *VisiTrend/VisiPlot* still selling at a healthy rate, VisiCorp, anxious to bail out of a steep royalty deal, decided to buy out that old contract for $1.2 million. With that money, Kapor started a company that he called Lotus and, inspired by the elegant design and outstanding success of *Visi-Calc*, then set out to produce a real blockbuster.

But Kapor was one of those programmer–entrepreneurs who were visionary enough to conceive of a new kind of software, yet smart enough to realize that to make that vision a reality would require more than they could provide as programmers. He had reached the limits of his own programming skills, and he knew it. Although he still calls himself "the best BASIC hacker in the world," he knew in 1982 that the days when one could write a serious commercial program in BASIC were numbered.

Kapor's forte was now program design—that is, knowing what kind of program he wanted, and how he wanted the computer to present it to the user. He was particularly adept at designing that part of the program called the "user interface," where the person meets the machine. But creating a good program takes more than a knack for design. It also takes an ability to translate that design into compact, efficient, fast programming code. Assembly language wizard Jonathan Sachs had just that ability, and Kapor's collaboration with him on the new piece of software Kapor had envisioned led to a success that dwarfed Kapor's previous triumphs.

Kapor knew that he wanted to put together a package of related programs that would help businesspeople with every aspect of preparing a presentation—a spreadsheet program, a graphics package for preparing charts, and a database manager. Sachs already had the rights to a spreadsheet package. With the IBM PC now out on the market, Kapor and Sachs knew that the PC's microprocessor made possible the new level of program capability they were seeking. They also decided that the software publishing game had matured. It was time for a large-scale product introduction—the way the hardware boys did it.

Expensive booths at the major trade shows and more than a million dollars' worth of media advertising prior to the new program's release were only the beginning. More money was spent flying around the country making personal presentations to key figures, such as the management of the Businessland computer stores, to get the key retailers on the bandwagon before the program was offered to the public.

It certainly would have been possible for Kapor to bootstrap his new product, *1-2-3*, on the proceeds of his VisiCorp deal, and to buy his advertising and promotion as the profits rolled in, as they were virtually certain to do. But he decided that the only way to gamble was to gamble big. In order to put on the publicity blitz he envisioned, and to turn out the number of copies he was aiming for, Kapor had to resort to venture capital. Fortunately, he remembered one of the old-time users of *Tiny Troll*, a fellow named Ben Rosen who, Kapor knew, was a partner in a venture capital firm.

Kapor contacted Rosen and told him about his idea. Rosen was intrigued enough with it to ask for a simple précis of Kapor's business plan to show his partner, L. J. Sevin. Nothing happened at first. Nothing ever happens at first with venture capitalists, because they do what they call "due diligence," which means checking every single one of the fifty separate business references you provide. But finally, six weeks later, Rosen and Sevin took Kapor to dinner, and over salad they mentioned that they would like to invest in Lotus. How much did Kapor think it was worth? They put together a deal over dinner.

Rosen and Sevin put in $600,000 for the first round of financing, and other venture capitalists made it an even million dollars, for which the investors received 30 percent of the stock. Sevin-Rosen put another two and a half million dollars into Lotus before *1-2-3* was announced in the fall of 1982— accompanied by a million dollar-plus publicity campaign. The gamble worked spectacularly well—the company was profitable from the day *1-2-3* went on sale. The principals re-couped their investment in record time. When they took Lotus public in late 1983, the investors made themselves and Kapor and Sachs millions more.

As for Electronic Arts, its very name evokes an unlikely juxtaposition of images in the mind's eye. Indeed, Electronic Arts had little more than an image when it got started, but by the time its well-thought-out story hit the media, it was exactly the right image at exactly the right time—the best products of hot young programming stars, packaged by savvy marketers, backed by the winningest venture capitalists, all of them out to change the software landscape and make a for-tune. The age of the programmer was over. The age of the "software artist" was not in full swing. Like Activision before it, EA adopted the metaphor of the software publisher as a kind of record company—with the programmers as the recording stars.

"Simple, hot, and deep," was the slogan Electronic Arts' founder and guiding spirit, Trip Hawkins, used to describe the kind of software Electronic Arts wanted to publish. "Ful-filling the promise of personal computers" was another slogan he used to describe Electronic Arts' goals. EA has always been good at creating slogans. It billed itself as the first of a new generation of software publishers that would share a vision of the computer-enhanced future and a burning com-mitment to advance the state of the programming art. And EA told programmers that they were going to make software artists famous as well as rich.

In my opinion, EA had a lot more hype than substance when it started. Of course, I'm a competitor, so you'll have to consider my analysis in that light. But I felt that many of EA's products, particularly its early stuff, was mediocre. The company's hype was superb, however, and the quality of its marketing has always been unusually good.

EA certainly did its best to fulfill its promises to pro-grammers who wanted the same public recognition that musi-cians, writers, and other popular artists were granted. It hired a photographer from the rock scene, announced itself in the computer media with full-page group portraits, and put Bill Budge's face in full-page ads in national magazines. EA packaged its software to look like record albums, complete with programmer biographies, liner notes, and attractive graphics. Its very modern logo was designed to be stylish enough to put on posters.

The birth of Electronic Arts did represent the advent of a more advanced approach pioneered by Activision and others— a new kind of software publishing business that was rooted not in the early days of technically oriented enthusiasts but in the personal computer industry that had grown up around homebrew-spawned enterprises like Apple. EA's management group shared a vision of the changes computers were going to bring to the world, but EA's heavily marketing-oriented Silicon Valley vets weren't exactly a bunch of dewy-eyed hobbyists. Trip Hawkins had been with Apple since 1978, where he had most recently been in charge of marketing for Apple's Lisa computer. Although the machine flopped in the market, the job brought him into contact with a lot of talented programmers, and his relationship with them became a bankable asset when he left Apple in April 1982 to hang out his own shingle.

The spring of 1982 was a golden time for somebody like Trip Hawkins to look for venture backing. Atari was still raking it in. Activision was performing phenomenally well. The shakeout wasn't even a cloud on the horizon, and venture capitalists were salivating over the phenomenal profits that people like Arthur Rock had made by backing start-ups like Apple. Obviously, software was the next gold mine for these investors. Hawkins drew up a business plan around the idea of a company that would publish innovative high-quality software slated for the home market and created not by anonymous employees but by contract artists who would be as potentially promotable as rock stars.

The start-up money became even easier to find when Hawkins signed up Richard Melman, then director of marketing for VisiCorp, as Electronic Arts' marketing director. (Venture capitalists like track records and pedigrees.) To ice the cake, EA moved its start-up operation into the office of its backer Don Valentine, one of the most successful of the software venture capitalists. And the cherry on top of the icing was put into place when Steve Wozniak, co-founder of Apple, joined EA's board of directors.

With Wozniak, Melman, and Valentine in place, Hawkins sold his vision to the people who could put some product out there to fulfill the image—top-notch programmers. He had at least one great programmer from the beginning—Bill Budge. Woz was one of Budge's heroes, and EA gave Bill the full treatment, showing him mock-ups of the product packaging and media ads that would turn him into a star, and it convinced Bill that his participation was essential to the success of the enterprise. Electronic Arts obtained the original rights to the Atari version of *Pinball Construction Set* and then later picked up the Apple version, originally published by Budgeco.

The metaphor of the software publishing house as a kind of record company wasn't invented by Electronic Arts. The original "software artist" house, Activision, was started by Jim Levy, a marketing whiz from the record industry, and a group of programmers from Atari who felt that Ray Kassar's approach to software marketing didn't give programmers the recognition they deserved. The essence of Activision, since its inception, was therefore its programmer orientation; and before long its central group of programmers succeeded in living their dream of being part of a company that was run by and for programmers. They achieved the recognition they wanted and did very well for a number of years.

The Activision magic was unbeatable for a time. Everything the programmers touched turned to gold. Then the video game fad began to diminish, and with it, Activision's chief market. Because Activision had so emphasized its programmer orientation, and had intentionally isolated the people who created its products from the people who sold those products, it failed to respond quickly enough to the change in market conditions. The programmers' distrust of marketers had simply led them to lose touch with their market. Activision's director of product development once told me proudly that its marketing people were not permitted to have any input into product development. Marketing wasn't allowed to get involved until the product was finished.

Activision had sales of more than $150 million in its biggest year, but things started going downhill with the demise of the Atari cartridge market. The company went public in June 1983. The stock quickly fell from its opening price, and as I write is priced at less than one-twelfth of its initial value. The company has lost virtually all of its top management.

Electronic Arts, on the other hand, was as firmly committed to the importance of marketing as it was to the importance of programmers. It started out much smaller than Activision, and it aimed itself at the growing home computer market rather than the diminishing video game market. It was one of the companies that survived the software shakeout of 1984.

Sympathetic as I am to the programmer's need for creative freedom, I know that if a company is so fanatical in its perception of programming as a kind of sacred art, it can, like Activision, cut itself off from changes in market conditions. Like the book and record businesses, software publishing must, in order to work well, achieve the proper balance of art and business interests. Many game programmers would still be writing shoot-'em-up games, and far too many business-productivity programmers would still be turning out spreadsheets, if it weren't for the marketing people who told them that people just weren't buying the old stuff anymore.

Indeed, the metaphor of a software publisher as a kind of relative of a record company goes beyond the idea of the programmer as star. It involves as well a number of simple rules on how to run a record company properly—rules that do seem to translate well to the software business. Hits are identified in advance and promoted heavily. Classics are identified that are going to give a company a catalogue that can run year after year, but that are not expected to be hits right away. And a company develops an ability to respond very quickly to the sleepers that it didn't spot in advance but that just seem to blossom; a company picks the sleepers as early as possible and promotes them into hits.

The software publishing industry is still so new that no single model or metaphor has proved so successful that it has dominated all segments of the market. The record-company metaphor has not proven to be the only model for the way a software publishing business ought to be run, nor has it been the most successful one.

In the early days, there was no such thing as a metaphor or model for running a software company. *Packaging* and *promotion* were foreign words in the era of the homebrew enthusiasts. A booth at a trade show consisted of a card table or two. The first instance of an image or model that shaped company styles seemed to be the rise of VisiCorp, the business-oriented marketing company. VisiCorp software was the first microcomputer software to be taken seriously by the business community, and VisiCorp people dressed themselves like the customers they wanted to sell their product to—dark three-piece suits, white shirts, and dark ties. By contrast, home computer software companies seem to have maintained a less formal style than that of the business-oriented companies.

When Atari came along and turned an electronics and software start-up company into a billion-dollar profit center, the metaphor for a software publisher became one of a producer of consumer goods; Kassar preferred people from Procter & Gamble and Clorox over people from Apple. Atari's fatally flawed vision of software publishing concentrated on software as a mass-market commodity that can be packaged and sold like towels or detergents. It neglected to notice that software is a kind of intellectual property as well as a marketable commodity, and care must be taken to hire and nurture the very best programmers.

Atari's spin-off, Activision, went to the opposite extreme and forgot that it was putting out something which was a commodity as well as an intellectual property. Electronic Arts, in my opinion, went to the extreme of promoting its image above its substance (although the substance has improved dramatically from the first year). Activision is in decline, but Electronic Arts is very much alive, so the verdict on the success of this metaphor is still not in.

9

Enter the Software Marketers and Developers

Another metaphor for software publishing grew out of the educational software market. Venture capitalists were entering the software industry in a big way at the same time market researchers started predicting phenomenal growth in the area of educational software. This led to the idea of the software publisher as a marketing company, an idea that is similar to the metaphor of the record company, except that it glorifies the company instead of the programmer. The company name is the focus of attention, not the individual products.

Driven less by promotion of its individual titles than by promotion of its overall reputation, a marketing company creates a public awareness of its position in the market, an image that makes people want to buy the company's product almost regardless of what it is. The goal is to persuade the consumers to buy the newest software "flavor" of their favorite "brand" on a regular basis. Spinnaker is probably the best example of a purely market-driven company. It even uses different names for its different software lines—like General Motors' Chevrolet and Cadillac divisions—for different market segments.

Most of the significant new companies in 1982 and 1983—that is, those, like Spinnaker, that appeared to have lots of money behind them—weren't especially interested in games.

Their mandate was educational software, especially for young children. The futurists had said that educational software would be the area of greatest growth for the next few years (in an industry where phenomenal rates of growth had become commonplace), and it seemed auspicious that there were so few companies taking advantage of this particular market.

A billion-dollar pie was therefore waiting to be cut up. Today's start-ups in the educational software field were bound to be tomorrow's success stories. Let MicroPro and MicroSoft and VisiCorp carve up the business software market. Broderbund, Sierra On-Line, Sirius, and other companies that were founded in the hobbyist days were welcome to the entertainment software market. The fortunes of the near future were going to be made in educational programs.

Furthermore, educational software was respectable. The only thing respectable about video games, for example, had been the amounts of money *Pong* and *Pac-Man* had magnetically attracted from the pockets of teenagers around the world. But that respectability was based on nonsense—inscrutable worlds of alien invaders and munching cartoon characters that made a game hacker's paradise. No, educational software would be a rational market, one in which serious programmers could implement designs formulated by professional educators and could bring out products that could be sold by truly professional marketers.

Why, just look at Spinnaker—everybody's idea of what a professional, marketing-oriented, home software company ought to look like. It was carefully planned and well capitalized, and it had a rapidly growing professional management. Founders William Bowman and C. David Seuss had seen the vacuum in the educational software field and moved to fill it. Their ambitious plans had called for a rate of growth that was regarded as phenomenal even by the somewhat jaded standards of the software industry. They confidently predicted that they would grow from $700,000 in revenues in 1982 to $10 million in 1983 to $74 million in 1984.

By the end of 1983, it was clear that Spinnaker was not just meeting these sales projections but actually exceeding them! Not only did 1983 revenues top $11 million, but the company showed a (small) profit to boot. With revenue growth like that, Spinnaker might make the Fortune 500 by 1987!

A commonplace notion in the industry says that sales are eventually going to be driven more by effective marketing than by outstanding products. It stands to reason, for as products proliferate, technological gaps will narrow and the market will become increasingly confusing. In such an environment the companies that should prosper are those that most effectively convey their message to the consumer.

And Spinnaker's marketing was superb. Its product packaging and media advertising were highly stylized and drove home the company name. It was hard to miss the Spinnaker name in magazines. According to an article in the August 13, 1984, issue of *Infoworld*, Spinnaker spent $1.5 million on advertising in 1983, more than five times what Broderbund spent. In fact, it was advertising in magazines we never even *dreamed* of advertising in—like *Good Housekeeping* and *Better Homes and Gardens*. The company name was everywhere.

Some of Spinnaker's marketing strategies appeared to be borrowed from much larger corporations. In order to increase its share of shelf space and give the consumers a sense of a greater degree of choice, Spinnaker adopted a "branding" strategy whereby the company marketed its products under six different brand names, each of which defined a particular kind of educational software. "We will get much more shelf space with six brands," Bill Larson, director of business development, declared. "Just like General Motors aims each of its cars at a different target market, from Chevy to Cadillac, so will we."

This strategy seems to be generating high sales figures, but it is still too early to tell whether Larson's pronouncement amounted to a prophetic declaration or famous last words. High sales are profitable only if they can offset expenses—and this marketing strategy is expensive. It remains to be seen whether or not the market-driven company will end up as the dominant metaphor in the software publishing industry, but there is little doubt that marketing considerations will remain an important part of every software publisher's strategy for success.

I like to think that Brøderbund incorporates the best features of all the various models that have so far defined the software industry, but if there is any single metaphor that is closest to our self-image, it is that of a book publisher. We like to work with independent authors who nevertheless establish a close relationship with us as regular contractors. We like to help authors develop their prototypes into finished products. We pay advances against royalties, and our product managers serve as editors who help guide a product through the process of creation, production, and marketing.

But software publishing is not the only way to get into the industry. Another way is by means of a "production team"—that is, a group or company that concentrates on creating marketable products but leaves the actual sales of the product to another company that is geared up for a large-scale marketing effort. This side of the business, strictly speaking, is known as software development, and the companies that do it are known as developers rather than publishers. The idea behind such a company is to totally eliminate the marketing division and focus on developing all the talents, skills, and resources needed to create high-quality software that is so attractive and appealing that publishers will bid against one another to get it.

There are developers and there are developers, and their approaches are as different as their products. One of my favorites is Joyce Hakansson, who is neither the marketing czar nor the programming wizard of her outfit; the phrase most often used to describe her role in Joyce Hakansson Associates is that of "den mother." It is an apt description in several senses. Her primary focus is neither on marketing nor programming, but rather on software's potential as a tool for awakening, nurturing, and stimulating the growth of our nation's most important resource—the minds of our children.

The atmosphere inside the headquarters of Joyce Hakansson Associates is like the style of the company's products—colorful, whimsical, full of exuberance, with music in the air and the sound of children's laughter in the background. In a bright airy Victorian house in Berkeley, a team of programmers, education experts, graphic artists, musicians, writers, game designers, and children of various ages works together to produce programs for computer users between the ages of three and thirteen.

To walk around this software company for a few minutes is to notice the customary variety of computers and floppy disks on desks, the people staring at computer screens or toying with joysticks, and the mock-ups of product packages and galleys of documentation lying around—all the usual signs of software production. But given the extraordinary nature of the company, there are several not-so-usual features in evidence as well.

First of all, a distinct majority of the staff members are women. Most of them are mothers and have been teachers or child psychologists at one point in their careers. And the children aren't there just for atmosphere—they are an integral part of the design process and help the production team design and test the products. Fun seems to be one of the key tenets of this company's philosophy of life.

A half a dozen projects in different stages of production are often going on at the same time in one of the several rooms down the hall from the common room, where the secretary/receptionist's desk, the bulletin board (a source of in-house humor as well as information), several computers, and the coffee machine are located. The atmosphere, apart from being upbeat, is one of controlled chaos. In the middle of it all is Joyce Hakansson, infecting everyone with her intense enthusiasm and sense of fun.

A middle-aged dark-haired woman with a ready smile, she serves as a kind of director for all the talented people she has assembled in the production team. Neither she nor her co-workers pay much attention to the fact that her mobility is somewhat limited because of a degenerative muscular disease. She is very much the leader and guiding spirit of her team. Like a film director, she uses storyboards to weave together the various educational, aesthetic, and technical components of the programs the team produces. Along with her experience and charisma, Joyce Hakansson brings to the group a reputation for excellence, and long-standing relationships with publishers like Spinnaker, Milton Bradley, CBS, and Simon & Schuster.

Joyce got into the software business not because she was a homebrew enthusiast, an avid programmer, or an entrepreneur, but because she was a concerned mother of two children whose education she thought needed supplementary attention. In fact, her involvement with children and computers in general predated the Altair by a couple of years. Even before that, in the 1960s, she had first become acquainted with the same generation of mainframe, batch-processing IBM computers, now utterly obsolete, that had hooked me on programming. She was in college at the time, and the man who was to become her husband, then an IBM research assistant, had introduced her to the mysteries of a data-processing center.

Joyce still recalls her reaction to the experience: "Like most people, I thought computers were colossal electronic brains that only geniuses could operate. I saw them being used and watched the whirling tape drives. I saw all the people running around in their white coats and badges. When I got to know them I found out that, golly, they aren't godlike at all. They are intelligent and have certain abilities, but they are ordinary mortals. I found that even I could sit down with a stack of computer cards and make this formidable machine print out a Snoopy calendar for me."

Her husband left computers in the early 1970s (to teach economics at the University of California), and so, for a brief time, did Joyce. Her initial enthusiasm for computing had by then been dampened by the feeling that computing just wasn't within her intellectual grasp; she thought she wasn't "mathematical" or "logical" enough for it—an assumption most people made back in the days when it seemed that all computers could do was solve complicated equations for scientists. Still, it was Joyce's concern over her so-called lack of mathematical aptitude that in time led to a deeper concern with the educational process in general and her children's education in particular. And that, in turn, eventually brought her back to computers.

As Joyce describes it: "I stayed away from mathematics courses in school, but what I didn't realize at the time was that the science courses I was enjoying required mathematical and logical reasoning skills. The problem was that I didn't identify what I liked to do with what I called 'mathematics.' I always saw math as restricted to calculating skills and the formal kinds of things that happen when you are in a class and have pencil and paper and problems to solve. It was only much later when I had children of my own that I realized that math is a much broader discipline than calculation.

"I realized that I had been thinking and reasoning in mathematical ways all my life and that I was actually fairly good at it. I guess I felt I missed out on something, so I got involved with my children's education when they were in elementary school. I saw that they weren't teaching children any differently than when I had gone to school, and children were going through the process with that same fear of math and that same feeling of inadequacy that I had experienced. So I asked the school if I could start a math lab, with lots of things that would be attractive to children—puzzles and colorful pictures and art tools and music."

The seeds of Joyce's career in children's software were planted when the school agreed to let her have her math lab. Of course the school couldn't provide any funding, so Joyce and a friend recruited volunteers and raised money. Pretty soon, the volunteers started discussing all the things they wanted for the math lab, and somebody brought up the idea of computers. That made sense to Joyce, who happened to be the only one who had any computer-related experience. So they called IBM and said they wanted to buy a computer.

"I'm sure the salesman thought we were representing the school district," Joyce recalled, smiling mischievously while she recounted the event to me. "He came racing over to sell us this $200,000 computer and found these suburban housewives with chocolate brownies and white wine, wanting to talk to him about computers. He was charming. He told us that what we really wanted was an educational time-sharing system that we could access through a remote terminal. We didn't know what all those terms meant, but we went about trying to find such a thing."

Joyce was living about thirty miles from Berkeley at the time, and it happened that just the kind of system she wanted was located at the Lawrence Hall of Science, an interactive science museum in Berkeley. The Hall, as it is called, is associated with the University of California and sponsors special science education programs for children. Lawrence Hall had a large computer that could actually be connected, through a kind of telephone hookup, to a terminal that was located at Joyce's suburban school.

One of the conditions that Joyce insisted upon was that all the teachers and volunteers in the math lab learn how to run the system so that they could all be available to help the children learn how to use it. A class would have to be set up. The people at Lawrence Hall thought that this was a terrific idea and in the summer of 1973, the first computer training classes for lab volunteers started at the Hall's computer lab. First, Joyce taught herself—with the help of Lawrence Hall personnel—and then she taught her fellow volunteers.

"Basically, what we did was play games on the computer," she remembers of those early days with the clunky, loud teletype terminals. It was a grand beginning. But it was only a beginning. Compared with the color video screens and sound capabilities of today's computers, teletype terminal technology was closer to a telegraph machine than what we now know as a personal computer. The equipment needed to be upgraded—an expensive undertaking. And it still cost money to operate the computer training as well as the classes for the children.

Joyce went to her school district and asked for funds. They were reluctant to give her tax money because the computer education curriculum she and her friends had set up hadn't been properly evaluated. So Joyce went back to the Hall and said, "We need an evaluation tool"—a way of testing whether the new kind of curriculum had a positive effect on students. Joyce volunteered to help take over some of the administrative burden of developing and evaluating the curriculum so that the tool could be written and the volunteers could get a computer and math lab funded.

She started hanging around the computer room at the Hall, learning and teaching not only children who were attending the Hall's other programs, but also her fellow volunteers. At the end of the summer the people in charge of the Hall asked her to continue her work with them on a part-time basis. The math lab and the Hall never received the evaluation tool that got Joyce into the Hall as a staff member.

In 1975, Joyce began working as director of Lawrence Hall of Science's computer education project, which involved introducing schoolchildren to the principles of computer programming. In 1978, she was instrumental in getting some state-of-the-art replacements for the old teletype terminals—a dozen Apples. By the time she left in 1979, the Hall was teaching 30,000 to 40,000 people a year how to use computers, and those people included everyone from very young children to senior citizens.

Back in 1978, while Joyce was still at the Hall, a group of people from Children's Television Workshop (CTW)—the creators of "Sesame Street"—came to the Hall, looking for help with an electronic theme park they wanted to create, to expand their educational efforts beyond television programs. The park, to be called Sesame Place, was intended to be something like Disneyland—a place for parents to bring young people for the sheer fun of it, but with a technological and education theme. The CTW people knew they wanted to use electronic components, but they weren't sure what that might mean. They had talked to Atari and realized that arcade games weren't what they wanted. When they saw what was going on at the Hall, they signed up Joyce and her colleagues as consultants to CTW's Sesame Place project.

A year later, in June 1979, impressed with her work as a consultant, CTW asked Joyce to come to New York and direct its children's computer park project. They still weren't certain about which direction the project ought to take, but they knew that with Joyce in charge it would crystallize. They were asking a lot from Joyce, who had two children in school, a husband who couldn't have his work at the university, and a physical handicap—muscular dystrophy—that would make life in New York City difficult.

Joyce still remembers how scary it was to make that decision: "I had children and a husband who couldn't just up and leave. I had married very young, so I literally had never lived on my own. I had never lived in a metropolitan city. I am disabled. I thought that the whole idea was crazy. I also thought it was the opportunity of a lifetime for someone with my background and my interests. At the Hall, we were able to introduce thirty or forty thousand people to computers every year. Sesame Place was expected to draw a million people a year. My husband told me what I had known all along—that I had to do it or I would always regret it."

Joyce's idea, which CTW approved, was to create a permanent large-scale version of the pioneering computer education project she had directed at the Lawrence Hall of Science. Collecting the best of the computer educators and programmers that she had met over the years, and commuting between New York, Berkeley, and the site of the park in Langhorn, Pennsylvania, Joyce gave shape to the project. She was originally hired to oversee the production of the software. When she arrived and asked where the hardware person was, CTW told her that the person they had hired wasn't able to take the job after all. Did she think she could do that too? She did. Ten months later the park opened, with more than fifty microcomputers and specially designed educational games.

In those days, Joyce was one of a small, dedicated, growing network of parents, educators, and microcomputer enthusiasts who thought that computers could revolutionize education the way they were transforming business and entertainment. Because of that, she stayed with CTW for another year to see that the software her group had produced for the park reached the commercial market. She went to software publishers such as Science Research Associates, Macmillan, Random House, Milton Bradley, and Personal Software and rounded up contracts for what became Children's Computer Workshop Software in 1980. Originally a division of CTW, it has since become a separate corporation that was renamed again—it is now called Children's Television Workshop Software.

In 1981, Joyce moved back to California. With a track record of more than sixty programs produced by her CTW software team, and with her reputation among the people who were looking for high-quality educational software (including, but not limited to, the publishers she met in her CTW work), she felt that now she could build her own production team and turn out products on her own. Like many of the other software developers who came into the business in the early 1980s, Joyce saw the computer as having real potential to become a device that could help bring about social change in general.

In her view, computers could be particularly useful in bringing about significant social change in the field of education. The dream she had for her production group was an outgrowth of the same feelings that had led her to start a math lab in her children's school eight years prior. She dreamed that her group's software could bridge cultural worlds that in the past had been separated. As she said to me recently: "I could see that the machines were getting smaller and more powerful and less expensive, and the software was making the computer more accessible to people who weren't engineers, but I didn't see many people building bridges between the potential of the computer and the artists, musicians, literary people."

When I asked her to describe her notions of what children or artists or musicians would want to do with computers, Joyce answered by first pointing out that personal computers were initially introduced to businesspeople because of spreadsheets—programs that allow business people to ask "what if" questions and thereby make financial predictions. Similarly, Joyce said, "The magic of a computer to an artist or a child is the ability to draw something on the screen and play 'what if.' What if it's purple or green or blue? What if it's bigger here or smaller there? What if I stretch it or shrink it? You an do these things with paper, pencil, and conventional media, but it's so much slower and tedious that it isn't worth playing. The computer eliminates those barriers to the creative process."

She firmly believes that this kind of systematic imagining is as important to the fields of science and business as it is to creative thought: "That's what research is all about. That's what people are doing in universities—thinking about 'what ifs.' If kids can be taught to play 'what if' games, then they can build their intuitions and begin to trust themselves when it comes to other kinds of intellectual exploration—because they have already played that kind of game. This is *discovery*, not rote learning, and it is a far more powerful kind of learning because children do it naturally, on their own."

In order to develop a kind of computing that would naturally serve as a tool for trying out intuitions and playing "what if" games, Joyce knew she had to build a team capable of creating software that would appeal to very young children. In fact, the programs had to be appealing before they could be educational, and as such they would require a very different approach from that taken by a program designer who wants to produce games or business tools. Joyce's idea was to provide something that would be "whimsical and fun and engaging, that would say to kids, 'This is a neat world—enter it, try it, play with it.'"

As for why she needed a team in the first place to handle software design and production and, in short, to make the kind of software she envisioned a reality, she explained: "I don't have the talents to do it alone. I am not an expert programmer. I'm not a professional graphic artist. I have no musical talent whatsoever. I studied history in college, not education or child development. But I knew that if I could get people with those skills to join me and bounce an idea back and forth, we could envision our creations from our different perspectives and put our different viewpoints together in such a way that the idea would become bigger and more complete as we bounced it around."

Such was the concept behind Joyce Hakansson Associates (JHA), which opened its doors for business in May 1982. First came the programmers and graphic artists and musicians. Then came the writers. The children, drawn from Berkeley public schools and private preschools, joined the enterprise after the child development specialists suggested that bringing potential customers in to help them build the software from the ground up would be more effective than using the children only as a test market for the programs after they were developed. In the midst of the software gold rush, Joyce and her associates made an unusual decision: They decided to go about their business carefully. Undoubtedly, that decision was responsible for the critical acclaim from educators, parents, and computer software commentators that greeted JHA programs. But in practice it meant that their first programs would hit the market in 1984, just as the bottom dropped out of the software boom.

Together, the group decided to take the time not just to make a batch of software to throw into the home computer market but to craft the kind of truly effective educational programs they had envisioned in the first place. Like a television production company, they would create the product, then contract with the software equivalents of the networks or syndication outfits to publish and distribute it. They would become a software developer, rather than a publisher.

A typical JHA product is *Ducks Ahoy!*, published in 1984 by CBS Software. The setting is a brightly colored cartoon version of Venice, with canals, gondolas, piazzas, bridges, and houses in which there are quacking ducks who have the habit of hopping out doors into the canals. Children between three and six play the game, complete with animation and silly sound effects, by using a joystick to steer a gondola through the canals, under the bridges, and alongside the ducks' houses. The initial goal is to predict which duck will jump next, and then to move the gondola directly under it. If the duck lands in the boat, you can deposit the duck on a beach or look for another duck.

Ultimately, the object of *Ducks Ahoy!* is to catch and carry ten ducks to the beach, allowing as few ducks as possible to land in the water. There are obstacles, of course, and one of them is a submerged hippo that likes to capsize boats full of ducks. All in all there is real humor in the game—its characters look and sound and act *funny*, and this makes them fun to play with. And by the time a child has mastered the game, he or she has gained important counting, predicting, and hand-eye coordination skills. The child has also learned that a computer world can be fun and rewarding to explore.

Other JHA products include its first and highly acclaimed little game, called *Alf in the Color Caves*. A program for very young children, it was published by Spinnaker in January 1984. Other programs, with names like *Bubble Burst, Sea Horse Hide and Seek*, and *Kermit's Electronic StoryMaker* were contracted for by CBS and Simon & Schuster. But most of the products that represent JHA's first two years' worth of effort weren't published until early 1985. As a result, it's still too early to judge JHA's impact on the educational market, or even to say with certainty that this market will ever grow at even a fraction of the extraordinary rate that was initially predicted by many industry analysts and market researchers.

In fact, a full appraisal of JHA's long-term influence on the market may never come to pass, because, unfortunately, JHA's timing was off, and unforeseeable events began to overtake everyone in the software industry. By 1985 it didn't matter how good one's software was, or how much critical acclaim JHA's or any other developer's programs garnered in the media. The microcomputer software market was overcrowded with products, the buying public was confused, the popular media were jaded with the microcomputer phenomenon, and software publishers were going out of business. When publishers are in trouble, developers like JHA are in trouble.

In the spring of 1985, several of the software publishers that had survived the shakeout of 1984 were still feeding JHA money to develop programs, but the royalty stream Joyce and her team had anticipated when they started their enterprise was barely a trickle. People were still buying educational software, but there were many products to choose from, and the vast majority of potential buyers had no way of knowing that JHA products were superior to any one of a dozen competing programs. If the company is still in existence in the spring of 1986, Joyce Hakansson and her associates will be among the ranks of the pleasantly surprised.

What happened to the gold rush? Where did the shakeout come from? In retrospect, it is much easier to see the roots of the disaster in the midst of the boom years. The software shakeout didn't happen all at once, nor was it caused by one simple event or situation. In order to understand what happened to developers like JHA, it is necessary to go back to the end of 1982, when the tide turned.

10

The Shakeout

The fall of 1982 was an extraordinary time for Brøderbund, the Brotherhood, Apple, IBM, Softsel, *Softalk*, programmers, and just about everybody in the microcomputer software industry. Barely two and a half years before, my brother Gary and I had been sitting on the living room floor of our house in Eugene, Oregon, busily copying cassettes of my *Galactic Empire* program, hoping to produce enough of them to fill our first $300 order. In late 1982, we were operating out of a converted liquor warehouse in San Rafael, California. Our forty-five employees did the copying (and a lot of other things as well). And our sales revenues amounted to many thousands of dollars every month.

But it wasn't just the company itself that was doing well by this time. Some of the monthly royalty checks for our top programmers were large enough to buy houses. I don't just mean that one of those monthly royalty checks could cover a down payment; I mean that a programmer could (and often did) buy the whole house for cash on the basis of one month's royalties. And other companies besides ours were doing even better. VisiCorp was getting very button-down. Sirius and Sierra On-Line were fighting for dominance of the computer game market, and in the November issue of *Softalk* magazine, On-Line even took 17¼ pages of advertising space. Little did we realize that November 1982 was the beginning of the end of the software gold rush and that an entirely new era was about to dawn on the horizon.

In retrospect, the first tremors of the great software shakeout of 1984 can be traced back to a single day in 1982. By this time, the home computer software business had grown from a loose confederation of hobbyists into a genuine industry, but it was still dwarfed by such video game giants as Atari and Activision. While Brøderbund, Sirius, and Sierra On-Line were celebrating revenues of hundreds of thousands per month, Atari was nearing a hundred *million* dollars per month in sales.

And then the tide turned. On December 8, 1982, Ray Kassar announced that Atari's sales had dived and that earnings had fallen more than 50 percent. There were suspicions of stock manipulation—a couple of officers had sold substantial amounts of stock a week before the disclosure. Even more suspicious in the eyes of many industry observers was the timing of the announcement. A new and highly touted competitor, Imagic, had been planning to go public only a week later. Atari's announcement scrubbed any possibility of Imagic's successfully launching its public stock offering.

But the bad news had only just begin. At first, only the game machine companies suffered. Mattel pulled out of the video game business in January 1983. Games by Apollo collapsed in June, resulting in that company's owing its advertising agency $24 million. The Quaker Oats subsidiary U.S. Games was the next to go, in July 1983. Even Activision, the leading video game software independent, only barely succeeded in going public that summer, and if the public had known then what it was to discover over the following six months, Jim Levy, like his counterparts at the other video game companies, would have been left in the hands of his venture backers too.

It would be some time, however, before this fallout would descend upon the home computer industry. In fact, home computer software people watched all the carnage in the video game industry with considerable complacency. Nineteen-eighty-three turned out to be a banner year for most of us. "Naturally the game machines are doomed," we said to one another. "How can any game machine even begin to compete with a real computer?" And even though companies like Activision (with annual sales of $150 million at one time) were ten or twenty times the size of the home computer software companies, these video game–based businesses were still seen only as software dinosaurs, mired in a market without a future, turning out trivial products for increasingly sophisticated consumers.

That image turned out to be accurate. What those of us in the home computer industry failed to foresee was that the collapse of video game software portended an eventual depression in sales of entertainment-oriented software for personal computers as well. Indeed, in 1983 it was hard to imagine that the woes of Atari and the video game business would touch the computer world. The home computer market was expanding at an unabated pace. The personal computer was featured as *Time* magazine's "Man of the Year." And more than 150 magazines had sprung up to serve the home computer industry, each one of them sporting hundreds of pages of advertising promoting an incredible array of products.

Flipping through a copy of *Softalk* in 1982 or 1983 was like walking through a crowded video arcade. Hundreds of four-color full-page ads shrieked for one's attention, promoting everything from floppy disks to competitors' magazines. Discount mail-order houses were heavily represented, as well as business-oriented software companies like Software Arts, the creators of *VisiCalc*. Dozens of little hardware companies were manufacturing peripherals that added extra features to computers—clocks and fans and extra-high-resolution-graphics. Lots of new software companies started showing up. And there were computer games. Hundreds of them. The market expanded faster than the competition.

The microcomputer software market in 1983 was especially boosted by the efforts of educational software publishers like Spinnaker. Spinnaker's sales department was doing its job to fulfill the marketing department's master plan. The product line *looked* like a line, and Spinnaker was able to persuade retailers to display its products in the most visually impressive manner—side by side, at eye level. Spinnaker's apparent success at pursuing this strategy was one of several factors (the huge profits raked in by independent software publishers in the previous three years being most prominent among them) that drew larger established companies into the microcomputer software business.

Spinnaker provided the kind of model for a software division that corporate management could sell in its own boardrooms. Here was one new division that investor relations departments wouldn't scream about. Major book publishers and television companies observed Spinnaker's success and resolved to emulate it.

CBS Video Games had been organized in the summer of 1982 as part of the parent company's toy division. CBS Software, organized at the same time, was a separate operation, not connected with the toy division. Initially, CBS Video Games appeared to be modeled after Activision. Its products were games. Its competitive advantage, CBS evidently thought, would lie in the complexity and sophistication that CBS, with all its financial resources and media savvy, could bring to the products by "loading" the game cartridges with expensive additional memory.

But CBS Video Games *didn't* prosper, simply because the video game market was shrinking at the same time the number of competitors was expanding. The president of CBS Software, Ed Auer, decided to strike out in a different direction—away from games for the sake of games. He decided to move the company toward educational software. He signed up top-flight educational software developers like Joyce Hakansson to produce a whole new lineup of products. By the summer of 1983, most of CBS Software's products were presented as "educational." Even his games were thinking games, like *Bridge* and *Forecast*, a weather forecasting game.

CBS wasn't the last of the major corporations to enter the microcomputer software market; indeed, it was one of the first of many. With CBS in the game, major media corporations, from Simon & Schuster to Reader's Digest, began to look hungrily at this new market that seemed to have appeared overnight. In 1983, the rumor that soon became common wisdom among software-industry watchers held that the big corporations were going to move in soon, pay top dollar for the best products, put on an advertising display that would blow the cottage-industry folks out of the water, and dominate the industry by the end of the year. As early as 1982, that was what people like John Brockman believed was bound to happen.

Brockman was a new phenomenon in the software world— a milieu in which flamboyant characters and new phenomena were hardly rare. For starters, Brockman wasn't a software person or a marketing expert or even a venture capitalist. He was a literary agent. He didn't live in Silicon Valley; he lived in New York (with the obligatory weekend place in Easthampton). He and his partner, Katinka Matson, had represented such serious nonfiction literary luminaries as John Lilly, Gregory Bateson, and Stewart Brand.

Back in the 1960s, Brockman and Matson had been involved in the "counterculture" scene in New York, Berkeley, and Cambridge. Brockman himself had organized "happenings" and had had a kind of new-age literary salon called "The Reality Club." Then, during the 1970s, he and Matson concentrated on building a successful literary agency. But they missed the action, the excitement, the sense of community that faded away with the end of the Woodstock era. In November 1982, when they attended a computer trade show, they noted that a similar kind of excitement could be found in this new, little-understood industry. Something was brewing in the software world, and it looked to be as potentially profitable as it was exciting.

"I'm getting into software," John had told his skeptical colleagues back in the "early days" of late 1982. "I can make more money on one software deal than I can make on a year's worth of literary deals." The real stars of the coming software revolution wouldn't be its chroniclers and manual writers but the programmers themselves! So he set out to find them and represent them. He started combing the aisles of the big trade shows like COMDEX and the National Computer Conference and even the once-tiny, but now huge, West Coast Computer Faire.

To whom would he represent these new media stars? To the customers Brockman knew best, of course—the book publishers and other East Coast corporate giants who were watching the success of outfits like Spinnaker and were indeed contemplating the expenditure of enormous sums in order to break into this unbelievably lucrative software publishing business.

And as Brockman predicted, the biggies started to buy, beginning with a contract he negotiated between Bruce & James, a software developer, and Simon & Schuster, for *WordVision*, an inexpensive word-processing program that Simon & Schuster planned to sell through bookstores. When the word spread around that this New York literary agent was able to sell software to big publishers, the inquiries came pouring in, and some of them panned out spectacularly well.

Brockman's biggest star was Sat Tara Singh Khalsa, a blond, bearded programmer–software publisher from Montana who was a convert to the Sikh religion. With his all-white suits, white turban, red rose boutonniere, and diamond stickpin, he was just the model of the programmer–as–media hero that Brockman was looking for. He also had a very attractive product in *Typing Tutor III*, a program that taught touch-typing skills by using, among other devices, a kind of shoot-'em-up game in which the alien invaders could be destroyed only by pressing the correct key.

Brockman rented a suite at New York's posh Carlyle Hotel, set up a computer, and invited the heavies from the newly created "electronic publishing" divisions of the biggest publishers to come and see *Typing Tutor III* in action. He ended up selling the program to Simon & Schuster for a reputed seven-figure advance and a royalty arrangement that could make his client as much as $20 million in the near future. (By early 1985 the program was selling moderately, but far from spectacularly well, and Sat Tara had been ousted from a position of leadership in Kriya Systems, the company he had founded.)

Indeed, for a time, the publishers were on a buying spree. Millions were spent, not just through Brockman—

although he did garner his share of the early sales, and more than his share of the early publicity in his self-created role as "software agent." Although the most respected developers—Joyce Hakansson foremost among them—went direct to publishers, the idea of a "software agent" had captured the imagination of the small army of journalists who had turned their attention to events in the software world. Every publication from *InfoWorld* to the *Wall Street Journal* and the *New York Times* published pieces on Brockman.

Then Brockman began representing the authors of computer books, which were one of the most lucrative spinoffs of the microcomputer boom. Most of the instruction manuals that came with both software and hardware—known in the trade jargon as "documentation"—were so awful and incomprehensible that a few professional writers were beginning to make good money by writing how-to books to supplement the manuals supplied by manufacturers. A cottage industry had sprung up around these books, with small publishing houses on the West Coast turning out profitable titles month after month. Brockman's clients were among the first to get serious attention from the larger East Coast publishing houses like Simon & Schuster, Doubleday, and Harper & Row.

In his characteristically immodest fashion, Brockman began sending out press releases, trumpeting his latest triumphs in the computer-book field. Among those triumphs was an $800,000 contract for a series of books by the editors of *PC World* magazine, followed within a matter of weeks by a $600,000 contract for another book series to be created by the editors of *InfoWorld* magazine. Then came his biggest coup. In April 1983, he negotiated the largest advance in the history of trade paperback publishing—$1.3 million from Doubleday based on a ten-page outline by Stewart Brand, the principal author of the hugely successful *Whole Earth Catalog*. The proposed book was to be titled *The Whole Earth Software Catalog*.

The big-figure blockbusters announced by Brockman were only the most spectacular examples of the book deals publishers were making at a frantic pace throughout 1983 and 1984. Booksellers estimated that, based on the rate at which publishers were signing up authors, computer books would outsell fiction in 1984.

By 1983 and early 1984, the book publishing houses were racing, lemming-like, to sign up their own software superstars. Bookstores were seen as the natural place to sell software, and the new buzzphrase in book circles was "electronic publishing." As the electronic publishing divisions grew more sophisticated, they found their way to many of the software development groups springing up around the country. And there they advanced millions of dollars for products that did not yet exist.

It must have been in April or May 1984 that software publishers began calling around to their friends in the industry. "Are you folks experiencing something of a slowdown?" they asked, slightly euphemistically. Most said yes. Some said that *slowdown* was too mild a word. One of the computer magazines noted that advertising pages were down 50 percent from the previous year. That's quite a slowdown.

The venture capital firms were getting edgy too. The bloom was off the software rose. All the software public offerings, even those from the phenomenally successful Lotus, were selling at less than their initial public offering price. Talk of an industry-wide shakeout started appearing in the trade media. People inside the industry and out in the software-buying world were no longer assuming that today's spectacular product announcement would turn into tomorrow's successful product introduction and next week's sales bonanza.

As it turned out, some of the highly touted, richly funded, anxiously expected new products—particularly those of the big publishing corporations—would never exist. A new word came into the vocabulary: *Vaporware*, which seems to have been first applied to VisiCorp's ill-fated *VisiOn* system, was defined as software that disappears like mist before your eyes as its delivery date approaches. And sometimes when a product *did* appear, the investors and publishers almost wished that it hadn't. The market ended up being more sophisticated than they were, and some of those long-delayed, over-advanced products simply didn't sell when they hit an overcrowded market. It was humiliating. Some of the corporate entrants started to make their exits from the software game.

Reader's Digest pulled out relatively early. Prentice-Hall was rumored to have advanced nearly $10 million in new product development and had almost nothing to show for it. Simon & Schuster—long after it had contracted with Bruce & James for *WordVision* and after it had included the title as part of an extensive advertising campaign for a new line of productivity tools—did finally get the program, and it was, finally, acceptable enough to publish. But it was nearly a year late in its arrival, by which time the market for word-processing systems was glutted. Sales were abysmal. The Bruce & James partners split up, and the rest of the planned Bruce & James line was quietly shelved. What was going on? How could savvy and well-funded outfits like Reader's Digest, Prentice-Hall, and Simon & Schuster fail so spectacularly where "amateurs" like Microsoft and Brøderbund had made millions?

Part of the problem was the collective inexperience of the corporate entrepreneurs. It not only hurt them in choosing and evaluating software, but it hurt equally when it came to selling and distributing the product. They just didn't know how the software distribution pipeline worked, and so they missed most of the best opportunities. The book publishers made their biggest mistake when they assumed that bookstores would become the next big marketplace for software, and that the channels used by the cottage-industry companies would diminish in importance. By focusing their efforts on book-related distribution channels, the book publishers weren't prepared to play ball with the people whose business was exclusively involved with selling computer products—specialty store distributors.

Still, the book publishers were particularly insistent on the prediction that bookstores would soon become the principal distribution channels for software. "Software," many of them would repeat, "is just a form of literature that happens to run on a machine." They overlooked the fact that few bookstore employees know anything about these new products and that it is indeed risky to order half a dozen copies of a product that might sell for anywhere from $50 to $500. How many books sell in that price range? Ultimately, however, the book publishers might be right. Bookstores might well become important distribution channels for software. But not in 1985. Probably not in 1986. And certainly not at $500 a pop.

But another part of the problem was that book publishers didn't know the real size or nature of the market. They paid too much for products because they thought the real market was much larger than it turned out to be. When friendly representatives from the cottage software companies suggested that the market wouldn't support such high software acquisition prices, the corporate entrepreneurs merely assumed that the cottage companies had failed to address most of the market because of marketing inexperience.

And the corporate newcomers talked a lot about "installed base"—the millions and millions of home computers that had already been sold. The managers of cottage companies who didn't buy into *this* myth, either, could have told them from experience with the long-vanished Commodore VIC and Texas Instruments markets that installed base doesn't make a whit of difference when the principal channels for the sale of software are stores that still make most of their living selling hardware. If they aren't still selling Widget Computers, they don't really want to bother selling Widget Software, even if there are a billion Widget Computers already out there.

So until independent software channels become the principal channels for the sale of software, the size of the real software market depends on the rate of sale of computers, not the installed base. And the installed base was going up every day in late 1983 and 1984. But the rate of software sales wasn't. For while the installed base increased, the *rate* of increase was decreasing, and since most software is purchased with the computer or soon thereafter, software sales are tied to the rate of computer sales, not to the number of machines that have already been sold.

The corporate biggies weren't the only ones to be caught with their assumptions down. More than a few of the cottage-industry folks missed this point, too. The sudden demise of the

Commodore VIC market hurt companies like Human Engineered Software. The virtual disappearance of Atari made life difficult for Atari-oriented companies like Synapse. The installed base was large, alright. But it wasn't buying new software. As a result, many software publishers that had been in the business for years started to go under.

In January 1984, a small advertisement appeared in the *Wall Street Journal*, offering a software company for sale for $500,000. The company was not named in the ad. Interested parties were directed to Box WP736. Tom Measday, Brøderbund's vice president for sales and marketing at the time, saw the ad and responded to it. We were looking for good acquisitions, and who knew what products might be involved in this mystery company?

We were in for a surprise. We soon learned that the ad had been placed by none other than our old friend Jerry Jewell. The company for sale was Sirius, once the largest of the companies in the loose association of Apple-oriented software companies known as the Brotherhood.

We met with Jerry the following week to talk about the situation and find out what had gone wrong. The figures painted a grim picture, indeed. Sirius was under the gun. It owed its creditors a half million dollars and had virtually no assets left except its inventory of old game titles and the possible proceeds from its lawsuit against 20th Century-Fox for failing to publish Sirius VCS games. Sirius had not been able to afford to purchase disks since December, so the company had not been shipping products for almost a month. As a result, its products had all disappeared from the best-seller lists, which made it hard to determine which products were still alive and which were dead.

Among those Sirius programs that apparently were still active in the market was a typing program, *Type Attack*. But was it, and the few other programs that were still selling respectably well, worth half a million dollars? We at Brøderbund didn't think so, and apparently neither did anyone else. In the summer of 1984, Sirius filed for reorganization under

Chapter 11 of the bankruptcy laws. In September, Scarbor-ough Systems, a venture start-up in New York, picked up *Type Attack* for a reported $60,000.

Jerry Jewell worked hard for months to tie up the loose ends—or clear away the wreckage, depending on how you look at it—from Sirius Software. Gamely, he started a new soft-ware company, Softprose, which found 1984 to be a pretty tough year. It turned out to be a decisive year for many com-panies in the old Brotherhood of Apple-oriented software pub-lishers. Ken Grant and Ihor Wolosenko looked at the future prospects for their company, Synapse Software, during the summer of 1984 and decided that it was time for profit-taking. In October, they sold Synapse to Brøderbund.

By the end of 1983, only three consumer software mar-kets in the United States were worth spending much time on: those for IBM, Apple, and Commodore. And there were those who thought that Apple's days were numbered. IBM was about to roll out its long-rumored "Peanut" computer and was universally expected to grab a huge chunk of the home com-puter market away from Apple, just as the IBM PC had wrested more than half of the small-business market away from Apple in the previous two years. Apple had a new pro-duct in the works, too, however. It was called the "Macintosh," but it was not getting anything like the press that the Peanut got. After all, Apple's two previous products—the Apple III and Lisa—hadn't been box-office smashes.

Ken and Roberta Williams decided to bet their Sierra On-Line farm on IBM. Their company, after an unbroken string of successes in their first three years of operation, began suffering its first losses in mid-1983, and Ken, in his inimitable way, was looking for an opportunity to turn the company's fortunes around. The new IBM home computer, the Peanut, didn't seem like a bad bet—lots of retailers decided the same thing when the machine was announced. In the summer of 1983, Ken told me that he had two-thirds of his programmers working on a secret project for IBM.

You see, Ken Williams understood about installed base and rate of sale. He knew that if the Peanut took off, his one-year advantage in software development would be worth millions. He is a gambler by instinct. I suspect that he also likes to be seen in the company of the rich and famous, and IBM is certainly both. The IBM deal was made to order for him. Then, when the Peanut was released into the market under the name PCjr, in January 1984, several things nobody expected to happen, happened.

I am something of a sports fan and so, even though I was traveling on the day of the January 1984 Superbowl, still managed to join the crowd in an airport bar to watch the game on television. I don't remember much about the game, but I do remember watching the most riveting television commercial I have ever seen. In a gray, futuristic amphitheater, hundreds of colorless, zombie-like skinheads were pictured watching a Big Brother–like character on an enormous video screen. Suddenly, a healthy-looking Amazon, who was the only figure in the scene whose face was depicted in flesh tones, wearing a vividly colored T-shirt, ran into the amphitheater, chased in eerie silence by a phalanx of robot-like guards. She carried a sledge hammer in her hands, and as she broke into the center of the room and the guards closed in on her, she lofted the hammer up at the gigantic screen, shattering it into a thousand pieces.

It was the pre-announcement for Macintosh. Like David challenging Goliath, Apple announced that it wasn't about to roll over and die before the IBM juggernaut. With imagery that was a skillful blend of George Orwell and H. P. Lovecraft, the company whose guiding spirit and patron saint was not the businessperson but the midnight computer hacker announced that it would fight IBM in the only way it knew how—with superior and boldly innovative technology.

The Macintosh was everything people had expected of IBM's PCjr. The "Mac," as it soon came to be known with affectionate familiarity, was a brilliant piece of engineering, incorporating dozens of novel and intriguing hardware and software concepts. Whether or not it was responsible for the

PCjr's lackluster performance in the market (and there is little reason to think the two machines competed head to head, since Macintosh was substantially more expensive), comparisons between the two January market entries were inevitable. The fact was that the PCjr just didn't move. IBM the invincible had come up with a dud. This meant that PCjr software didn't move either. Months later, after the jr's keyboard had been roundly trashed by virtually every reviewer in the computer press, IBM did something it almost never does—it fixed the keyboard, which was widely perceived to be one of the major sources of the machine's problems in the marketplace. Once the Mac came along, jr had another, less fixable problem—it was boring, compared with the excitement generated by the Mac. By mid-1984, jr was in trouble. By the end of the year, despite efforts at resuscitation and a brief upswing in sales, it was still in trouble. And that meant that Sierra On-Line was also in trouble. When IBM finally announced in March 1985 that production of the jr would cease, Ken managed to soften the blow by cutting good deals for the software with Tandy, whose Model 2000 computer was compatible with the jr software, but the jr venture was still far from the bonanza he had hoped for.

Sierra had already taken two rounds of venture financing, the last in the summer of 1983. And Ken had hoped that if his company needed any more before going public, it would be at a valuation far higher than that. But the venture capitalists were not in a mood to put much of anything into software in the spring of 1984. And when Ken went back to his venture people to explain that he was going to need another couple of million because IBM sales weren't up to snuff, he got the shock of his life.

His investors didn't want to have to write off the money that had already put into Sierra, but they weren't very happy about the previous year's valuation either. So they agreed to put up the money, but only if the company's valuation were cut to half of what it had been before *and only if the previous year's financing were recomputed at the new valuation too!* Ken was aghast. Still, there was little alternative. Banks wouldn't grant him a line of credit until *after* he had secured the venture money, so he was more or less out of options.

By the end of 1984, Ken and Roberta had restored profitability to the company by drastically reducing their costs. Staff was laid off. Their previously lavish expenditures were cut to the bone. However, the founders barely had a majority interest in Sierra, as their company was now known, and we at Brøderbund kept hearing rumors that some of the investors were trying to ease Ken and Roberta out.

I wish that all stories had happy endings—a personal weakness, I suppose. The fact that many of us cared about one another's welfare, allies and competitors alike, was one of the things we believed to be different about the microcomputer software business. *Softalk*, in particular, had been the heart and soul of the Apple part of our industry since the magazine's beginning. And as I've already mentioned, Al and Margot Tommervik are among the small number of people whom I personally credit for helping Brøderbund survive and succeed. They are wonderful people, and *Softalk* was a wonderful magazine. There never were any magazines quite like it.

I saw their place of business only once. It all started with a football game that gave me the opportunity to visit *Softalk* while I was in the Tommerviks' neighborhood. When Iowa won the Big Ten football conference championship in 1982 and 10,000 delirious Iowa Hawkeyes descended on Pasadena for the Rose Bowl, our parents and various Carlston siblings, including Gary and me, were in the throng.

The game was anti-climactic—at least for Iowans. Even though I hadn't lived in Iowa since 1965, I was disappointed that so many of the fans in the Hawkeye bleachers didn't even *look* familiar. But New Year's Eve, the night before the game, wasn't anti-climactic at all. That night we made our first and only visit to *Softalk* in its cluttered North Hollywood headquarters.

The whole company was located in a house that at one time had been converted into a storefront. When the *Softalk* people moved in, they pasted Fiberglas insulation over all the huge glass windows to save heat in the winter and keep the place from broiling in the summer, so the front room glittered with the scattered reflections of a dozen lights, bouncing off the insulation's aluminum backing.

The house was a rabbit warren of desks, miscellaneous piles of paper, and narrow pathways connecting individual domains. In one corner, a grand piano was buried under a mountain of books, clippings, magazines, and coffee cups. When we all retreated to Margot's office in the rear of the building to show her our latest game (the pinball simulation called *David's Midnight Magic*), a careless elbow tipped over an already-teetering bookshelf by her desk, triggering an avalanche of half-empty coffee cups, overflowing ashtrays, and floppy disks onto Margot's sleeping bag, which was unrolled on the office floor.

That was *Solftalk*—unruly, disorganized, operating at full-tilt even on New Year's Eve. It amazed me that such a well-crafted, highly polished magazine could come out of such a jungle. But it did, and for years it was one of the most popular computer magazines in the industry. The creative souls who were drawn to the place loved it, and even when the staff grew to seventy people and had to move to larger quarters, the ambience of the place stayed just as funky, informal, and chaotic.

But from the start there were problems with *Softalk* as a business, even though the problems were not visible to the outside world. Nobody in the organization had much real business experience. As a result, *Softalk* went for years without computing a profit-and-loss statement or a balance sheet. When they finally got around to figuring out their profitability, in April 1984, they were horrified to discover that they had been losing money—a lot of it—for quite a long time. *Softalk* had been running on its cash flow. And that works only as long as revenues continue to increase.

In 1984, however, revenues were way down. Advertising pages were off by more than 50 percent, given that companies struggling to find the cash to meet their payroll don't place a lot of ads. There was a lot of competition for those dwindling ad dollars as well, for it seemed that everyone in America wanted to start a computer magazine. In the meantime, the shakeout had made many of whatever receivables *Softalk* had uncollectible. And then there were the other magazines in the *Softalk* empire—*ST Game, Softalk for the IBM,* and *St Mac.* Compared with *Softalk,* they were poor, starved-looking little creatures that siphoned off funds from the parent magazine and diluted the efforts of the staff. It all added up to trouble.

Softalk had always disdained acquisition offers from large publishers like Prentice-Hall and ABC. It turned to them at this point but was told that it wouldn't receive any money for the company. The best it could hope for would be the continued survival of the magazine. Margot wasn't sure she wanted that. It was one thing to work for herself for peanuts; it would be quite another state of affairs to work for somebody else for next to nothing. In the end, Margot reconciled herself to the sale. A couple of *Softalk*'s shareholders could not be, however, and so, on August 30, 1984, *Softalk* closed its doors.

The employees held several wakes that week. There was an oddly festive air about the place at the very end. David Durkee's long-suppressed boom box, which had always been turned way down so that others could work, was shaking the offices with hour after hour of old Beatles tunes as the staffers cleared out their desks. Maybe it was just the relief of having some resolution of the situation, even if that resolution was the magazine's demise. After all, life goes on even if magazines die. At the week's end, the former employees scattered. Among them was my youngest sister, Erin, who had been working for *Softalk* over the summer.

Right near the summit, a lot of people discovered that the top of the software mountain was a slippery slope. When the shakeout started, it didn't seem to matter which hardware market they staked the future of their software company on. Sirius and *Softalk* had hitched their fortunes to those of Apple. Synapse was essentially an Atari company. Sierra had moved into IBM's orbit. And the Human Engineered Software (HES) comet waxed with the rapidly rising fortunes of Commodore and just as quickly waned.

In 1980, a twenty-five-year-old programmer from River-side, California, Jay Balakrishnan, founded Human Engineered Software as a means of selling a programmer utility that he had written. After two years of working at it, Jay discovered that he didn't enjoy running a business nearly as much as he enjoyed programming, and that in fact he was also a far better programmer than businessman.

So far, this doesn't sound like your entrepreneurial legend. But strange Fortune is about to step in, as she so often seems to do in the software world. Jay just happened to be ready to sell his minuscule company when USI International, a privately owned supplier of microcomputer components, decided that it wanted to get into software. A software company that already exists has certain advantages, even if the company's assets are very small. And besides, "Human Engineered Software" is a pretty jazzy name. Jay sold his company to USI.

HES operated as a division of USI for about sixteen months, with Jay staying on as vice president. By the summer of 1983, USI was in deep financial trouble, for reasons largely unrelated to the software division. USI needed cash to stay afloat. Software companies were still hot items that summer, so USI "spun off" HES and persuaded three investors to kick in more than a million dollars each for equity in the new independent company. Of the millions of dollars invested, most was immediately spent to pay off short-term debts incurred previously by USI/HES. The new company really received only $1.3 million for its own needs.

This new HES was a far cry from Jay's original creature. Indeed, although Jay was still a vice-president (of licensing and acquisitions), he was no longer seen as one of the "line" officers of the company. He owned only about 1 percent of the new HES. A new professional management team was brought over, headed by Ted Morgan, previously general manager of the Computer Products Division of USI. Before that he had spent thirteen years at Xerox in sales and marketing positions. He is an impressive figure, tall with gray-flecked hair, and he looks the part of a chief executive officer. Morgan was a salesman, and his purpose all his life had been to get revenues up. Period. He was able to do this at HES as well. In his first year at the helm he raised that all-important statistic almost tenfold to more than $12 million. At the same time, however, the company lost millions.

HES was caught unprepared by the demise of the Commodore VIC market and suffered a bloodbath of returns. Unlike the book publishing and record industries, which have for years factored into their projections the possibility that products that don't sell fast will be sent back by retail vendors, HES and other software publishers didn't fully learn about the economics of returns until 1984. Compounding the problem was the fact that these HES programs were all cartridge products rather than floppy disks. Cartridges cost the publisher five to ten times more than disks. And if they come back, they can't be recycled.

But not only had HES been selling exclusively cartridge products—it had also been making them with chips known as EPROMs rather than with ROMs. EPROMs have the advantage that they can be built in about half the time as ROMs (usually five to six weeks instead of ten to twelve weeks). But they are terribly expensive.

In June 1984, Egil Juliussen, chairman of the market research firm Future Computing, was quoted as calling HES the "number one independent software company in 1984." By the end of the summer, however, HES was on the block. In October, HES filed a bankruptcy petition in federal court. But the biggest surprise didn't come until the week following the Chapter 11 announcement. Another software company announced that it had acquired HES by purchasing all of its common stock in a straight cash deal. The company? Our old friends from Eugene—Avant Garde. Shortly before this book was published, Avant Garde's offer was blocked by the judge in bankruptcy court. The deal fell through, and HES disappeared.

By the end of 1984 several of the software people had put a close on their careers in the home microcomputer industry, voluntarily and otherwise. Others, far fewer, managed to survive and even to grow. All the survivors saw their enterprises evolve into something quite different from what they had started out to do. Software people, with very few exceptions, weathered drastic changes, for better or worse, in 1984.

Dan Fylstra and Peter Jennings's VisiCorp, the first of the quick-growth giants of the software industry, publisher of the program that transformed Apple from a hobbyist company to a serious competitor of IBM, disappeared—absorbed by a start-up company called Paladin. Fylstra left the company and the microcomputer industry. Co-founder Peter Jennings, creator of that chess program I once sought in Boston, took off for Europe. And in April 1985, Lotus announced that it was buying Software Arts.

Bob Leff and Dave Wagman continued to capitalize on their blend of luck and business savvy that made Softsel successful in the first place. In contrast to all the business disasters of 1984, Softsel managed to increase its annual revenues by 70 percent over those of 1983 while increasing its inventory by only 7 percent.

MicroPro continued to be the top-grossing software publisher through 1983, but its flagship product, *WordStar*, had slipped from its position of dominance in the word-processing field, and its long-awaited upgraded version, *WordStar 2000*, was greeted with lukewarm reviews when it was released in 1985. The company weathered the shakeout, but not without major reductions in force.

Microsoft, the giant that grew from the hobbies of a couple of teenage hackers, was no longer a whiz-kid company. Microsoft BASIC continues to be the first computer language most microcomputer users learn, and MS–DOS, its operating system for IBM PCs, continues to dominate the operating-system market. But the company's newest efforts have been greeted with less overwhelming success.

Microsoft's display booth at the 1984–85 Winter Consumer Electronics Show was a collaborative effort with all of its Japanese partners—Kay Nishi's ASCII/Microsoft Japan notable among them—to promote MSX, a standard operating system for a new kind of low-cost computer manufactured by more than twenty different Japanese vendors. The manufacturers were being coy about whether or not they were actually going to launch the product in the United States. After inflated claims of a new coup in the global operating-system wars, MSX had enjoyed only moderate success in Japan, and the jury was still out on Europe. More ominously, Microsoft's long-awaited big project, a monumental production called *Windows*, touted to be an entirely new kind of operating system, was late and getting later—in the manner of *VisiOn*, the program that helped lead to the demise of VisiCorp.

The troubles of 1984 were not confined to the home computer software industry. They originated in the computer hardware shakeout that started in 1982. The problems extended across the software spectrum, from the tiny cottage companies to the corporate entrants to the much larger business software companies. During the summer of 1984, virtually every software stock listed on the public exchanges was down.

The troubles spread to the surrounding industries too. The computer magazines, with their advertising revenues dramatically diminished, experienced their own shakeout. And there were rumblings that even the venture capital community might not be immune. With so many firms chasing deals, more and more had to overbid on increasingly risky investments.

The first and most obvious fundamental reason for the software shakeout was a lack of business management skills on the part of many of the formerly hobbyist entrepreneurs, in particular their failure to remember the one thing required of all business ventures—that they return a profit. Many firms, however, feeling no need to be profitable *today*, since they were going to be phenomenally profitable tomorrow, spent money foolishly. For example, many entrepreneurs built organizations that were appropriate in size and structure for the large company they *hoped* to be rather than the small firms they actually were. And many got so wrapped up in this process of "building a company" that they stopped studying the market carefully and so lost the speed and flexibility that had made them successful in the first place.

One has only to look at the companies that ended up with huge inventories of product for dead machines or that failed to support the wildly successful machines when they came out. Or the companies that turned out the same kind of product year after year despite changing public tastes and increasing technical expectations. At Brøderbund we took pride in the fact that although we started as an Apple game company, Apple games constituted only 13 percent of our sales in 1984. Games for other machines accounted for 11 percent; productivity software accounted for 75 percent; educational programs were 1 percent of our sales.

If the lack of business skills that caught up with many of the hobbyists who founded software companies was one reason for the software shakeout, then the second reason—one that did in so many of the corporate industry participants— was an inability to develop and handle new sources of quality products. The reason for this shortcoming is a little hard to comprehend. Perhaps it was because hackers have such a huge advantage (in that they are more imaginative and more obsessed) over the more orthodox, properly trained programmers preferred by corporate publishers when it comes to dealing with very small computers. It's a vicious circle—if you are going to work with hackers you have to be able to speak their language, but orthodox publishers don't like hackers, partially because of their propensity for speaking their own language. Unfortunately, both the very best and the very worst programmers come from their ranks, but if you can't communicate with them well enough to tell the difference, you are going to get into trouble very quickly.

The same inability to develop new sources of quality products also plagued many cottage-industry companies, some of which were founded by programmers who in turn seemed to have trouble working with new programmers. This difficulty probably stemmed from the fact that ex-hacker executives were at some level competing with these new programmers. This competition can be deadly, since hackers-turned-executives quickly lose many of their hacker skills, but many are loathe to admit that their hacker employees are more skilled than they are.

Developing new sources of product on a regular basis is critical to success because, in the final analysis, it is still the caliber of its product that determines a company's success. Marketing is important. But the software consumer's grapevine is phenomenally effective and can fairly quickly disrupt an aggressive marketing campaign for a faulty program.

The third reason why many companies failed is that they didn't understand whom their market consisted of. I often had occasion to talk with people who were thinking about jumping into the computer software business. They would talk about the "installed base" of a certain type of machine, and I would nod sagely. "The Atari video game machine has the largest installed base," they would say, and I would agree. "And among the computers, it looks like the Texas Instruments and Commodore VIC have the largest base," they would continue.

They could not have chosen three less attractive software markets for 1984. The truth is that installed base isn't a very important concept, as said earlier. What *is* important is that a particular kind of computer is selling well at the time that a company is selling software for it *and that it is expected to continue selling well for a long time into the future!* Indeed, these expectations are probably more important than actual rates of sale. For example, during the summer of 1984, Apple's Macintosh was probably outselling IBM's PCjr by only three or four to one. However, Mac software was outselling PCjr software twenty to one. The Mac was seen as a winner, but the PCjr was perceived to be a loser.

By contrast, many companies that entered the business late suffered from the "Future Computing Syndrome." They sent scouts out to the thinktanks to find out what kinds of products could be expected to sell well in future years. The thinktanks told them, and they all went home and started working on identical products. The first ones to reach the market may have done reasonably well, but as more and more products flooded that market segment, all the companies suffered. The area of young children's educational entertainment products (sometimes known as "edutainment") was opened and then filled in this manner in 1983 and 1984. By the summer of 1984, it was a terrible market for most companies. The fourth reason for the shakeout was the extreme availability (*not* unavailability) of money. There was lots of money, tons of it, invested in just about every software idea under the sun. So we not only got too many competitors; we also got lots of companies with soft underbellies.

Companies should usually be undercapitalized. It's good for them because it helps them to remember the essential purpose of their business—to make money, not to spend it. The very existence of the venture capital community with its vast investment resources changed the way many companies did business and in a way blurred their vision of their purpose. There was incentive to posture, to try to show the greatest rates of growth and most positive financials at a very early stage in a company's life. Many of my associates took to fudging their numbers slightly upward when they talked to investors, sometimes doubling or tripling their actual sales. Maybe they just changed the time frame a little. A question was asked about last year's sales, and they would answer with next year's expectations.

The fudging that I'm describing was never intended to be a form of deception. If anything, we were deceiving ourselves, or instead, falling prey to a kind of delusion that was relatively well founded in fact. After all, we were in an industry where a company could start with revenues of several hundred dollars a month and grow to a million dollars a month within a couple of years. Look at Microsoft, MicroPro, Brøderbund, Sirius, Sierra—all started on shoestrings, and all soon were doing business in the tens of millions of dollars annually. *Of course* next year's sales figures would be a healthy multiple of this year's. That's just the way it worked in the software business—at least during the boom years.

The reason these overestimates were harmful was that many companies failed to set up contingency reserves, which not only save taxes but also furnish a cushion to soften the impact of downturns in the industry (and it must be remembered that this was an industry in which the word *downturn* was seldom publicly mentioned before Atari introduced it).

Furthermore, many of the early software companies tended to believe the fantasies about our business that we and the media had created, and to act accordingly. Outsiders, viewing the mouth-watering "make a fortune and have fun" fantasy, wanted to be a part of it. Some of them joined and helped glut the market.

When companies discover that they are in trouble, they sometimes look for a single solution to their problems—the "big score." In the microcomputer world, that usually meant one gigantic contract with one of the hardware vendors, a million-dollar deal that would magically turn red ink to black ink and restore the dream. This is the final reason many companies failed—they counted on the big score, and the major partner failed to deliver. Sometimes it was because the major partner backed out of the market, like Texas Instruments. Sometimes the partner had troubles of its own, as did Atari. Sometimes the software companies had unrealistic expectations of what these major players would do for them.

Synapse counted on Atari to provide a good deal of Synapse's revenues and ended up being disappointed when Atari failed to pay for millions of dollars' worth of software that it had purchased from Synapse. Broderbund signed a contract with Texas Instruments that might have provided millions in revenues. When TI pulled out of the market, we considered ourselves lucky to recover our out-of-pocket costs.

The shakeout will probably continue through 1985, but as the word implies, it is just the end of an era in which everybody seemed to flourish—not the end of the industry. After the next chapter I'll take a look at a few of the directions software and software publishing are likely to take in the future. But first, I'd like to introduce you to another software industry, one that has striking parallels with the software world I've been describing, and equally striking differences.

11

The Software People
of Japan

Although the personal computer revolution began in the United States, it has become a global phenomenon. In fact, in Japan a hobbyist community has evolved into a full-scale industry, a process that has been similar in some ways to the growth of the microcomputer software business in the United States. This chapter is probably the first word to come to many people regarding the Japanese software milieu, but I can guarantee that it won't be the last. Japanese software doesn't sell in the United States. But neither did Japanese steel, automobiles, cameras, or electronics . . . at first.

My first encounter with the software people of Japan took place in the very early days of Brøderbund, and the wholly circumstantial nature of the meeting is a prime example of the importance of the random factor: Our company's business relationship with the Japanese software industry and my personal friendships with many software people in Japan began casually, when one of the occupants of the microbooth next to ours at the 1980 West Coast Computer Faire borrowed Brøderbund's Apple to demonstrate some new game programs.

That software was from a Tokyo company called Star Craft and was so popular that after we returned to Eugene Gary and I made an agreement with one of our booth-neighbors at the Faire, a man named Mioshi, who was representing Star Craft at the time, to sell those programs ourselves. As it turned out, that chance meeting helped ensure the survival of our young company, for Gary and I ended up selling more and more of those game programs in the early months of Broderbund's existence. Moreover, that encounter eventually led to our introduction into a whole network of Japanese microcomputer entrepreneurs.

Of course, long before this encounter took place, a part of the Japanese software community had influenced the microcomputer industry in the United States for several years, particularly in the days of the video game machines that preceded microcomputers. Although arcade games were not computers because they could not be programmed by the people who used them, they contained microprocessor chips, and that meant that the most important element in the video game systems was the software that instructed each chip to play the game designed for it. The arcade game business brought young programmers into the Japanese electronics industry before microcomputer hobbyist communities surfaced in either the United States or Japan.

The size of the computer hobbyist culture in Japan—the network of technically sophisticated enthusiasts who put together their own hardware and create their own programs for microprocessor-based computers—may be twice as large now as it was in the United States during the homebrewers' heyday, even though Japan's total population is half that of this country. Although the hobbyist population in both countries is a small fraction of the total computer-using populations, the hobbyists have exerted a disproportionate influence on the software industry. Just as Microsoft, Apple, and other microcomputer companies in this country were started by intense young hobbyists, a very significant part of the Japanese software industry was created by similar enthusiasts.

It was these hobbyists' predecessors, however, who were Japan's first software people—the young programmers whose video games were instantly popular with and enormously profitable to the Japanese hardware manufacturers of arcade game systems. These programmers were also culture-free in a strange way: Handling a joystick and shooting down alien invaders with bolts of purple lightning appears to be an equally hypnotic experience in Scandinavia and Indonesia, L.A., and Yokohama. A significant fraction of the world's coinage began to flow through these addictive, hypnotic new devices. Indeed, the Japanese arcade game industry was most responsible for triggering the video game craze in the United States when the Japanese exported *Space Invaders*—the original "shoot-'em-up" game—and followed it with dozens of other arcade hits, including the phenomenally successful *Pac-Man.*

Although the games may have transcultural appeal, the business of creating and marketing them is very different in each country. In Japan, for example, the most popular *magazines* are also software publishers! The position of the programmer in the economic hierarchy and concepts such as software entrepreneurship are perceived very differently in Japan. Programmers, especially young ones, never became wealthy and famous the way they did in the United States, unless they were among the very few who decided to strike out on their own instead of working for one of the large companies—an action that meets with far less approval in Japan than it does in this country.

The personal computer software industry as we know it is still relatively new in Japan because it took a little longer for the Japanese hobbyists to turn into industrialists. The first microprocessor programmers weren't the same people as the first microcomputer hobbyists, and neither group rushed out *en masse* to manufacture and distribute hardware and software, the way they did in the United States. Nevertheless, both software entrepreneurship and a very healthy microcomputer market have grown up in Japan.

Outside the brief but enormous impact of video games, Japanese-created software has not been successful in this country, except for the early games for the Apple we sold at Broderbund, and the game market in the United States has long since declined from its peak in the early 1980s. Indeed, Japan has become a growing market for American-originated microcomputer software—particularly games.

I have a theory about the continuing success of computer games in Japan—as opposed to the rapid decline in the game software market stateside. It has to do with the American taboo against adult participation in the same kind of games that children play, a taboo that doesn't seem so present in Japan. I never fail to notice, for example, that the majority c the customers in Japanese arcades are not always children and teenagers, as they are here, but are often young and middle-aged businessmen, as well. I have also noticed that in Japan, commuter trains are filled with adults, many of whom are utterly absorbed in comic books that emerge from brief-cases the way copies of the *Wall Street Journal* appear in American commuter trains. In the United States, no self-respecting accountant or account executive would ever read a comic book while commuting on the 8:15. Similarly, to Americans, playing games in public or even in the home is considered "immature" or "childish." In Japan, for some reason, that attitude is not as prevalent.

My theory on the Japanese fascination with comic books and games doesn't mean that I'm an expert on Japanese culture. Although I'm not a student of the cultural differences between our two countries, I do know something about differences and similarities between the American and Japanese microcomputer software industries. My acquaintance with the Japanese software world dates back to that coincidental meeting the first time Gary and I attended the West Coast Computer Faire. Eventually the agreement we made with Mioshi was superseded by a direct arrangement with Star Craft's founder, Minoru Nakazawa. In time, our original contact with him not only contributed significantly to Broderbund's early growth, but it also led to other connections and friendships in the Japanese software industry.

In fact, personal contacts, as I later discovered, are the only manner in which one can become involved in Japanese business in general and in the Japanese software business in particular. Japanese business, in short, is purely a person-to-person contact business, and a cold call seldom works there. One often goes through a series of strictly ritualistic meetings that end up producing nothing "tangible" in Western terms— the kind of trips that would be considered failures in our country. But the real intent behind all these meetings is for prospective business partners to establish some kind of personal relationship. As it turns out, the most important step in doing business with a Japanese company is when top management from both companies get to know and trust one another.

Of course, I didn't know how this worked until after our business with Nakazawa led to business with other figures in the Japanese software world. And since he was our first contact in that world, it is only fitting that Nakazawa's story should introduce the stories of other Japanese software people I have come to know.

The Nakazawas are a very old merchant family that has been doing business in the Tokyo area for hundreds of years. Our associate's two brothers now run the family silk business, and it was Nakazawa's experience in that business—particularly his attitude toward personnel policies—that eventually led to some problems he had in the software business.

In the silk industry, many small farmers bring their silk harvest to companies like the Nakazawas'. There the raw material is spun into silk, usually by young girls whom Nakazawa recruits from the poorer, rural northern area of Japan, where Japan's indigenous people, the Ainu, live. These rural girls have difficulty finding good husbands in more prosperous areas of the country. Their marriage prospects are improved, however, by their working in the Nakazawa silk mill. Nakazawa recruits attractive twelve- and thirteen-year-old girls and brings them to his factory, which is near the silk farming areas around Tokyo, and where there are male farmers whose situation is handily complementary to that of these females. Very few marriagable young women who live near Tokyo want to marry farmers. The young farmers have a hard time finding wives. So the silk farmers gravitate toward the Nakazawa silk mill to court the silk spinners, who by the age of sixteen and seventeen are delighted to trade in their jobs for the role of farmers' wives.

The young ladies' families are happy, the girls and the farmers are pleased, and the Nakazawas are especially fond of the arrangement because their industry pays spinners on the basis of seniority. Since the company recruits the girls at twelve and since they usually leave by the end of their teens, the population of silk spinners rarely gains enough seniority to receive high wages. The perpetually youthful presence of a marriageable female population also brings more farmers (and their silk) to the vicinity of the Nakazawa factory, and the cycle repeats itself.

This has been a lucrative arrangement for the silk mill for hundreds of years. A similarly autocratic attitude toward his employees gave him trouble, however, when Nakazawa got into the software business. Programmers aren't sons and daughters of poor farmers but rather upper-middle-class kids of the electronic generation. Programmers also tend to have very strong opinions of their own, a trait that always leads to conflict when anybody tries to impose any authoritarian structure on them.

After several years, our relationship with Nakazawa's software company came to a sad end. This is unfortunate, since he is a loyal friend and an honorable and energetic businessman who has a nose and an eye for talent. Star Craft, founded in 1979, made its name on the strength of its programs—which meant that the company's chief resource was the talent of its programmers. Among the young programmers of very high ability that Nakazawa found was Tony Suzuki, who wrote *Alien Rain*, a Brøderbund-licensed product that was the first entertainment product in the United States to knock *VisiCalc* off the number one position on the *Softalk* chart.

Nakazawa's business acumen and ability to spot programming talent were, needless to say, extremely beneficial to us. We still remember him as one of the three people most responsible for our initial success. He might have brought his software to any one of a dozen bigger companies, but he stayed with us, and we won't forget the time he worked with us through the night for a solid week, sleeping in shifts on our couch and helping us perform the monotonous labor of duplicating copies of his software for distribution.

Unfortunately, Nakazawa's relationship with his own programmers wasn't always as successful as it was with us. He made the mistake of keeping most of the revenue he obtained in foreign royalties and giving his programmers what amounted to allowances. This was entirely in accord with Japanese custom, since it isn't appropriate for nineteen-year-olds in Japan to have a lot of money. But nineteen-year-old programmers in the United States were making hundreds of thousands of dollars a year, and in time the word got around. The result was that Nakazawa had a revolt on his hands.

Nakazawa's problems with his programmers didn't get any better when he hired a translator and liaison between our two companies. She was Japanese-born but had lived in Berkeley for ten years. Nakazawa brought her to Tokyo, and while she was there she got to know all his employees. She is a very open person, and it wouldn't occur to her to refrain from speaking frankly about the software gold rush that was taking place in the United States at the time. Of course, she wasn't the employees' only source of this news. Eventually many of the dissatisfied programmers broke away from his company and started working independently.

When Nakazawa's programmers left, he didn't have any more products to sell. I hired Nakazawa's former translator, who had returned to the San Francisco Bay Area, to go back to Tokyo to see if she could find other opportunities for us in Japan. The programmers she already knew led us to a wider network of programmers who worked for different companies. We made contacts and began to license Brøderbund products to a few companies in Japan.

Our first contract to provide game software to System Soft, a publishing house in the city of Fukuoka, made front-page news in a major Japanese business daily in the summer of 1983. Microsoft had already begun to dominate the operating-systems market in Japan, so Brøderbund's incursion into games was seen by some Japanese journalists as a sign that the long-feared day had arrived when America would sell far more software to Japan than it bought from it. In fact, Brøderbund was licensing American software to a dozen Japanese software publishers in Japan by the end of 1984.

Although the microcomputer hardware market in Japan

is dominated by the huge companies that already manufacture and distribute electronic hardware, a very significant part of the Japanese software industry was created by start-up companies founded by the same kind of hobbyist–zealots who started the microcomputer revolution in the United States. Indeed, hobbies in general seem to have played an important part in the revolution in both countries. The microcomputer industry wasn't started by the computer industry or by big-business men, but by people who were fascinated by, obsessed with, and intensely engaged in computing for the fun of it. And a lot of those people had other hobbies before software came along. Among the computer entrepreneurs I know or have heard about, I have noticed a definite preponderance of three different kinds of hobbyists, in both the United States and Japan: Many computer enthusiasts in both countries share a passion for model trains, ham radios, and/or music.

Perhaps the explanation for this is that people who are so dedicated to their personal interests that they spend most of their spare time bent over soldering irons or hunched over their radio receivers are made of the kind of stuff that can create billion-dollar corporations in a few years. A case in point: Among the key software people in Japan is a hobbyist extraordinaire, Yuji Kudo, who is so fascinated with model locomotives that he named his company Hudson Soft, in honor of the Hudson—his favorite kind of steam locomotive. Kudo's company happens to be the largest microcomputer software publisher in Japan.

Yuji Kudo's office is filled with model trains, including a four-foot-long steam locomotive that sits on his desk. Stacks of one-foot gauge track are stored down the hall. Once a year, Kudo and his friends rent the parking lot of a huge shopping center and set up all their track and run their trains for impromptu audiences of several hundred onlookers. But Kudo is an inveterate entrepreneur as well as an astonishingly dedicated hobbyist. Since he is closely associated with so many other key figures in Japan's software world, Yuji Kudo's story is a kind of history in miniature of the microcomputer revolution in Japan.

In 1967, while he was still a university student, he started

Hudson Productions and sold the work of various commercial photographers—an enterprise that prospered for a while and then went under after six years. But commercial photography wasn't his sole passion. He was also an ardent amateur radio operator. In 1973, the same year his photography company filed the Japanese equivalent of Chapter 11, he started Hudson Company Limited. At first, he sold ham radio equipment. Then in 1976 he saw the first advertisements in American electronics hobbyist magazines for the microprocessor chips.

Although hailed as "computers on a chip," these microprocessers were far from usable computers. But Kudo, an accomplished amateur electronics engineer, wasn't dismayed by the prospect of getting involved with this hardware. He wanted to know more about the potential of the chips and was drawn to the idea of building and using his own computer. He didn't speak English, but, with an adventurousness that is characteristic of other legendary microcomputer entrepreneurs, he flew directly to Silicon Valley in 1976 to obtain one of these mysterious new devices.

A young man at Stanford University, Harry Garland, a member of the homebrew movement who would later become co-founder of *Cromemco* (named after a Stanford dormitory) showed Kudo an 8008 chip. Kudo had read about the chip and was fascinated by it, so he bought a one-board computer manufactured in Berkeley—the SBC80—for $1200. Kudo took the hardware home and played with it until it broke. When he came back to the United States less than a year later to buy an IMSAI, he was astonished at how quickly the technology had advanced since his previous trip. He was burning to be part of this new hobbyist renaissance, so Kudo persuaded his younger brother Hiroshi to run his ham radio store while Kudo studied programming at Hokkaido University. His intention was to gain enough expertise in programming so that he could expand his company's interests into the microcomputer field.

Hiroshi was for a time seriously opposed to Kudo's plan to expand their venture into a field that was then so unknown. But he relented when he realized that to Kudo this wasn't strictly a business matter. Like his locomotives and his radio equipment, computers were objects of endless devotion, study, and wonder to Kudo, who continued to pursue his studies and to buy and program new varieties of microcomputer from the United States.

After he switched from Hokkaido to Waseda University, during a time when most of the nation was still fascinated by the single-purpose nonprogrammable arcade video games, Kudo was finding out all about their successors—personal computers. He had taught himself enough about his IMSAI to give seminars for hobbyists in Hokkaido. He bought several more computers and wrote the system software to make them run. He wrote other programs as well and then began selling them to other hobbyists. At first, business wasn't exactly booming, since few people in Japan outside the hobbyist community had machines before 1979, but sheer enthusiasm for the subject kept Kudo creating and publishing software and writing articles for *I/O*, the first Japanese microcomputer magazine.

Throughout 1978, Kudo wrote games. By this time he had started Hudson Soft, his software publishing company. He also bought a PET and an Apple in the United States and produced his own version of BASIC for those machines—Hudson Basic. he even designed FORTRAN and PASCAL interpreters. He also began to train an assistant, a man named Nakamoto, who shot right past his teacher in programming expertise and became in time the leader of his development team. By the end of 1978, Kudo had seven employees.

Hudson Soft really got off the ground when Kudo made deals to provide software for such major hardware manufacturers as Sharp, Panasonic, and National. These manufacturers distributed Kudo's software with their machines (an arrangement known, colorfully enough, as "bundling"), and as a result he never had any reason to build his own distribution network. But in 1981, he met someone who persuaded him to change his mind—another software entrepreneur named Jung-Eui Son, who was a student at Berkeley. A discussion about Son is appropriate here, for his story is closely linked to Kudo's and others'.

In 1980, while Son was studying economics at Berkeley,

he devised a business plan for a portable language translator, then hired a University of California physics professor to build him a prototype. Son took the translator to Japanese hardware manufacturers and sold the idea to Sharp, which gave him a fair amount of operating capital. Son then formed a software publishing company, Unison World, which still exists in wonderfully mutated form in Berkeley. Then, in 1981, when he returned to Tokyo, Son started a software distribution company called Soft Bank.

When Soft Bank began to dwarf his software publishing business, Son sold Unison to another Berkeley student by the name of Hong Lu. An energetic and amiable fellow who was in his mid-twenties when he acquired the company, Lu now occupies a ninth-floor suite with a panoramic view of the Berkeley hills. In the warren of programming and brainstorming rooms outside Lu's office, is one of the largest and most determined collection of eighteen-year-old hackers west of the Charles River. What with wild-haired and wild-eyed teenage programmers mingling with delegations of Chinese computer scientists, and development models of next year's Japanese computer hardware locked away in small cubicles from which the sound of punk rock is often heard, Unison's office has indeed become a kind of software carnival to behold.

But Unison was only a sideline as far as its founder was concerned. Son's jackpot was Soft Bank. His most brilliant move after establishing his distribution company was to identify and enlist the real star in Japanese software, Yuki Kudo, then persuade him to let Soft Bank handle Hudson Soft's distribution. It was a beneficial arrangement to both parties, to say the least. Both Kudo and Son were still in their twenties when they made the deal that would earn them small fortunes in a few years.

After settling on this exclusive distributorship for Hudson Soft, the hottest software publisher in the country, Son then went to a company called Joshin Denki, which sold around 10 percent of all software sold in Japan, and cut an exclusive deal to sell Soft Bank's software in its stores. A distributor can't do much better than to have the largest chain of stores in the country in one pocket and the best software company in the other.

It would be nice, however, also to have advertising in the big, colorful hobbyist magazines like *I/O* and *ASCII*. But both magazines were either involved in software publishing, (*ASCII*) or planned to get into it eventually (*I/O*) and saw Soft Bank as a potential competitor, so they wouldn't take Son's advertising. Son reacted by starting his own magazines; he enlisted major hardware manufacturers to finance magazines dedicated strictly to their machines. Then he ran his own ads for free. Eventually at least one of Son's competitors changed its policy toward him. By 1984, Soft Bank was distributing *ASCII*'s software. Needless to say, *ASCII* magazine also began carrying Soft Bank's advertising.

Soft Bank is now the biggest microcomputer software distributor in Japan. Around 70 percent of the micro software in Japan is sold through distributors, and around 70 percent of the distributed software is sold through Soft Bank. This means that Son controls around half the software sales in Japan—a far higher share of the market than Leff and Wagman's Softsel controls in the United States. Although Kudo didn't mention it to me when I talked to him about his and Son's history together, Son told me that Kudo bailed out Soft Bank in the early days when they were out of money. Son also mentioned that Kudo is one of seven people who are honored at an annual company thanksgiving festival in gratitude for helping Soft Bank attain its dominance of the market.

Kudo has certainly shared in his friend Son's success. At first, more than 80 percent of Soft Bank's sales were Hudson Soft products, but Kudo's share of the overall market has since dropped to around 35 percent. The reduced market share doesn't necessarily mean reduced revenue for Hudson Soft, however, because the size of the software market in Japan keeps growing at such a phenomenal rate. (Does this sound like a familiar story?) Hudson Soft has about one hundred employees now. It is starting direct sales and has purchased a distribution company.

Not all such partnerships between the early microcomputer hobbyists ended up as amicably as Kudo and Son's. Consider, for instance, the tangled histories of three other important figures in the Japanese software culture: Masaaki Hoshi, Akio Gunji, and "Kay" Nishi. Their story is an example of how businesses as well as people seem to be more closely interconnected in Japan than in the United States.

In Japan, the distinctions between magazine publishers and software publishers, and between publishers and distributors, are not as clearly defined as they are in the United States. Besides ASCII, such companies as ENIX and Joshin Denki distribute or retail as well as publish as software. In the beginning, Hoshi, Gunji, and Nishi were involved in magazine publishing as a labor of love. The lure of big money was remote from their most immediate and driving interests. In fact, Gunji and Nishi were volunteer writers who wrote for Hoshi's magazine *I/O* for free until they started their own magazine, *ASCII*. The ultimate fate of their association is still a matter of dispute.

Hoshi started *I/O* in late 1976 as a service to the small but rapidly growing number of Japanese hobbyists who, like Kudo, wanted to get their hands on microcomputer hardware and software. At the time, he was working for a publishing company that produced technical documents for scientific and commercial customers. The first issue of *I/O*—at the beginning, little more than a catalogue—was only thirty-six pages long, and only 3000 copies were printed. It was respectable for a hobbyist publication, but nothing to base an industry on. The number of subscribers was up to 6000 by the second issue, however, and grew to 12,000 by the third issue. Hoshi quit his job and took over full-time management of his magazine business.

Money, in ever-increasing amounts, began flowing in from what had started out as an avocation. Now that he had a healthy subscriber base, Hoshi hired people to contact advertising prospects—who in turn were eager to present their products through this unique medium. When some of the hobbyists started their own companies, they turned to the established magazines as their primary means of reaching their market. One of the first of these early companies was Hudson Soft.

The raw enthusiasm of microcomputer hobbyists worked to Hoshi's benefit. One of the keys to his early success with the magazine was the fact that he found himself with a large business and a very small staff. Hoshi was knowledgeable enough to handle the publishing operation himself. All he needed to do was hire people to sell advertising. Scientists, engineers, and other hobbyists were only too happy to provide articles for free. Which is where Nishi and Gunji entered the scene. While still a student at Waseda University, Nishi became a volunteer contributor to *I/O*, after having spent some time just hanging around the magazine's headquarters and looking for ways to put his love for microcomputers to constructive use. When his friend Akio Gunji was out of a job, Nishi suggested that he, too, write articles for *I/O*, which Gunji did. At this point the disputed section of the history of these three men begins.

When I talked to Hoshi about his association with Nishi and Gunji, he told me that the less-than-amiable rivalry between him and the other two competitors dates back to the time Nishi and Gunji worked for *I/O*. The story Hoshi told me is hard to believe in the context of normal, tough-but-polite Japanese business, and even in the context of the most cutthroat American businesses. Nevertheless, I'm not close enough to the situation to be able to make a judgment about which party's story is accurate.

According to Hoshi, Nishi and Gunji took advantage of a time during which he left them in charge of his magazine while he was gone for a while to attend a wedding. In his absence, he alleges, they announced to subscribers that the *I/O* offices were moving. When Hoshi called to see how they were managing the business, they assured him that everything was fine. When Hoshi returned, he claims, he discovered that his former volunteers had set up their own magazine—located at the new address they had sent to *I/O* subscribers!

Nishi and Gunji's new magazine, started in 1977 and

named *ASCII*—which stands for American Standard Computer Information Interchange, a code used to represent alpha-
numeric characters in microcomputers—was also an immediate success, and they soon branched out into software
production and distribution as well as into other magazines.
By the end of 1984, ASCII rivaled Hudson Soft in size as a
software producer, with approximately $20 million annual
sales from its magazine and its software.

As for the circumstances preceding ASCII's formation,
Nishi of course tells a different story. In all fairness, I must
state that I did not interview Nishi about this matter, but it is
a matter of public record that in the August 1984 issue of
Creative Computing magazine, Nishi was quoted as saying
that he "decided to publish a magazine of games and other
electronic products. That was my first magazine, *I/O*, which
is today primarily a hobby magazine." In other words, according to that interview Nishi claims total credit for starting *I/O*
as well as *ASCII* magazine.

Like many of the microcomputer entrepreneurs in the
United States—Steve Jobs, Steve Wozniak, and Bill Gates, for
example, who were each personally worth hundreds of millions of dollars before the age of thirty—Nishi was a college
dropout. In Japan, however, dropping out of college is not
taken as casually by the student or the whole society as it is in
the United States. Instead, most of Japan's young people
devote years of their lives to preparing for the entrance exam
for the top schools that will help them obtain lifetime jobs as
employees of any one of the large companies in the country. In
addition, a large number of the major entrepreneurs in Japan
all come from families whose businesses stretch back hundreds
of years, and who have established a tradition in which wild-
catters are discouraged. A dropout wildcatter like Nishi,
then, is doubly rare.

Gunji is very much an active partner in *ASCII*, but Nishi
is the one who attracts all the public attention, both positive
and negative. Because of his aggressive, almost "Western"
approach to doing business, "Kay" Nishi ruffles feathers here
and there in the Japanese microcomputer industry. He made
an audacious move early in his career, one that contributed

greatly to ASCII's growth and that also made him one of the few Japanese software people who are well known in the American microcomputer industry. Nishi did something a traditional Japanese businessman would never do—he made a cold phone call to a foreign country, then followed up a rebuff with an unannounced visit.

Nishi was just beginning to get into software design, which meant that he needed a BASIC interpreter. At that time, August 1977, the best known BASIC interpreter available for microcomputers was sold by a company that had just changed its name to Microsoft and was then located in Albuquerque, New Mexico. (This was not long after the era when Gates and Allen were the software arm of MITS, creating software for the Altair.) Nishi called Albuquerque and asked for the president of the company, which got him to Bill Gates. In the course of the conversation, Nishi strongly suggested that Gates come to Japan immediately to join Nishi in the software business. Gates declined. So Nishi flew to New Mexico and literally showed up at Gates's doorstep.

Gates still didn't want to do business, but he eventually succumbed to Nishi's persuasive frontal assault—and Bill Gates is hardly what you would call a pushover for a sales pitch. By late 1978, Gates and Nishi had a contract with one of Japan's largest hardware manufacturers—NEC—to design the hardware and software for the NEC PC–8000. It was a phenomenally successful product launching. Nishi now sits on the board of Microsoft and has another company in Japan, unrelated to *ASCII* magazine, called ASCII-Microsoft.

Nishi has long been a legend in the American microcomputer industry. One of the most often-repeated Nishi stories is about the time he described to the person sitting next to him on an airplane flight what his "dream computer" would be. The fellow passenger turned out to be the president of Tandy, the company that owned Radio Shack, the manufacturers of TRS-80 microcomputers. Their airborne discussion led to the design and production of the first and extremely successful "laptop computer"—the Radio Shack Model 100. In general, Nishi stories all seem to be related to the fact that he spends so much time in the air. He virtually commutes between

Tokyo and Seattle (site of Microsoft's suburban Bellevue headquarters), and chief executives of American computer companies have been known to get on planes to Tokyo and then Seattle in order to have a business meeting with Nishi, literally "on the fly."

Perhaps it is not so much that Nishi's style is "Western" in its outlook but that he sees things as a "hobbyist." In Japan, as in the United States, microcomputers were never of much interest to the management of established computer companies until enthusiasts like Nishi—whose efforts matched those of his American counterparts Wozniak, Jobs, Gates, Kapor, and others—started industries of their own. To me, this indicates that the key cultural divisions in the microcomputer world might have less to do with nationality than with personal orientation to the technology. In my opinion, if you want to find out whom you are dealing with, the first thing to know about a microcomputer company, either Japanese or American, is whether the founder ever spent time working and playing with computers for the sheer intellectual thrill of it, or whether he sees computers as "consumer electronics"—just another product to sell, like so many bars of soap.

The prevailing wisdom in the microcomputer industry has been that Japan is a formidable competitor in electronics in general and in the production of mainframe computers, but that the Japanese are far less formidable in the microcomputer field—and when it comes to microcomputer software their significance has been as a market for U.S. products rather than as a potential competitor on the world market. The facts, as evidenced by the absence of Japanese software from any of the charts, certainly seem to support this case—for the present, and perhaps for the intermediate future. But I'm sure there are people in the American steel, automobile, and consumer electronics industries—or who used to be in those industries—who would advise caution to anyone who discounts Japan's role in the future of the software business.

What Lies Ahead?

One of my programmer friends was in a bit of a hurry as he drove me into Tokyo from Narita Airport one time, and he consistently exceeded the speed limit. At regular intervals the radar detector on his dashboard would sound an alarm and he would slow down. The one thing that puzzled me was that I never saw any police cars. Finally I asked him about it, and when we drove past a large metal box, fixed squarely in the middle of the concrete highway divider, he pointed to it by way of answering my question. It turns out that this box has made highway patrol cars virtually obsolete in Japan, at least as far as speed enforcement is concerned. The box automatically checks drivers' speed by radar and photographs their license plate if they are going too fast. The ticket is then mailed to them. Low confrontation, high technology. I could see why such a system might appeal to people in Japan.

At the 1985 Winter Consumer Electronics Show—an annual extravaganza in Las Vegas that dwarfs even such popular trade shows as COMDEX (and the increasingly commercial West Coast Computer Faire)—I saw what might well be the next escalation in this techno-legal war on the highways. An exhibitor was showing a product that not only detected radar but also sent out a phony signal to convince the radar that a driver was going at the legal speed. When this product reaches the market, it will mean that machine will be pitted against machine, and it will seem that the human drivers no longer will be a factor—even though they will still cause virtually all of the traffic accidents. This prospect was a little chilling to me, as the founder of a high-technology company, and I felt a little nervous in general about the latest, inevitable technologization of our lives.

It isn't news that high technology tends to beget higher technology. In the software field, the bootstrapping effect has been unusually powerful and rapid. In the days of the first generations of tube-powered computers, the beasts were programmed in raw machine code—long strings of zeroes and ones. Throughout the early 1950s, there was much debate over the future of "automatic programming"—the term used then for programs such as assemblers, compilers, and interpreters for higher-level languages. Most programmers of the day were skeptical about whether these translators could do the job any faster or more efficiently than human programmers— and virtually everybody agreed that programming was too highly technical for anybody but the most highly trained mathematicians and engineers.

It turned out that these special-purpose programs actually made a higher level of programming possible and transformed the programming population from a tiny elite to a rapidly growing profession. These programming tools indeed proved to be much faster and more efficient than unassisted human programmers and made it possible for some scientists, many college students, and even high-school wizards like Bill Gates, Paul Allen, and Steve Wozniak to learn how to program.

The automation of programming has not abated in the age of the microcomputer; indeed, the creation of increasingly sophisticated programs to help programmers write other, increasingly sophisticated programs has continued to accelerate. It may be that the software of tomorrow can be written only by other software, perhaps administered and guided by a team of designers. In that event, what will happen to the current generation of software people?

The answer to that question depends upon the way businesses evolve as well as upon the way technology changes. In the process, entrepreneurs and programmers face somewhat different adjustments. For the former, the evolution of the software industry thus far—from an underground swap meet to a consumer industry—has so changed the nature of many dominant software companies that it has put pressure upon many software entrepreneurs to move on.

In general, entrepreneurs, especially in the software business, tend to become entrepreneurs because they are uncomfortable with the normal roles afforded them by society and the business world. Their inner lives are usually far richer than their external surroundings, and they may prefer to elaborate their own visions than to work out a compromise with "normal" society. When entrepreneurs succeed, they may find that their sudden social acceptance (and monetary rewards) causes them to drift away from those behavior patterns that drove them to be entrepreneurs in the first place. By becoming more "normal," they may discard their spark of originality as well. Or they may simply become uncomfortable as society co-opts the entrepreneur's world and turn their attentions to some field that is not so popular.

After attaining a major success, many entrepreneurs push on to other risky enterprises, because success was never really their goal at all. Rather, it was to create a world in which they had some measure of control. For this reason, some of this breed may push on to the outer frontiers of technology as large firms move into the software arena. After all, microcomputers as we know them aren't the be-all and end-all of technological achievement in the field of personal computing. There are other achievements to come—optical computers, rather than electronic ones, and dazzling new visual displays and artificial intelligence applications to explore and to build industries around.

The changing environment in the industry has had drastic effects on the destinies of programmers as well as on those of entrepreneurs. If you ask the two young programmers who wrote Brøderbund's latest hit, *Print Shop*, you'll discover that the era of the teenage millionaire programmer is not over. But the competition is certainly a lot tougher than it used to be. Whether or not the era of the individual programming genius has come to an end is a matter of debate. Nevertheless, even old hands like Budge and Lutus and Draper are going to have to work much harder to make the kind of money they made in the early 1980s.

For in time, programming will be done more and more by teams of programmers and less by individual hackers. It is true that teams are not always faster or better than a lone programmer when it comes to creating programs of moderate size. But with the huge programs that will inevitably evolve as the capacity of computer hardware expands, it won't be possible for lone hackers to produce competitive software in a reasonable amount of time.

Undoubtedly, some hackers will make good use of the new programming tools that will be emerging, and some will move on to artificial intelligence programming and other software frontiers. But the day of the hacker as the superstar of the microcomputer software industry is probably on the wane. Hacking as a creative process is less organized than intuitive, less purposeful than persistent. When computers first spread to college campuses in the late 1950s, programmers tended to sort themselves according to their programming methodologies. Those who truly studied their machines and used them to accomplish orthodox programming goals, who organized and planned and structured their work, called themselves programmers, not hackers.

Many hackers, on the other hand, were generally drawn into programming for the sheer visceral and cerebral pleasure of it, without first understanding exactly what they were doing much of the time, and without organizing their work. They often begged, borrowed, or stole access numbers so that they could program and then play games like *Spacewar* on multimillion-dollar machines until dawn. They had no "serious purpose," and they not only knew it, they flaunted it.

What the first hackers did have was raw talent, as well as a community of like-minded ne'er-do-wells, and a few mentors who were smart enough to let the hackers play their games in return for the creation of some fast, brilliant system software like the operating systems for the first time-sharing computers. Above all, they had an intensity of purpose that comes only from truly enjoying what one is doing. Without really ever intending it to be so, these hackers became the real experts. When time sharing and interactive computing came along, they were the people who built the prototypes of the systems that would eventually bring programming out of the temple and to the masses.

When a marketplace for microcomputer software emerged, the hackers often knew the machines better than the engineers who had built them. They knew all the programming tricks—primarily ways and means of putting more code in less memory space and having it run twice as fast as "structured code." They often broke all the rules of good programming technique, but then most of them had never been taught good technique. Nobody had ever taught Steve Wozniak how to create a disk operating system, so he went out and built one so much more efficient and economical than any existing disk drives that it helped ensure Apple's success. Lutus and Draper and a dozen other self-taught programmers did things their own way and made fortunes.

The problem for hackers in an age of a changing marketplace and maturing technology is the demand for programs that are far more complex than those that were happily accepted by the software buying public only a few years earlier. Hackers tend to be short-haul drivers—they aren't usually organized enough and cooperative enough to participate in the kind of structured group effort needed to build an efficient large program.

Furthermore, the evolution of more powerful machines has made the hackers' favorite corner-cutting techniques obsolete. A talent for cramming code into a small memory space is no longer valuable now that huge memory spaces have become economically feasible. It used to take a hacker to make a microcomputer dance. That situation will change as the hardware evolves. Hackers will always be in style as long as computers based on 8-bit processors continue to be built. But there is so much power under the hood of a 16-bit Macintosh that a mere BASIC programmer can now put on a stunning display of visual pyrotechnics.

The new corporate culture that has taken over most of

the software world has brought different values that are often incompatible with the ones hackers remember from the early days. A software publisher can hope to survive and thrive only by making each program compatible across a spectrum of different machines and peripheral devices. This kind of time-dependent compatibility (you have to rush out the different versions of your latest hit program before your imitators can beat you to it) means that programming teams have to adhere to certain programming standards. And such standards are anathema to most dyed-in-the-wool hackers.

Support and revision of programs by people other than the original programmer are another requirement of today's highly competitive market, which is dictated by customers who no longer tolerate bugs nor attempt to fix programs themselves. These requirements can be met only if the original programmer observes certain protocols of programming style. In fact, projects get so big that they are designed and implemented by teams using sophisticated software tools designed by other teams. Programming protocols are therefore crucial in order to sustain this team interaction.

One day soon, the independent hackers will be forced to button down to stay in the ball game, or they will be forced to retreat from the mainstream of microcomputer software publishing and might end up without any niche—unless new and unexplored software territory opens up. In that event, pioneers are always needed to map the terrain and build the first roads into new computer technologies. As long as the capabilities of computer technology continue to expand beyond our present uses, we will need adventurous, perhaps undisciplined, trailblazers to chart the new capabilities for the rest of us.

What are the most likely new developments to come? Some of the hardware innovations of the next few years amount to a change in the *quantity* of something—the amount of memory, the degree of resolution of the display, the speed of a microprocessor. But a dramatic change in quantity can often make for radical changes in *quality*. (Microcomputer guru Alan Kay notes that when you put still photographs on a screen at a rate of twenty-four frames per second, you not only get more images, you get moving images—a quantitative change that creates a significant qualitative change.) Larger, faster memory technologies are the near-future developments that are most likely to make practical certain kinds of programs that were not before.

The microcomputer industry expanded to a whole new market when the older, slower cassette-storage technology changed to a faster, higher-capacity disk-storage technology in the early 1980s. Similarly, the advent of optically based storage peripherals, vertical magnetic storage, networking, and high-capacity memory chips with far greater speed and storage capacity than today's most advanced disk drives and RAM memories will permit practical mass-market use of computer applications that are now in the experimental (and expensive) stage. Among the most feasible applications will be even better high-resolution graphics, as well as practical and workable technologies such as speech recognition and synthesis by computers. Together with new kinds of human–computer interfaces—the means by which people command computers to carry out tasks—new voice and visual techniques are bound to revolutionize software.

Perhaps we are nearing the day when we may actually share in another person's adventurous experiences in the way futurists such as Aldous Huxley described in books like *Brave New World*. In other words, perhaps instead of movies, there will be such phenomena as "feelies," theater-like sensoria where one not only sees and hears what the characters in the films might have seen and heard, but also feels what they touch and smells what they smell. No such man/machine interface is currently under commercial development as far as I know (although top-secret defense technology is generally years ahead of commercial developments), but major increases in the quantity and quality of information that can be shared between humans and machines can be expected in the near future.

In the realm of machines like computers, the key to human–computer communication is that measure known as *bandwidth*—the capacity to send and receive large amounts of information back and forth very quickly. Humans are visually oriented creatures, and we have much larger capacities for individual information input than are being used by current computer displays. Simply look at the difference between a color television program and even the best microcomputer graphics and you will see the kinds of changes in visual displays that an increase in processing speed and storage capacity (*i.e.*, bandwidth) will bring in the near future.

And as our capacity to take in information from the computer expands because of advances in visual displays, our ability to put information into the computer will be hugely augmented by advances in voice recognition technology. But before voice recognition input technology—the capability of a computer to recognize and act upon verbal commands—will come a somewhat less difficult output technology, voice synthesis—the capability of a computer to generate an accurate facsimile of a human voice. This is truly one of the next areas for commercial breakthrough.

Voice synthesis, once deemed a very difficult problem, is virtually solved on the technical level; it needs only to become economically feasible for the mass market. Special sound-generation chips and speech synthesis software has already brought speech generation to the edge of commercial feasibility, and it is already being used, for example, to automate many of the telephone company's directory assistance services. The next time you ask for a listing, you will probably hear a computer-generated voice. Microcomputer versions of speech generation systems are already used by visually handicapped computerists, and in a few years "talking computers" will become more widely used.

Speech recognition—a means by which computers can understand a large number of spoken commands—is a more difficult scientific and software problem than voice synthesis. The problem is that the spoken word is terribly hard to decipher if you don't *know* what is being said. Speech is highly ambiguous because many words sound alike, so humans use a lot of contextual information to translate speech—a feat our brains do without our conscious awareness. For computers, however, the ability to know what is being said in every possible circumstance requires artificial intelligence techniques that are far from being perfected. In order to get a computer to recognize a human-sized vocabulary, very sophisticated, very complicated software must be created. And that requires large memories and fast processors. However, smaller vocabularies are an easier problem, and voice-commanded microcomputers will become commercially feasible very soon.

True speech recognition of very large vocabularies might be a difficult problem, but it also offers the opportunity for the next truly major increase in practical functionality for computers. When it is no longer necessary to know programming, or even simple keyboard commands, when one can actually control a computer's operations by talking to it, using a reasonably large vocabulary, then the true computerization of the world's population will take place. The need for a voice-controlled computer is perhaps nowhere more widely perceived than it is in Japan, where voice recognition is believed to be the key to the creation of a workable Japanese word-processing system. The Japanese written language has so many characters that the present word-processing systems are very slow and clumsy; speech-based word-processing systems would improve these capabilities.

Just as humans are used to taking in information in a visual form, our species has many thousands of years of experience communicating information in an aural form. Once computers are able to capture and process our normal spoken communications, our ability to feed information to the computer will increase suddenly, in both speed and quantity.

Besides the capacity for high-bandwidth displays, near-future information storage devices based on videodisk technologies offer the opportunity to supply enormous amounts of data to people in a software format. A typical floppy disk today can store a few hundred kilobytes—equivalent to a few hundred pages of information. A more recent rigid-disk technology can store millions of bytes, equivalent to thousands of pages of information. But when storage technology goes optical, the unit of storage can get as small as a wavelength of light, which means that a platter the size of a long-playing record can hold hundreds of billions of bytes of information—

including not only data like payroll records and bank statements but also books, symphonies, movies, lectures.

When cheap storage reaches the gigabyte level, as it is bound to do within the next few years, it will be possible to put entire libraries—huge amounts of video, audio, and text information—into the hands of individuals. Right now, these massive storage devices are used for certain specialized applications. The repair manual for a high-performance aircraft, for example, can be a half million pages long. A 747 would have difficulty loading and lifting its own repair manual! The same information can be handily carried (and accessed) by one repair person, however, if it is encoded on videodisks.

The way in which software is transferred from place to place is bound to change as well. A great deal of software will be brought to consumers by electronic means—via the telephone or television cable. Recent efforts by a variety of companies to make their mark by providing electronic distribution services have not met with the huge success predicted for them. But it is inevitable that electronic distribution will eventually succeed in areas where the software has a very high service component, as with a payroll program that needs to be changed every time the tax laws change at the city, state, or Federal level, or where large databases are involved.

Some of the most impressive accomplishments of the next few years may not even depend upon changing technology, however. Instead, they may derive from the ability of talented young men and women to push existing technologies to new limits. The most consistent efforts so far have been in the research conducted on artificial intelligence, the results of which are only beginning to emerge into the commercial markets after decades in the laboratories and thinktanks. The most prominent current example of this spinoff is the advent of "expert systems," programs capable of transferring expertise from one human to another, which are already used commercially to locate valuable mineral deposits, and experimentally to diagnose diseases! Although true "thinking machines" might still be far off (or not possible), advances in many areas of artificial intelligence research have already guaranteed revolutions to come in microcomputer applications. And it is worth noting that artificial intelligence research is where hackers have tended to produce their most brilliant efforts (such as Richard Greenblatt's pioneering chess program and Carl Hewitt's ultra-high-level computer language named HACKER).

It is hard and often foolhardy to speculate about some of the more futuristic aspects of artificial intelligence research. But it is reasonable to expect that programming efforts based on new knowledge gained from past and current research soon will permit computers to respond more and more similarly to natural human communication. The area of natural language understanding—whereby computers would not only recognize words but would be capable of figuring out what sentences mean—is considerably more difficult than voice recognition, since understanding involves knowing a great deal about the world. (How can you tell the difference between "I am going to see" and "I am going to sea"? When you say "I saw that oil can leak," do you mean that you watched oil seeping out of a can or that you realized such an event can happen?) But techniques for emulating humanlike communication, while falling short of true understanding, are bound to bring computing to an ever-wider population.

The nature of communication, the way in which people transfer information and knowledge, comes into play when programmers attempt to create software capable of emulating that communication. As it is, the recent effort of trying to figure out how to get a machine to respond in a humanlike manner to human input has already taught psychologists a great deal about how human thought and speech are organized. It has demonstrated how difficult it will be to program even the most advanced computers to emulate the kinds of feats normally accomplished by the human brain. It will surely be no loss to the public if the next great achievements in software come first from the social rather than the physical sciences.

As we all know by now, technological advances bring problems as well as opportunities. Our increasing reliance on the electronic storage and distribution of information opens doors for a whole new criminal class who lack the daring to engage in the kind of crimes that require their physical presence. Long-distance, telephone-mediated, computer-assisted thefts of information from data banks, including telephone and bank credit card numbers and personal, confidential credit information, are already occurring on a massive scale. Some of the software tricks for burrowing into bodies of data and removing information have been tagged with names like "worm programs" and are passed on from one hacker to the next as tokens of programming prowess. Indeed, to many people the word *hacker* has only this one, recent connotation of software thievery.

The use of programming talent for criminal purposes increases the need for law-enforcement people to have software skills, ar.d so we see another effect the software revolution is having on our society—the rise of a new literate class. Just as the spread of literacy was largely responsible for the rearrangement of the class structure of medieval Europe, the rise of a new class whose skills are needed and valued throughout our society (and entry into which is not restricted by age, sex, or race) may help to break down traditional employment and class barriers.

Of course, there is nothing in the nature of the technology itself which guarantees that the new class will come into being in a strictly egalitarian manner. So far, boys have been far more interested in learning about computers than girls have been, and upper-middle-class white children have had far more access to computers than lower-class or nonwhite children. The impact of the software revolution could therefore serve to increase rather than decrease class and racial differences, particularly if public schools are unable to afford to become more involved in fostering computer literacy. The inevitable decrease in prices will make "low end" computers more widely available, but the latest, most capable personal computers will always tend to be more expensive.

Whatever the social impact of the software revolution may turn out to be in the long run, the software people I have known are delighted that it began during their lifetimes. In fact, most of them can't imagine what their lives would be like right now if it hadn't been for that revolution. Most of them expect to be exploring the frontiers of new technology five and ten years from now. People don't change that much. Sometimes history spotlights them for a while before the focus of events moves on to something else. The shakeout was the end of the microcomputer software gold rush, but by no means was it the end of the software industry.

What is the software industry really like, once the dangerous delusions are stripped away? If you remove the rose-colored glasses, peel away the whitewash, and discount the extravagant rags-to-riches tales of some of the participants, what you will find is a decent industry, filled with good and fascinating people, that usually offers better-than-average growth and average rates of return on investments. It is a very volatile industry and will continue to be volatile and less than totally predictable, in part because it depends upon creative efforts (like the film, record, and book industries) and in part because it is a secondary marketplace that follows and reacts to changes in the hardware marketplace.

Still, microcomputer software publishing is fundamentally a fair industry. By that I mean that it isn't completely controlled by corporate marketing giants. Anyone who comes up with a great product can be a part of this industry, and that's what makes this particular business—and the people in it—so special.

Index